MW00979320

M W
& R

ONE MAN AT A TIME

ONE MAN AT A TIME

(Secrets of a Serial Monogamist)

ELIZABETH SIMPSON

Dear Moira,
You will find
yourself in here in Mexico &
at my table. As Bing Crosby
sang, "Thanks for the Memories,"
they make looking back to that
time bearable. Enjoy! Love,
Elizabeth ♡

Macfarlane Walter & Ross

Toronto

Copyright © 2000 Elizabeth Simpson

All rights reserved. No part of this book may be reproduced,
transmitted in any form or by any means, electronic, mechanical,
photocopying, recording, or otherwise without written
permission from the publisher (or in the case of photocopying or
other reprographic copying, a licence from a licensing body such
as the Canadian Copyright Licensing Agency), except by a
reviewer, who may quote brief passages in a review.

Macfarlane Walter & Ross
An Affiliate of McClelland & Stewart Ltd.
37A Hazelton Avenue
Toronto, Canada M5R 2E3

Canadian Cataloguing in Publication Data

Simpson, Elizabeth, 1941–
One man at a time : secrets of a serial monogamist

ISBN 1-55199-041-5

1. Simpson, Elizabeth, 1941– – Relations with men.   2. Wives –
Canada – Biography.   3. Authors, Canadian (English) –
20th century – Biography.*   4. Authors, Canadian (English) –
20th century – Marriage.*   I. Title.

HQ1455.S55A3 2000   306.872'092   C00-932218-3

Excerpt from *Fugitive Pieces* by Anne Michaels. Used by
permission, McClelland & Stewart, Ltd. *The Canadian Publishers*.

Macfarlane Walter & Ross gratefully acknowledges support for
its publishing program from the Canada Council for the Arts, the
Ontario Arts Council, and the Government of Canada through
the Book Publishing Industry Development Program.

Printed and bound in Canada

Dedicated to my father
Robert Simpson
and
to the mothers
who gave birth to me and my husbands
Daisy, Irene, Clara, and Lily

No one is born just once
If you're lucky, you'll emerge again
In someone's arms . . .

Anne Michaels, *Fugitive Pieces*

CONTENTS

ACKNOWLEDGEMENTS

Thank you to the men with whom I have shared variations on the theme of love; to my sisters – one dead, one remaining – for the bouquets and arsenals of childhood; to the many friends with whom I commiserated and argued; to Gary Ross who got me started and Jan Walter who kept me going and knew when to quit; and to Noel, my destination. Where necessary, names have been changed to protect aging mothers and children.

PROLOGUE

I HAVE always been loved by men. Even now in middle age, I
have found love again. It is the *again* of love that defines my world,
a serial monogamy that hints of murder – murder of the heart.

The fault may abide with my father who taught me to seek and
expect a particular devotion from men, and to think of the word
husband or *father* as synonymous with *family*. This expectation has
proven a surefire way to acquire male affection and to consider
lasting love my due. Taking my father's love for granted meant I
could put my trust in his unconditional loyalty as I gave him mine.
But transferring this faith to a husband can be dangerous. Some
men do not cope well with the gift of trust. My father's ability to
take his own marriage for granted spoke of an innocent exchange
less common in my generation. He depended on the affection he
and my mother shared. She, in turn, discovered her womanhood by
nurturing it.

At the end of the work day and at the sound of Father's footsteps on the porch of our Winnipeg bungalow, Mother would
stop whatever she was doing and slip into their bedroom. As a
child, I watched her brushed her light brown hair and toss her head
back. Dipping her baby finger into a jar of rouge and with quick

strokes on lips and cheeks, she made roses bloom. Giving her reflection a coy smile, she turned to greet her man. This ritual drew weariness from Father's face, his eyes becoming tender and vulnerable. Three decades would pass before I understood a healthy portion of Mother's beauty came not just from her form and flesh, but also from my father's delight in them.

Father's awareness of love's significance came with his parents' early deaths and from Mother's devotion and eventual illness. I loved my father even though he couldn't cook or remember birthdays. I was his favourite daughter of three, and I imagined I would one day be like my mother, one half of a perfect whole, having waited for the other half to join with me when I grew up to be as beautiful in some man's eye as my mother was in Father's. Mine is the story of learning to accommodate surprise.

MY FATHER'S FACE

I FELL in love with my father in August 1947 when I was five years old. It began shortly after dinner with a drive to the local store for next day's breakfast groceries. Father pulled up to the curb on the far side of the road. I was barely able to see out the window of our Chevrolet but could look up and across the street to the familiar sign – Stanley Foods. My father suggested that I cross the street and ask Mr. Stanley for the cereal and eggs Mother had sent us to buy. He told me I was to give the grocer our two-dollar bill and return without spilling the bag of food. All this seemed possible with my father watching from his car window. My eagerness to please him was directly connected to his allowing me to contravene Mother's rules about having my hair brushed and my hand secured. Mr. Stanley remembered me and I remembered the color of the cereal box and the fact that my mother liked brown eggshells. I came out of the store just as a bus stopped between me and my father's face across the asphalt. Bus passengers smiled and moved around me as I peered over the grocery bag.

Father praised me for waiting until the bus had gone before I ran onto the road. He reached into his pocket for a nickel, shining it on his sleeve before giving it to me. When we arrived home, Mother was waiting at the door. Mrs. Stanley had phoned to say I had left the change on the counter. My parents' laughter confused me, but Father did not ask for the return of his nickel. I was smitten.

My parents had enrolled me in kindergarten the previous year because my head looked so big it needed something to do while my body caught up. My grandfather said my head would be filled up with thoughts. He told me a thought was like an idea, and I would be able to carry hundreds of them around as I walked to and from school. When I grew tired, I could spit them out like orange pits. My birthday fell near the end of September, and Father explained that each of my birthdays would allow me to catch up to other students during the first month of school. Birthdays became markers for autumn classes and prairie Indian summers when the elm trees became umbrellas of orange and yellow leaves.

Each morning, after my father caught the bus for work, Mother propped me on a wooden stool and brushed my hair. Having given up on a page boy, she wound the curls around her finger, afterward telling people, *All those curls are natural*. Sometimes she licked the tip of her thumb and index finger and slicked a stubborn strand into place. *Okay*, she'd whisper, and I'd jump down off the stool. The prairie wind blew my hair into a jumble as she walked me to class. Once there, she stooped to kiss my cheek while reorganizing my curls and promised to return at noon. I sat with other students at wooden desks, coloring pictures with crayons, listening to stories with hands clasped, and lying on mats for nap time. When I folded my jumper beside my shoes on the first day, the teacher told me we didn't have to take off our clothes or put on pajamas.

At mealtimes my father made up funny or wise stories to make us laugh and learn, and Mother asked us questions and told us not to answer when our mouths were full of food. At school the teacher hushed us while she read stories from books. During recess, students who already knew the tales would blurt out the endings before the teacher had arrived at them. In this way I learned Alice in Wonderland was dreaming, and Santa Claus never forgot poor people, and Lassie found her way home alive. Knowing the stories ended happily, I left off worrying.

The teacher sent me home with a report for my parents, and Mother shared it with Father and my older sister, Joyce, when we sat down for dinner. *Elizabeth*, she read aloud, *is the sweetest child in my class*. I knew I was sweet because my father called me *sweetheart* when he was proud of me. He'd never been to my class, but he knew everything about the world outside our house. He knew before our teacher told us that I should finish school because it would make me proud of myself. Kindergarten forecast academic success.

No one explained that in grade one I would have to return after lunch to the classroom where I had once spent only mornings. I hated being inside all day. The school toilets were at the end of the hall and down some steps among concrete and pipes. After I hoisted myself onto the wooden rim, hands clutching its sides and feet dangling above the terrazzo floor, the horror of my pants being around my knees made me blush. The teacher told us we must return to the bathroom if we didn't remember to flush, but I hesitated to pull the wooden handle on the end of the dangling chain because a noisy torrent of water would gush from the tank above and sweep everything into a whirlpool that disappeared into the earth below.

In the second week of school, I raised my hand to go to the bathroom, walked past the stairs leading down to the cubicles, and hurried outside. I turned the doorknob quietly when I reached home. Mother stood ironing clothes she picked from her wicker basket. She moved her shoulders as she sang along with Caruso on the radio, sweeping the iron up and down in time with the melody. *Because God made you mine, I cherish you*, she sang in a louder voice than I had ever heard her use. She was soaring into the second verse when I startled her, and I realized she was not as happy to see me as I was to see her.

After my third escape, the teacher sent a note home. Mother returned with me after lunch to stand by the classroom window with two other mothers. They leaned on the painted iron heating ducts that hissed and knocked when cold weather set in. I loved to look up into her familiar face even though she would not look back into mine. She seemed tired and disappointed, and I suspected she didn't like the afternoon in school any more than I did. At the end of the week, Mother told the teacher about the new baby who would come after Christmas, and the two women agreed I would have to learn to manage without her. On our way home, she told me it was nonsense to worry about the basement toilet and that I should take a friend down with me. The spinning water was just *doing its job*, and I was supposed to do mine.

At bedtime Father said I couldn't come home until the school day ended because it upset Mother. The next day I didn't bother my mother or the baby she carried inside her tummy. Instead I went to a neighbor's to use her bathroom. While I was behind the closed door, I could hear her dialing Mother on the phone. I arrived home to silence, until Joyce spoke up: *Why do you have to be so stupid?* The day after, I bypassed both home and neighbors to find my father's office, but I had only imagined I knew where it was. The principal offered to give me the strap.

According to Mother, this was not like the strap on my Sunday shoes, but more like Father's belt. The strap was used to smack children's hands to make them sorry for what they'd done. Father objected, *No one's going to hit her*. In the soft voice she used to win him over, Mother reminded him I was on a busy street when the policeman picked me up and sat me in the side-seat attached to his motorcycle. *Anyone could have run off with her*, she warned. At the kitchen table, my father put his face in his hands for a moment before he rolled up his trouser leg to remind me of the difference between his two calf muscles. A hollow of flesh about the size of an ice-cream cone distinguished the right from the left. A jagged scar ran through it from the knee to ankle. I had seen this misshapen limb at the beach but it had seemed somehow natural to me.

Father, who had been orphaned at thirteen, told me he had lost this part of his leg when he was fifteen years old. A man had been teaching his girlfriend to drive and she was sitting on his knee, *behaving foolishly*. Their car had hit him and his right leg had been mangled with his bicycle. I listened to Father's story and wished he would come to school with me now that Mother was too tired. As he talked, I heard her sigh, the closest she had come to tears. Alone in bed, I decided I would stay in school until the new baby was born and my parents had returned to their old selves. As it happened, I never left the classroom again, except when the bell rang. The weariness in my father's shoulders that day as he bent down to roll his pant leg over his scar, and the quiver in the corners of my mother's mouth as she watched him, may be why I am still in school today, a half century later, having simply moved to the other side of the desk.

After Christmas, Mother went to Misericordia Hospital to give birth with the help of Doctor Picard, who had brought Joyce into the world twelve years earlier and me six years after Joyce. In Mother's absence, my maternal grandmother, Grandma Blore, came to feed and bed us, bringing with her a bosomy and bottomless affection. The following week, our mother came home. Without a son to name Robert after Father, she called the baby Roberta Lynne. When I clambered onto the bed to look under the flannel blanket, my mother cautioned me not to smother the baby. I saw in Mother's face the expression I had been looking for when I had come home early from afternoon classes.

My new sister had a moving mouth that seemed attached to her curled fists. Lynne was warmer and more interesting than my doll. After the first week, Mother confessed she'd only wanted a boy to please my father, but he was happy enough she had survived what Grandma called *a difficult birth*. In the late forties, birthing was a ritual hidden from fathers and children, so I knew none of the physical details, nor about the pain and tears. I knew only that a part of me claimed Lynne for my very own and I was certain I would be able to keep her safe for the rest of her life because I was so much bigger and older. I leaned against Mother's knees while she breastfed the baby, but when I tried to cuddle them both at the end of the feed, the baby would wail and my mother would turn away. *I fed you for a whole year, and now it's the baby's turn*, she said, tucking her swollen breasts back into her blouse.

Mother shifted her attentions back to me and Joyce the year following. For Easter, she made coats of soft green felt with matching tams and purses. Our tams sat at a saucy tilt on our heads, our purses dropped to our hips from shoulder straps, and our coats had large buttons and long knotted waist ties. After she had dressed us in our new outfits and told us to show them off to our father, Joyce and I wore our coats to church. This began a habit in our family of blessing each new outfit at the Presbyterian Church where we asked the Lord to keep us humble. We also put our shoes out for Father to polish. *You can see your face in the leather if you look carefully*, he would say.

After Lynne came into the family, Joyce had to walk to school with me. She didn't feel the same pride about our matching outfits as I did. Instead, she shooed me off when I managed to catch up with her, forcing me to walk with Marlene and Darlene, who were in my classroom. On the spring day I got separated from these friends after school, I followed two boys into a puddle that spanned the school yard. They were taller than I was and wore high black boots against the spring run-off. I dawdled behind them, cold water lapping over my boots. The bottom of my green felt coat floated on the murky water, and it slapped against the tops of my wool stockings. My calves had begun to ache by the time I slopped up the porch steps. I knew my mother would be unhappy, but I was too cold and hungry to stay outside. Longing for my after-school sandwich of peanut butter and banana, I opened the closet and hid in my soggy coat. When Mother found me, she spoke quietly. *Let's just wash all that mud off your stockings and coat, and we'll hang them up to dry*. While she crouched down and rubbed my legs with a warm towel, I clung to her shoulder and cried for all the lonely homecomings I'd known since my baby sister had come to live with us.

Our home changed again when Mother took an office job. Grandma and Grandpa moved into our house for a year to look after us when school ended each day. Grandma Blore was more cuddly than my mother and she spoiled us all, including her son-in-law, my father. In grade three I discovered her unconditional love for family meant that whatever her grandchildren did she would forgive as long as we stayed healthy and loved Grandpa. Staying healthy was easy, loving Grandpa Blore was harder. The smell of pipe tobacco clung to his face and his breath felt hot on my nose. Father seemed pleased when I refused to sit on Grandpa's knee or let him dab his beery kisses on my face. His drinking annoyed my father and me, although we never spoke of it, and I always wondered how I could overcome my reluctance and love him for Grandma's sake. *Don't you fret about it*, my father said when I asked him how to change my heart.

Grandma's whole being hummed with happiness when she spoke of Grandpa. She was grateful that after he emigrated from Britain to Canada, he had not forgotten to save his pennies until he could bring her and their two sons to Manitoba to join him, *You'll never see him again*, her sisters had warned. She even found joy in the memory of his leaving her on the homestead with their growing family while he built a shoe business in Winnipeg on the corner of Portage and Main. Mother adored Grandpa too, even though she once confessed that Grandma had spent much of her life waiting for him to come home.

Grandma folded laundry, cut vegetables, and dusted in corners while she waited. Sometimes Grandpa came home so late we were all asleep except for her. He came in with breezy stories, waking Joyce on the couch where she slept to make room for our grandparents. Once Grandpa knocked over the empty milk bottles on the porch, sending them to the bottom of the steps in a heap of broken glass. Reliable or not, Grandpa had a special power because he remembered Grandma's birthday roses, made Yorkshire pudding with gravy on Sundays, and grew a vegetable garden in summer.

Mother said that before Grandpa's hair had turned silver, it had been as blond as our aunt Winnie's and my sister Lynne's. When Mother had a glass of wine, she made it clear that blonds might be bad but they were easier to forgive in a British heart. Father disagreed. He thought Winnie was *idle and cranky*, that Grandpa spent too much time *at the damn racetrack*, and that Lynne *fussed over nothing*. Grandma was happy with us all, as long as we were on the warm side of the grave. She had never forgotten her first-born, who had died at the age of five in his third year on Canadian soil. His blond hair hadn't saved him from the neighboring child's smallpox.

Only two things could drive away Grandma's joy. If we stepped too close to a horse her serenity disappeared: *Sing gently*, she would say, *so you don't make him jumpy by surprising him*. She had seen her father trampled by a startled horse in Yorkshire, and she kept sacred a newspaper clipping from the 1800s that told the story of his death. Perhaps her family had put a high value on fatherhood after the only wage earner had been cracked in the skull by the hooves of the horse that pulled the neighborhood ice wagon.

Grandma's other cause for upset was more of a mystery. She went wild when she imagined some other woman coming between her and Grandpa's eyes. Unlike my mother, who seemed incapable of feeling threatened by any woman, Grandma would grow anxious when Grandpa swung his polished cane as he walked down the street. *She gets beside herself over his antics*, Father would say. Grandma thought his dapper cane attracted women who peered from cars or watched from their front porches.

After one Sunday dinner of Yorkshire pudding, gravy, roast beef, mashed potatoes, and lemon pie, we bundled up in scarves and lined boots while Grandpa hooked his cane over the inside of his elbow. I walked behind with my parents, Grandma and Grandpa leading the way through the snow. Under the street lamps we could see Grandma's stiff walk reflecting her unhappiness. Suddenly, Grandpa cracked his cane over his knee, its snap breaking the quiet of the pristine night. For a moment he looked back, perhaps surprised at his own strength, perhaps sorry for the loss. Before anyone could speak, he tossed the pieces of wood into a snowdrift. While Father shook his head in dismay, Grandma slipped her arm through Grandpa's, and they continued along the street as though the world had become a better place.

In the summer following, I sat between Grandpa and Father in the front seat of the car on our annual August pilgrimage to the beach. When I reached behind me to shift myself back, I placed one hand on a small furry marble and something jabbed my palm, making it numb and painful at the same time. Mother and Grandma cooed at me between their instructions from the back seat while Grandpa pulled out a bee stinger. As Grandpa massaged the spot with his thumb, Father sang his train song to distract me. I raised my voice to join in and tried harder to love Grandma's man:

> In the wreck he was found
> Lying there on the ground
> And he asked them to raise his weary head.
> As his breath slowly went
> This message he sent
> To the maiden who thought she would be wed.
> There's a little white home
> That I built for our own
> Where I dreamed we'd be happy by and by.
> Now I leave it to you
> For I know you'll be true
>   Till we meet at the golden gate
>   Good-bye.

Grandpa was the first to say good-bye, and Grandma at sixty-nine remained true until she joined him in her nineties. In widowhood, Grandma Blore impressed the females in our family with the notion that we would be able to love our husbands without effort, bury them with courage, and outlive them for a long while.

In grade three, I climbed onto the roof of a skating shack with my girlfriends at recess. Since I had been chosen to skate solo at the Christmas festival and was enjoying a new popularity, I believed myself invincible. It seemed exciting when the boys removed the ladder and left the girls to jump down. I was last to jump and first to be injured. I leaned against fences as I hopped homeward, protecting my ankle and reaping sympathy from the neighborhood mothers. Grandma hugged me, propped my leg on a footstool, and brought me hot chocolate.

Mother's patience had ebbed with three children and a part-time job. Over breakfast next morning, she told the family I had ruined my chance of performing in front of my friends and their parents. *You could have broken your neck*, she said. Knowing I would have to miss skating practice, she wrote off my performance. Even though Father was annoyed with me, he suggested I be given a second chance: *Let her rest at home a day or two*. Grandma said, *She's just a wee thing that meant no harm*.

I was quick to blame the boys who took the ladder, but Mother advised me I would be better off if I stopped judging people by my own behavior and opened my eyes to their deceits. Like all her advice, I eventually discovered a certain fear and truth at the root of it. I was forced to hop back to school on my swollen ankle and ponder my father's silence. His compassion in the face of mistakes surpassed my mother's by a country mile, but his sympathy was complicated by another sentiment. He couldn't abide my being hurt or sick, perhaps fearing he would be separated from me as he was from his brother and sisters after his parents had died. Later when we talked, he said, *Failure only happens when people stop trying*.

After putting on my skating costume, I was able to pull my skate over the swelling, but the pain made me gasp for breath as I skated onto the ice. When I lifted my left skate high over my head, I put all my weight on the sprained ankle and veered south when I should have turned north. My free arm skimmed the boards, knocking me off balance. As I struggled to keep from falling, I heard the music slip ahead of me. Thereafter, the skating tricks I had learned by heart were executed slightly behind the waltz tempo being broadcast into the chill air by a raspy speaker. The skating instructor and Mother looked grim as I hobbled through the gate. I stared down in shame, their eyes belying their feeble praise. Father tried to elaborate on his earlier counsel: *Trying again doesn't mean being silly. You've hurt yourself again, this time on purpose. You needed to go at your second chance differently; that's the whole idea.* I wondered why he hadn't explained things properly in the first place, and I refused to laugh when he wiggled his left ear. The next winter he redeemed himself and saved my pride by moving us to another province.

In 1950 Father was promoted by the General Steel Wares Company to Western Sales Manager. Having begun his career as a delivery boy on a bicycle, he saw the promotion from clerk to manager as a reward for his years of company service. The promotion came with a transfer. Mother would have to leave behind Grandma and Grandpa Blore, Aunt Winnie, and their brother Uncle Maurice. She looked for our new city on a map: North Battleford was a tiny dot in northern Saskatchewan. Mother became silent with the strength of purpose she had learned from my pioneer grandma. Eventually Father realized she was not about to pack a single teacup unless he convinced his company to send him to Regina, a capital city on a similar latitude as Winnipeg. Regina was a long day's drive from relatives, but it had a population large enough to support music teachers and an Eaton's store.

Father went ahead to buy a house for the five of us on Queen Street in Regina, and Mother stayed behind to sell the home on Clifton Street in Winnipeg. The Manitoba flood of that year and my father's absence gave her time to grow more pliable about moving. But when Father drove us to the new place, Mother discovered our street had a wooden sidewalk. Her lips narrowed when he explained that the pump beside the kitchen sink brought rainwater up from the basement after it collected in a rare Saskatchewan rainfall or when melting snow filled the enormous water drum beneath our kitchen. Even my father's abundant hair became unruly in Regina's hard tap water, and Mother feared running out of the rainwater that made her daughters' long tresses manageable.

Before the stove was hooked up, Mother heated our dinners in the coal furnace. Cooking in the basement came to an end when she forgot to puncture a can of beans. All her unhappiness at being forced to leave her familiar home exploded when sixteen ounces of brown beans splattered the basement walls Father had just covered with whitewash. He wore her disappointment like a harness, rounding his shoulders and tensing his neck. Her only sources of delight centered on having an open fireplace and hardwood floors in the living room. It was a sign the day had gone well when she praised these features.

When the milkman took me for a ride in his horse-drawn cart and slipped his fingers under the elastic of my panties, even the fireplace and hardwood floors couldn't console Mother. I had no idea he had committed a naughty deed because my mother saved her point of view for my father's ears. I told her he'd made me uncomfortable because his breath was *stinky*, and I asked her to let me stay home if he wanted me to go with him again. Father told me never to go with men I didn't know unless my mother was with me. When I reminded him, *Mom said I could*, my words were met with silence. Father told me he couldn't be *around all the time to look after me*. When I promised him I would never marry a milkman no matter what, my parents laughed and promised me a puppy from the litter next door. A new milkman arrived at our door the following day.

My older sister, Joyce, refused to accept our move to Regina, even after I offered to share my puppy. Although the move had been Father's idea, Joyce blamed Mother. Father had insisted we move as soon as possible, preferably at Christmas, rather than waiting until Joyce and I had finished our school years. In Regina, we sat next to strangers who were already friends with one another. One boy whistled at me, and I knew this was good because my father always whistled at Mother when she asked him how she looked. But no one whistled at Joyce even though she was glamorous and was allowed to wear lipstick. Mother explained that boys only whistled at girls who smiled once in a while.

Father's job took him away from home three days a week, traveling about Saskatchewan. He returned every week to a hero's welcome. Once home, Father spent long hours in his basement room, an office just big enough to hold a desk, chair, and filing cabinet. We were not allowed to enter this cubbyhole where my father typed up sales invoices, his two index fingers banging out pages at great speed. From the kitchen we could hear the tap tap tap of keys hitting the old steel roller with its rubber covering. Surrounded by stacks of files on his desk and balls of crunched paper around his feet, he inadvertently telegraphed the notion that idle hands belong to the unfulfilled.

When I was nine and Joyce fifteen, we distanced ourselves from Mother's wary eye and Father's compassionate ear. Mother was busy organizing the house, and Father arrived home Thursday nights tired and preoccupied. Neither of our parents grew accustomed to these separations. They seldom complained, but every time they said good-bye they looked sad, and each time my father came home they happily ignored us. When I walked into their bedroom one day, I appreciated there was a difference between the milkman slipping his hands under my skirt and my father slipping his hands under Mother's dress.

In Winnipeg, Joyce and I had dressed the same from Monday to Friday in long-sleeved white shirts, pleated navy tunics, and dark stockings. The mandatory uniform camouflaged the distinctions between families who were rich and those who were not, families who had one child and those who had many. Students sought attention through grades and sports rather than with pretty sweaters and matching skirts. Beyond her school uniform, Joyce's wardrobe consisted of the blue dress she wore on Sundays and to birthday parties, a brown wool skirt, several sweaters my grandmother had knit, a jacket, and her winter coat. In Regina, where no one wore uniforms, she went to school in the same clean but slightly worn skirt day after day. Her lovely face and good grades impressed none of the other fifteen-year-old girls.

Joyce took out her anger on our parents. She smoked behind the garage and in full view of neighbors across the back lane. They didn't hesitate to phone and complain she was about to burn down their garage. Having completed grade ten, she refused to return to school. Instead she took a secretarial course and began work as a filing clerk, just as our father had done at the same age. One night, after a terse discussion with Mother about her future, Joyce slammed the bedroom door and caught Lynne's thumb in the jamb. Over Lynne's wailing, Mother called Joyce *a stubborn and selfish girl*. Joyce shouted from the top of the stairs, *And you're a* bugger!

When Father arrived home to hear the story, he dropped his newspaper on the table, bounded up the stairs two at a time, and grabbed Joyce by the arm. He took her to the dictionary on the book shelf beside the fireplace and told her to look up the meaning of the word she had used. *So what's sodomy?* she asked. *Look it up*, Father ordered. The definition silenced her and she crept back up the stairs to our shared bedroom. When I asked my mother what the word meant, she said, *It doesn't matter now*. I knew two things for certain: When I was a mother I would give my daughters lots of clothes and I would help them understand the meanings of new words.

During school recess, when the baseball team captains picked their players, I refused to be an outcast as Joyce had been. I told them I'd been known in my Winnipeg neighborhood as a home-run hitter. The truth was I had never played baseball and had only seen the game when my parents took me to watch the grownups. Father told us they had begun their romance over baseball when Mother, fetching in a red skirt, nonetheless allowed the ball to roll between her legs. He soon taught her how to catch. When I swung and missed the pitch, I explained that in Manitoba baseball bats had one flat side and that if my teammates were patient, I would reward them with a home run as soon as I had accustomed myself to their *old-fashioned bats*. No one quarreled with me, and I made good my word the next time we played. Father had shown me how to move my swing into the ball. I tried to forget that he had also taught me *Never let anyone make a liar of you*.

Having come from Alberta where five children, a baby, and two parents had shared a two-bedroom farmhouse, Father had no understanding of Joyce's misery in sharing a large bedroom and one closet with two children who were six and twelve years younger. Lynne painted pictures on the mirror with the lipstick Joyce bought from her pay cheque, and she fussed when Joyce turned on the light. I stole dimes and quarters from Joyce's dresser and bought chocolate bars for myself and a kitchen garbage container with a toe pedal for Mother's birthday. *Where did you get the money?* Mother asked when she unwrapped the embellished can. *Off my dresser*, Joyce shouted, slamming the bedroom door.

The garbage can is really from both of us, I explained, and took Joyce a piece of cake on a birthday napkin. *You're always such a cheery chipmunk*, she said, ignoring her cake. When Mother came upstairs to reason with her, Joyce locked herself in the bathroom, yelling, *You make me want to puke.* I sat cross-legged outside the closed door, promising to pay her back from my allowance. *You dimwit*, she yelled. Soon after, Father started to travel four days a week instead of three, earning bigger pay cheques that would eventually buy a bigger house.

My Winnipeg teacher had read our class a story called *Understood Betsy*, about a girl my age named *Elizabeth Ann*, without an *e*. When someone began coughing in her city house, she had to move to a farm. There she was called *Betsy* and learned to speak up for herself. In Regina I practiced the same new name on the swing in our back yard, calling myself Betsy as I swung forward and saying good-bye to Elizabeth as I swung back. *Betsy's a cow's name*, Mother said, *and your grandmother already made that mistake when she named me Daisy and your aunts Winnie and Elsie.* After a moment's thought, Father said, *Your name's just fine as it is.* Grandma, visiting from Winnipeg, looked for the positive as she always did: *Elizabeth is the name of England's princess.* Before Mother carried our dishes to the sink, she said the same about me as she did about Joyce – I was *being stubborn.* When I insisted, they finally agreed to call me *Betty*, to avoid a cow's name. No longer Elizabeth, I became Betty, a girl who had something to say.

When Father's boss came to town before my father arrived home, I learned why people said Mother was shy. Her face grew red right down her neck and she excused herself to make dinner, allowing me to leave off cleaning cutlery in order to *entertain our guest*. I talked about everything I could think of, even asking him questions about himself. *I was so proud of you*, Mother told me later. *You sounded very intelligent.* She seemed as proud of my conversational skills as she was of Lynne's piano playing, and from then on I knew talking was the way to win her approval. The family accepted that *Betty* was curious and talked up a storm, whereas *Elizabeth* had been silent and timid.

I tried to think of things to say to Miss MacDonald, my grade four teacher at Connaught School in Regina. She was beautiful, and I couldn't help gazing at her even though my parents had told me it was rude to stare. On summer Sundays she came to Westminster Presbyterian Church and sat in the balcony with us, wearing hats with wide brims and dresses with full skirts. As she swished past our pew, I whispered to my mother about Miss MacDonald's beauty. *Anyone can wear big hats*, she whispered back, her glove hiding her mouth. *Why don't we get hats?* I asked. *It's what's under the hat that counts*, she said with the coy look she usually saved for Father. I noticed my father smile at Miss MacDonald as though he too appreciated the face peering out from under her brim.

Miss MacDonald chose me to dance demanding roles in the productions she organized at school and encouraged me to study to become a professional ballerina. After she spoke to my mother, I began dance lessons with a teacher downtown. When I sprained an ankle by leaping into the air in front of my bedroom mirror, Father was as upset by my vanity as he was by the sprain. I explained that Miss MacDonald had suggested we practice our dance steps in front of a mirror. He said he didn't want me to burden Mother. I knew she was pleased, though. Lying awake in bed, I heard her telling my father how I could bend over backwards and pick a rose off the floor with my teeth.

The next morning I asked her what oral sex was. She stopped

folding the clean towels and demanded to know where I had heard such a thing. I told her that while we were changing into our street shoes, the boy in our dance class had bet I didn't know what it meant. Mother was quiet for so long I thought she hadn't heard me. Finally she said, *It's something French people do.* When I asked if it meant kisses, she repeated, *It's French.* After class on Wednesday, I hurried home to tell her the ballet teacher had chosen me to do a solo, but Mother said she didn't like me taking the bus alone after dark. *You never know what kind of men hang around those places,* she cautioned. *There's only Terence, and he's fifteen,* I explained, thinking I had disqualified him.

That night Mother told Father she was concerned that the locker room in the basement where we put on our dance costumes was unchaperoned. At breakfast she told me we couldn't afford to pay for piano lessons for Lynne and toe shoes for me too. *It has to be one or the other,* she said. When the piano tuner arrived, Mother said, *You can take singing from the woman down the street, and put all those high notes to use.* Even though I knew pink satin shoes with wood in the toes and laces up the ankles cost ten dollars, more money than I had ever had even with Joyce's dimes and quarters, I would occasionally attempt to reintroduce the topic. I thought one of them would change their mind, and I held to this hope in spite of the invariable response, *Not right now, dear.*

I passed into the hands of two other female teachers in grades five and six. *The Teachers Grimm,* Father called them, as they spread misery like chicken pox. Miss Metherall and Miss Rutherford were middle-aged spinsters who seemed to dislike the children they taught. In grade five, I asked Miss Metherall why she didn't get married and have babies like my mother had done. Miss Metherall's face turned as red as a summer tomato, and she accused my mother of allowing me to walk in a way not proper for a young girl. We assumed she meant I walked with my feet splayed, as dancers do, or that I held my head high and my back straight as Miss MacDonald advised. I began pointing my toes in and curving my spine, but my grades spiraled downward anyway.

Just before I turned ten, I was passed on to Miss Rutherford for grade six. If I spoke up she criticized my choice of words until I could barely find any to use. I tried the hard words my father had taught me. *I appreciate your magnanimous ways*, I told her. *You don't know what you're talking about*, she snapped. When I remained silent as Elizabeth Anne, she accused me of being sullen. If I talked like Betty, she called me a chatterbox.

Matters reached rock bottom when I arrived at class wearing hair curlers. Usually Mother set our hair on weekends, but I was to sing a solo part at a church concert mid-week. She got me up early, washed my hair in rainwater, twirled it up in rollers, and covered my head with her favorite blue scarf. *It's paisley wool from Eaton's catalogue*, she remarked before sending me to school with a note.

Miss Rutherford demanded an explanation before the whole class. When I finished telling them about my church solo and the Eaton's catalogue scarf, she sent me to the principal, who seemed as afraid of her as I was. He left me to sit in a corner of his office with my mother's paisley scarf on my head and a library bible in my hands. After school I sat behind our garage until I knew it was too late to go to church. Father came home at the end of the week and phoned the school. Miss Rutherford told him I had *prurient interests*. These apparently resulted from Father's being absent most of the school week. *Why can't you be home like other dads?* I pleaded.

When Miss MacDonald decided to teach grade seven, I returned gratefully to her classroom. Good fortune lasted only until the end of the first week of school when the principal asked those of us whose names began with the letters S through Z to move across the hall. Miss MacDonald's class was overloaded. Mother was certain the spinsters had dredged up this idea. Father didn't hush me or wiggle his left ear when I cried, but he referred to Miss Rutherford as *Rubbertits* and made me promise never to repeat it. On Monday he didn't leave for work as early as usual, and in the afternoon the principal came into class. *Where would I find Betty Simpson?* he asked. He already knew who I was, but he seemed to want to enjoy the occasion. I was allowed to return to Miss

MacDonald's classroom. Father couldn't remember just what he had told the principal, but I forgave him for working out of town.

I was ten years old before I met my father's only brother, Uncle George, who lived in the countryside outside Medicine Hat. He had once stayed with my parents for a Winnipeg winter in the early thirties when they were newlyweds. Mother recalled that he had glued together a bone-china teacup with his rancher's hands, those same calloused hands that strummed the guitar after dinner. Father told us Uncle George had won prizes riding buckin' broncos in Alberta rodeos and could play a fiddle better than anyone on radio.

In 1951 Father planned a trip to Medicine Hat. In spite of our frequent visits with the maternal side of the family, Mother was as ornery as a country mule about the idea of visiting Father's family. According to her, Uncle George had made a bad choice when he had other opportunities: *He was so handsome back then, so handsome,* she said, her gaze elsewhere. The story unfolded in bits and pieces as stories do when they carve sharp edges around the dinner table. At the age of forty, Uncle George had married his girlfriend's daughter, Mildred, who was nineteen. *You can't expect a decent life with those people,* Mother said. Joyce translated for me: *Uncle George's girlfriend became his mother-in-law, get it?* But Mother interrupted to say, *It doesn't matter how young temptation is, it's still wrong when people cross God's boundaries.*

Eventually I understood the color of Mildred's skin stood between Mother and our family holiday. She assured us she would not have felt the same way if the girl had been nineteen and a pure-bred. *But Boots isn't purebred,* I interrupted her. We all turned to look at the dog, her black head resting on her two white paws. *She's just upset because Mildred is Metis,* Joyce told me. *What's Metis?* I asked. *She's an Indian girl,* Grandma said, bouncing Lynne on her foot. *Like Hiawatha?* I asked. *Hiawatha was a man, you bozo,* Joyce said. Our mother interrupted again: *If God had wanted the races to mix themselves up, He wouldn't have separated us in the first place.* Mother seemed beside herself that George and Mildred had four children: *It's bad enough they married, but it's an abomination to have children*. Yet it was easy to see that Mother had never thought of going without children herself. Father stayed silent and glum.

A month later he announced he would take Joyce and me to Medicine Hat without Mother and Lynne. Joyce had her own opinion: *I'm not spending holidays in an outhouse*, she said, hands on her hips. Perhaps emboldened by Joyce's refusal, Mother brought up the Metis children again. They chewed at her family pride like cutworms, but pride works in other ways too. It wouldn't allow Mother to stay home while Father and I went on holiday. We told her we'd have a good time singing car songs and eating makeshift sandwiches. The idea of our happy travels assured her we needed her company. Joyce could stay home, but she and Lynne would join Father and me.

On our way to Uncle George's ranch, Lynne and I sat in the back with pillows and blankets piled around us. I leafed through *Anne of Green Gables* and didn't get sick as Father said I would if I read in the car. *Are you sure my middle name has an "e"?* I asked repeatedly until Mother promised to show me my birth certificate. During the trip, I made Anne into an imaginary friend who had been orphaned like my father, and then I introduced her to Elizabeth Ann from *Understood Betsy*. Both girls loved their life on the farm.

What'll these half-breed kids say? I asked my father. *They're just like your school friends*, he told me, and paused before he said, *You don't have to call them half-breeds*. Before I could ask for the other word, it popped into my head. *Metis!* I said aloud, but that didn't satisfy him either: *They have names just like we do; Charlie and Mary are the older two*. Mother interrupted to tell us to wash up after we used the outhouse. *You too*, she said, looking at Father. *Mary was my mother's name*, he said, ignoring her. We knew that he had lost his mother and baby sister to a flu epidemic when he was eleven, but we weren't allowed to ask him about it. *Your uncle George was her first child*, he said. Suddenly, as though to cheer himself, he began to sing my mother's favorite song and I joined in: *Let me call you sweetheart, I'm in love with you. . . .* Mother turned away to stare out the window.

Father laughed out loud at the end of our drive through the Cypress Hills. We had turned onto a narrow road, and the car bounced over pot holes and between rocks. He slowed at the sight of a man churning up dust as he somersaulted toward us in the afternoon heat. Head tucked, he rolled over without damaging the hat he held in one extended arm. A cowboy rose in the mote-filled air to dance in circles, hugging an imaginary partner. He was wearing cowboy boots just like the ones I'd seen on Roy Rogers. When he reached us, he banged on our car hood. I heard my father whisper *George*, as though his brother could hear him through the windshield. Father never let any of us bang on his car.

Nor were we allowed to roll around in the dust. Father didn't seem upset to see his brother jam his big leather hat onto his head after using it to beat the dirt from his pants. Mother bent her head away when Uncle George leaned into her window, hat brim shading his eyes. I worried she might scold him. *He needs a good talking to*, she had said. Instead, her cheeks turned pink with happiness. I felt something magical stir in my belly when Uncle George's dark brown eyes pressed their soft look against mine.

Mother had cautioned us against blaming the children: *They didn't ask to be born*. It seemed she had decided Uncle George had nothing to do with their births either. Aunt Mildred had apparently done this terrible thing all by herself. Grandma had told me, *We're all God's children*, when I asked her where Metis come from. I figured she was probably right, but I also knew that *cleanliness was next to godliness*, and these Metis children didn't have a sink in their outhouse for washing up.

As the car moved toward the house, Uncle George talked with Father, holding onto the window frame as he trotted alongside. The house stood alone on a small crest where the road turned, and I saw the small outhouse off to the side and toward the back. There were children in the yard, one on the roof of a small shack and two others beside some stacked firewood. *Don't get any ideas*, Mother said. When I looked again, they were running toward the car.

I was almost as surprised as Mother to meet Uncle George's oldest son, Charlie. Like Lynne, he was four years old with blond hair the color of wheat. *He's a tough little bugger*, my uncle said. No one suggested he look up his swear word in the dictionary as Joyce had been forced to do. No one told him to take his cigarette out of sight either. It seemed Uncle George could do anything he wanted, and my father would still think he was wonderful.

A woman with a baby in her arms stood in the doorway, silent and watchful. She looked right at us, as though sizing us up. I worried that behind Mildred's eyes lived a witch who would pop out and surprise me when I was alone, perhaps as I sat in the outhouse. But she made no attempts to be alone with any of us. Instead she did everything with her baby tucked close to her chest, held in place by a long towel and some corner knots. She made humming sounds and the baby hiccoughed in reply. I wondered how I could get to hold the baby, but I wasn't sure what Mother would think of my holding a Metis child. I had also noticed that with a summer tan, my skin was no different than Mildred's and my hair was a whole lot darker than Charlie's. *Look, Mom, we're the same color*, I said, holding my arm against his. Mother threw me the look she gave when I talked during our minister's Sunday sermon.

Mildred spoke slowly as though she was thinking as she talked. *You're all here*, she said, as though she knew in advance Joyce and Boots weren't coming. Because she spoke slowly we all stopped to listen. In between her words, she seemed to be purring with a secret that had nothing to do with our arrival and everything to do with the sounds of her mewing baby and Uncle George's laughter. As he reminisced with my father at the kitchen table, my uncle puffed smoke rings toward the ceiling. I tried to put my finger through one, but it broke into pieces. When George saw my disappointment he puffed out two rings in a row.

My father's and uncle's elbows were bent at the same angle on the tablecloth, a double fist holding up each chin, the oilcloth cover held neatly at each corner with clothespins. Mother didn't allow elbows on the table, but Mildred didn't seem concerned. She told us where to find extra spoons and cups, untroubled by our sweaty clothes. *We brought our own bedding*, I told her before I saw my mother frown at me. In spite of the crowded kitchen, Mildred didn't rush. I thought how my grandma must have been on her homestead with a baby at her breast and another by her elbow. *She looks like Grandma*, I told Mother when we were unpacking. *Your grandmother's a saint*, Mother huffed.

We soon discovered Mildred was a saint too, at least to her children and neighbors. She had won her status in the early spring by leaping into the swollen river edging their land and saving her two-year-old boy from drowning or being crushed between the ice floes. It happened just days after she'd given birth to the new baby. *She come looking for the boy in the nick of time*, George said. Mildred shook her head as if to deny she'd done anything special. *She couldn't even swim before she damn well jumped in*, Uncle George grinned.

This Metis mother who had stolen Uncle George was not as straightforward a sinner as I'd figured. Her plunge into the icy river changed everything, even for my mother. On the second day of our visit, she and Mildred baked two berry pies for a picnic, and we ate them outside in the cool of the evening. Except for the mosquitoes, we were as happy as a family with normal relatives.

From the couch where I pretended to sleep, I could observe the grown-ups in the kitchen. Uncle George was sharing a bottle of something he called *hooch*. Once they had emptied that bottle, he brought out another. *Made from our own mulberries*, he said. He told a story about Father, how he had told my mother *she was going to marry him or else*, and how my mother replied he was going to marry her or *nothing else*. I didn't think Mother's reply was funny, but they all drank their berry juice and laughed until tears ran down their faces. Uncle George told how my father had escaped from his foster home in Winnipeg and hitched a ride on a boxcar back to Medicine Hat. When he couldn't find Uncle George, he'd painted his face with black shoe polish so everyone would think he was from the south and not send him back. *No Darkie ever got green eyes*, Uncle George slapped his knee and refilled his glass.

Father had promised Mother we would stay only three days. The time passed before we had explored the river bank or all the roads that forked off to other farmhouses in the foothills. As the two mothers walked through the summer grass and still heat, I heard mine confess to Mildred that she had grown up on a homestead sixty miles out of Winnipeg.

I don't think Father intended to hug his brother when we left. He never hugged anyone except us, and even then we mostly kept our hugs indoors where no one could see. But when he shook hands with his brother, they leaned into each other for a moment. I had a terrible feeling my father was about to cry. Then just as suddenly everyone was laughing, and no one knew what else to say. Father climbed in behind the wheel and started the car, and we waved out the open windows. Mother waved until a turn in the road made it impossible to see the small house and the family who stood in front of it.

The winter after our visit to Medicine Hat, Mother organized a collection of clothes at the Presbyterian Women's Church Circle for the Metis families on the outskirts of Regina. She looked annoyed as she served us dinner the night after her final meeting. *I'm not mentioning anyone by name*, she said, *but someone complained about getting involved with the half-breeds*. Mother said she had wanted to give the woman a piece of her mind, and tell her *we're all God's children*. I knew Grandma read the bible every night, propped on her pillow with my grandfather's reading glasses over her nose, but Mother must have been reading it when I wasn't looking.

I had to leave Boots at home again during the summer I was twelve and enrolled through our church in the Canadian Girls in Training summer camp. The night before I left, Father told me he'd been to camp when he was a fourteen-year-old foster child. A neighbor paid my father ten cents each Saturday morning to cut his lawn. One weekend, he surprised Father: *Well Bobby, I've just arranged to send you to a boys' camp for two weeks.* A few days later, he took my father to a bus where eleven boys his own age had gathered. The bus took them through the countryside to a campsite by a lake. Father told me all the chores were shared out equally among the boys, and after a day of baseball and swimming, they gathered around an open fire for their evening meal. It was a revelation to be able to take as many helpings as he wanted, and to discover there was an alternative to hunger and loneliness.

I also took a bus to camp, but it was full of girls I knew from CGIT. At camp I met other girls, eating and sleeping with them in spacious white tents with wooden poles. The following Saturday I talked to my parents through the mesh fence that protected the campers from outsiders. My parents hovered on the other side of the wire, able to touch hands by lacing them through the mesh, but unable to hug me. We girls swam every day before breakfast and again in the afternoon in water roped off to keep us in view of the lifeguard. At night, we were divided into groups of six, each group in its own tent with three bunk beds. We talked about the girls outside our cabin, exaggerating their faults and beauties. At some point each night, we would chant a secret camp poem:

When me prayers were early said
Who tucked me in my widdle bed
And spanked me till my ass were red?
    Me Mudder
Who took me from a cozy cot
And put me on an ice-cold pot
And made me pee if I could or not?
    Me Mudder
And when the morning light had come
And in me bed I'd dribbled some
Who would wipe me widdle bum?
    Me Mudder
Who did me hair so neatly part

And press me gently to her heart
And sometimes squeezed until I'd fart?
  Me Mudder

Finally we fell asleep in the middle of conversations that would erupt again mid-sentence the following morning, as we scrambled to line up at the outhouse.

That summer I tumbled blind toward the astonishing world of menstruation, the single most respected activity in my circle of friends. *Where did it go?* I asked my mother, after discovering a splash of blood and then realizing it had disappeared as mysteriously as it arrived. *It's called your "monthly" because it comes only once a month*, Mother explained. *I know*, I huffed, mimicking Joyce. I had thought the blood would come with every visit to the bathroom for the rest of my life. Voluptuous daydreams, combined with the desire to avoid parental intrusion, filled my waking hours. My parents spoke to me in loud and impatient voices. I considered silence a welcome alternative to communication with these old people over forty. I wanted to be left alone to concentrate on my womanhood. *I can have a baby anytime now*, I told my mother. *Not yet, I hope*, Mother laughed.

I was fully aware that the only girls my age who had babies were in *National Geographic Magazine*. They showed their bare breasts to the cameramen and to the boys in my class who thumbed its pages. The girls at school who were already menstruating kept their bodies covered and enjoyed high prestige. Each whispered announcement from yet another girl that she had begun to bleed was followed by a promise of secrecy that no one kept. Mother suggested I could learn about birthing by watching Boots, who was about to have a litter of puppies, but she hid in my father's office one night and had three puppies with no help from me.

When Mother said, *Your father thinks you should wear deodorant*, I was horrified. I began sniffing my underarms behind closed doors, certain everyone could smell me as they passed. We had been told in Physical Education we could shave our armpits for the school dance. I checked daily to see if a single follicle of hair would give me reason to ask for a razor, but every day blank flesh stared back at me from the mirror. *Just pretend you have to shave. Practice a smooth stroke*, Mother said, compassion in her voice. *You've been a woman for less than a year, dear.* I hated her pity even while I clung to her for a solution, imagining my hairless armpits a forewarning of future failures.

In early November, just after my thirteenth birthday, I sat at the top of the stairs listening to my parents' serious voices in the living room below. Mother was telling Joyce's boyfriend that he didn't have to marry her if he didn't want to because they would take care of the baby themselves. In a deep voice, he assured them he would have married her anyway. Joyce didn't talk at all, but when I saw her at bedtime, her eyes were red-rimmed. On Saturday, she and Mother went to Eaton's and came home with four dresses. They were all made of satin, our mother's in lavender, and Lynne's and mine in blue with puffy sleeves. Joyce's dress was the most beautiful of all: a long white gown with full skirt and veil. I asked her if she was happy now, and she said, *You don't understand anything.* She was grumpy with everyone but Grandma, who had contradicted Mother by saying, *No one is ever too young to be in love.*

Joyce married in late November, three days before her nineteenth birthday. Walking down the aisle behind Lynne as flower girl and me as bridesmaid, she held onto Father with one hand and a bouquet of roses with the other. I heard people sigh when they saw her, as striking as a movie star in white lace, her thick brown hair in an upsweep and her new earrings sparkling among the tendrils arranged artfully under the veil. The best part was when the minister told my new brother-in-law he could kiss the bride in front of everyone. When Joyce returned from her honeymoon, her tummy was rounder than on her wedding day. Mother said, *It must be longer than three months.* Joyce got angry all over again.

Four months after her wedding, Joyce gave birth to twins. The doctor was as shocked as she was and ordered the babies into incubators. They had arrived two months early. Father reminded Mother that Joyce had been telling the truth all along about when she got pregnant. But the truth didn't make it easier for Joyce to cope when one baby came home after two weeks while the other remained in hospital for a month. Once both babies were home, I went over to help her with dishes and housework, lavishing my love on the one who had come home last and who looked like a starving monkey. Proving she could manage without Mother's help, Joyce welcomed no one to her basement apartment but me. I had just begun to learn kitchen skills in my Home Economics class and Joyce's babies gave me a chance to practice.

In 1954, puberty was the point at which the schools readied young women for their future roles as wives and mothers. A woman couldn't possibly become either unless she had hair in her armpits and some smarts in the kitchen. The opportunity to acquire the latter was granted to our class of thirteen-year-old girls each Wednesday afternoon when we cycled to a neighboring school. The boys stayed behind in our home-school basement to weld metal into spatulas for their mothers and hammer wood into tie racks for their fathers. The boys called their class *Shops*, and we called ours *Home Ec*. The Home Economics room had three stoves, a fridge, four long cutting tables, two sinks with draining boards, and several sewing machines. With this equipment, Miss Wester prepared us for married life. She wore starched and embroidered blouses, and her fingernails were a source of fascination, each nail filed to the exact size and shape as the next and colored to match her lipstick. *All the better to point out your mistakes*, Miss Wester said when we stared at her manicured fingers. She uttered a tight-lipped snort we came to recognize as her laugh.

Our first task was to whip egg whites and sugar into frothy meringue peaks, turning the handles of beaters until our arms ached. These topped orange segments heated in liquefied brown sugar. We popped our creations under the broiler for just a moment to brown the curly white tips. Afterward, we sat at one of the long tables while Miss Wester inspected our finished desserts. The moment we all waited for came just before the bell rang when we spooned the orange meringue into our mouths.

We climbed back on our bicycles with recipes neatly written on lined foolscap, ready for testing on our families. Mine were willing victims, although I could see by the watery look in my father's eyes he liked the idea of my cooking more than the reality. Lynne was less charitable. She wolfed down a heaping spoonful, then spat it back into her bowl. When I tasted my masterpiece, I cringed at the flavor of moldy orange hidden under the browned peaks of beaten egg whites. All the joy of sugared citrus and lip-licking meringue was tainted by one aged orange. *Never mind*, Mother said. *Just keep your eyes open when you shop. Oranges aren't cheap.*

We learned to make peanut butter cookies by rolling the batter into small balls between our washed palms and then crushing them with a fork. *Lightly, mind you*, Miss Wester warned. On each cookie we placed a peanut before baking a batch until their centers popped back into place when we pressed them with a finger, taking them out before their bottoms burned. When I baked these at home, the family gobbled them up. I wanted to spend the rest of my life baking peanut butter cookies but my mother thought otherwise. *No one will appreciate them if they're always around*, she confided as Father pulled a cookie he had saved for me out of his cardigan pocket.

Next class we learned the secret of chocolate cake, which was to stir to the count of fifty-two beats. Miss Wester divided us into groups of four, and we each did thirteen strokes before pouring the batter into a greased tin and banging it on the kitchen counter to make sure the air bubbles hiding inside would rise to the top. *Holes are for moles*, Miss Wester snorted. We left our cakes in the oven until a hat pin stuck into the center came out free of sticky batter. Miss Wester checked our pins, purring at the ones she called *clean as a clock* and shaking her head at the rest.

As our cakes cooled on the counter, we wrote out the recipe for icing as Miss Wester dictated, and then slipped a knife into the space between the tin and the cake before flipping over the cooled cake tins and smacking their bottoms. If the cake didn't fall out in one piece, Miss Wester looked the guilty smacker in the eye, and whacked it herself. Once all the cakes were right-side up, she let us cut them horizontally and paste the halves back together with a layer of homemade raspberry jam. *Made on my own, and brought straight from home*, she bragged as we sawed and pasted. Finally each group beat into smoothness a sweet dark icing. Using table knives warmed with hot water, we smothered our cakes with thick chocolate, divided them into four pieces and ate the lot before pedaling home to our separate kitchens.

The following night I baked my own cake while I thought about feeding an imaginary husband and five children, filling their upturned mouths with dollops of chocolate. I hummed my piano homework, *Für Elise*, as I moved from pantry to sink, happy in spite of Mother's rule about the cook having to scrub pans and wipe off the counter. Miss Wester had taught us that washing up was part of being a grown woman or, as she put it, *A clean knife makes a good wife*. We knew she meant a clean kitchen, but no one ever argued with Miss Wester. Nor did we ask why she wasn't anyone's wife.

When the snow came, I stored my bicycle in the basement and walked in fleece-lined boots, carrying cooking and cleaning lessons in a cardboard binder that held notes about oven temperatures and how to rinse soap off cutlery. But just before Christmas I burned my *pointing finger*, as Miss Wester called it, the one I used to test cookies. I leapt onto a stool beside the sink to soothe the burn under a torrent of cold water. Miss Wester grabbed my arm, smiling her odd smile all the while and exclaiming, *Your finger's not on fire!* When she saw the black line of the oven rack branded onto the end of my finger, she rummaged about in the fridge for butter.

When I pulled off my buttered mitten at home, Mother sighed, warning me, *Always keep your wits about you when your hands are in the oven*. Her grasp was as gentle as her concern: *That'll take a few days to mend*. When Father came home from his week on the road, he told me to remember *if the oven's hot enough to cook a pie, it can cook a hand*. Somehow the image of a hand cooked and alone on a pie plate was enough to keep my attention focused.

We gave up cooking after the holiday and began sewing. A buzz of excitement filled the Home Ec room when Miss Wester gave every girl two squares of yellow felt and a piece of white flannel, each the size of a saucer. We cut the pieces into a pear shape from a cardboard pattern and layered them like a sandwich, yellow felt on the outside and white flannel in between. We embroidered green stitches around the edges and held the pieces together with a green stem at the top. We called it a pin cushion and hid our sewing needles inside to keep our fingers safe from nasty pricks.

What do we see, on a busy kitchen bee? Miss Wester asked. When one of the girls called out *an apron*, we could see by Miss Wester's mouth that she would have preferred to tell us the answer herself. During February we cut out our aprons, sharing three pairs of pinking shears *to keep our seams from traveling, as they go about unraveling*. In March we finished the bib and attached it to a gathered skirt front. Miss Wester showed us how to make a button hole to keep the waistline snug. We worked silently, tailoring these holes by making loops of thread to push the needle through. *The hole has to let the button through, but then keep it in there too,* Miss Wester chanted. She demonstrated the hem stitch and sent us home to hem our aprons, admonishing us to make our stitches *close enough to seal, so you won't catch a heel.*

Mother never rhymed her words but she told me, *Your finished sewing is only as good as your preparation,* and she showed me how to iron a hem in two folds before pinning it up. I was scheduled to begin ironing my own clothes at age fourteen, at the same time I entered high school and graduated from drying the family's dishes to washing them. I thought of the iron as an object of esteem, hinting of womanhood and still more dangerous heat. Father was away, and Mother not only lit a cozy fire, she also let me stay up to get a good portion of my hem finished in her company. We sat on opposite sides of the trilight, each with needle in hand. Every now and again, I would show Mother my stitches. *Lovely,* she would say and then go back to stitching Grandmother's chenille housecoat.

For the rest of the week I worked each night to get the stitches even, twice pulling out my evening's work to begin again. On Wednesday I folded the ironed apron, put it in a brown paper bag, and carried it to Miss Wester's class. My apron came back the next week with a grade of *D* and a note: *You must learn to do your own stitching.* I hid the note from my friends and watched Mother's face redden as she read it. After dinner she sat at the kitchen table and wrote her own note.

I walked alone to Miss Wester's school and, without a word, handed her my mother's letter in a sealed envelope. *An apology?* she asked, looking down at me without bending her neck. When she opened the envelope with her perfect nails, she made a small clucking sound: *Tell your mother she shouldn't lie for you.* When she walked out, I realized for the first time how big the Home Economics room was.

I knew Mother didn't lie, and in my shame and anger I went home instead of back to class. Mother hinted I should feel flattered the teacher thought my work was too good for a thirteen-year-old, but nothing could comfort me. Father came home at the end of the week and told me there was nothing we could do *to fix Miss Wester's troubled mind.* I had expected my parents to make Miss Wester see her mistake. If they didn't, I couldn't love them or my apron.

At the final class when we embroidered our initials on our apron pockets, I sat off in a corner working on my capitalized *E* without looking up. Miss Wester whispered as she came by: *I'm surprised your father fell for your tricks as well.* When Father came home, I refused to look at him. *All I did was call your principal to tell him about Miss Wester's mistake,* he explained. *It's his job to listen to parents.* After I had dried dishes, he pulled a miniature cardboard folder from his sweater, about the size of the face on my grandfather's pocket watch that now sat by Grandma's bed. It had a picture of a stove with the word *McClary* above the oven glass. The cardboard cutout opened onto green tinfoil, which held eight shiny sewing needles on one side and an advertisement for General Steel

Wares on the other. It wasn't soft like my yellow pear and there were no green stitches anywhere, but I kept my opinion to myself.

Father's voice softened as he covered my clenched hands with his own. I stared at the mound of our four hands to avoid looking into his face. *Sometimes it has to be enough for you to know you're right; don't let her make a difference in your life.* When I could no longer hold back tears, his voice became stern: *Give a person two chances, and if they blow both of them, to hell with them.* Looking up, I saw him staring out the kitchen window as though thinking of some other time. *She didn't give me two chances,* I sniveled. *No,* he agreed, *but we gave her two and that's what matters.* He called her *Miss Fester* thereafter, and though I laughed along with the family, I would have preferred that sticks and stones broke her bones.

In the September when I would turn fourteen, a boy from my grade eight class frightened me by knocking on the door of the house where I was babysitting. Alan had talked a barber into shaving his head into an Iroquois cut, bare except for the dark strip down the middle from his forehead to the back of his neck. We had been exchanging smiles since the Christmas party, and in early spring, on a bet, I brushed my hand along Alan's fringe, stopping suddenly as my stomach filled with butterflies.

On this evening, I could see Alan's friends leaning their bicycles against the fence as I stood in the frame of the opened door. When I turned back into the house, someone hurled a brown paper bag inside the foyer. The bag hit the floor and two handfuls of cartridges spilled out. Unsure whether they would explode, I rushed about gathering them up. The phone rang as I dropped them in the bag and the boys came inside.

Is something the matter? Mother asked; *you sound breathless.* Four boys stood silently around Alan, listening to my conversation. One boy brushed Alan's fringe and pretended to faint from excitement. I felt my face grow hot. *I was just finishing my homework, Mom,* I told her. *Do you want me to come over?* she asked. I had to turn away to recapture my normal voice: *Don't be ridiculous,* I bluffed. Alan helped me gather the cartridge shells as the others coaxed me to rob the fridge or drink from a bottle one boy pulled from his jacket and tipped into his mouth. *Firewater*, he said.

The children in the back bedroom slept through the noise, and the boys rode off on their bikes before the parents came home, but a cartridge rolled out from behind the front door as the children's father and I left for my house. I knew they would find it, but I feigned indifference. The parents had tried to pay me off with a slice of cantaloupe and a scoop of Neapolitan ice cream instead of the one dollar and twenty-five cents we had agreed on. They told me I was the only one they trusted with their eldest daughter, Angela, a four-year-old with thick blond hair and large blue eyes. Her legs had gone limp with polio the previous year, and she was bound up in metal braces. Father said I should feel proud of refusing their cantaloupe, and my parents assumed my refusal was the reason I was never asked to babysit for them again. Two years later Angela's father brought her on crutches to the Sunday school class I taught at our church. No one spoke of the past. It wasn't the Presbyterian thing to do.

In grade nine, my friend Kathy and I spent late afternoons chattering on the way home from school and early evenings talking on the telephone. Our parents believed telephone calls should be short and to the point. Kathy and I had not yet learned what *the point* was, and we talked at length about our changing bodies, the boys in our classes, and the restrictions imposed by parents. *What do you two talk about all the time?* Mother asked. *Nothing*, I said. To get away from their prying ears, I told them I was walking over to Kathy's house and would return before nine p.m. At five minutes after nine, my father phoned Kathy's house to remind me of the curfew. Her parents thought she was at our house.

Kathy and I had been lounging against a tree midway between the two homes. In the fading light, I looked up to see my father and waved to him as I said goodnight to Kathy. She didn't get a chance to reply because her father's car screeched around the corner and bounced onto the boulevard. The passenger door opened and a hand shot out, grabbing Kathy's wrist and pulling her onto the seat. My father slipped my arm through his and we walked toward home listening to Kathy's wails. I was frightened by her father's anger and grateful for my own father's gentleness.

When Father closed the kitchen door, he smacked my face with the palm of his hand, knocking my head into the door frame. I heard Mother whisper, *Don't hit her, Bob.* His hand fell to his side. As I slipped past them and up to my bedroom, I saw a pulse pumping in Father's neck. *Don't ever upset your mother again,* he hollered after me. Upstairs in the bathroom mirror I could see where his hand had reddened my cheek. Afraid, I slipped into bed and tried to warm my icy feet beneath the covers. For the first time, I felt drowned in resentment and longing.

Mr. Gillespie further hastened me into the adult world by hiring me at his shop, Gillespie's Flowers. He put me to work with carnations and roses over the Christmas holiday. I was sixteen, in grade eleven, and could finally hold a job beyond babysitting. I loved the colors and delicacy of flowers behind the glass cabinets, and I discovered a new confidence while I helped bewildered husbands, sons, and boyfriends choose flowers for wives, mothers, and sweethearts.

On the third day, Mr. Gillespie asked if I would like to work overtime to arrange bouquets in the basement and bring them upstairs for display. *More hours, more money,* he said. That night, in my pre-sleep fantasy, I became a floral artist with a shop of my own. *Don't tire yourself out,* Mother told me when I left for work in the morning. Grandma, who had come from Winnipeg for the holiday, called out after me, *Take time for a proper bit of food.* Mr. Gillespie hung around all day, chatting to customers and, in a quiet moment, showing me the storehouse of flowers in the cool cellar. He knew the names of blossoms and how to order them in various shades and states of openness.

The rose stems were damp, cold, and prickly; I held them carefully, laying the blossoms so their edges hung over the work table. I marveled that something so beautiful could have such an aggressive stem. Mr. Gillespie put his damp hand on my shoulder as I showed him I knew how to snip the end of each stem at an angle and to pluck off any tinged petals. It worried me that he had his hand on my pink angora sweater because it had cost most of my autumn babysitting money, and I had discovered how difficult it was to wash after I had splashed it with mustard during a basketball party.

When I left home again after dinner, Father offered to pick me up at nine o'clock. Mr. Gillespie was hanging his *Closed* sign and barely looked up as I went into the cellar to fill the vases lined against the wall. I divided the roses by color, twelve in each vase, and wrapped ribbon around the vases when I had finished. I didn't hear Mr. Gillespie come down into the cellar as I was telling the roses they would find new homes in sunny windows and I wouldn't hurt them when I plucked off damaged petals.

I was embarrassed that he might have heard me chatting to cut flowers, and I turned away to hide my blush. His arm bumped the back of my waist. Before I could move aside, I felt his hand slip down to my thigh. He grinned when I swiveled around to press my back against the cellar wall. When he threw his head back to laugh, I realized what a big man he was, bigger even than my father. He breathed loudly as he stood close to me, and I had to look away from his reddened face to catch my own breath.

Remembering my brief encounter with the milkman, I spoke up. *My mother will have you fired*, I said in a quavering voice, forgetting he owned the business. *She's a looker too*, he said in what my father called a Frank Sinatra voice. I couldn't imagine anyone other than my father thinking Mother was a looker. My shock amused Mr. Gillespie, and when he laughed again I could smell Christmas spirits. He winked as though we were sharing a joke before he slapped his open mouth on mine.

A wave of nausea hollowed out my stomach as I slipped from his grasp and leapt onto the table, jumping off on the far side. Two vases fell to the floor, trapping my feet among the roses, now mixed with water and broken glass on the concrete. The basement was suddenly quiet. *You clumsy cow!* he raged, looking at the damage.

Puffing up the stairs, he left me there alone. I stayed in the basement a long time, wondering how to get past him on my way to the street. But he remained in his office when I hurried through the store to the exit.

When I arrived home early by bus, I told my parents I had quit. *Something's wrong*, Mother said, suspicion in her voice as she looked into my eyes. *What's happened?* Father asked. My parents listened with grim faces while I described the attack. When I got to the part about jumping onto the table, my mother began to laugh and then Father joined her. Soon they had tears in their eyes from laughing so hard. *You can look after yourself*, Father said, apparently satisfied.

Stung by their laughter, I went to bed with my clothes on. Mother knocked softly on my bedroom door. *Just consider it a lesson*, she said, a hand on my cheek. *It'll happen again.* I imagined she thought I would be fired from all my jobs because I was a clumsy cow. *He's old enough to know better*, I told her, mimicking Grandma, *as old as you, Mom. Well*, she said, *that doesn't mean he's dead; he's actually only thirty-eight, dear*. I didn't see much difference between forty-six and thirty-eight, and I asked her how she knew his age. *I just talked to his wife on the phone.* Her smile was coy when she looked up at Father, who had appeared behind her, his hand on her shoulder. She reached up to cover it with her own hand. *I'll drive her to the shop in the morning to pick up her pay cheque*, he told Mother, as though I were not in the room. *He said Mom was a looker too*, I told my father, to upset him. *Well, I guess he saw your mother when the two of you were there for your interview*, my father said, missing the point. *But you're safe now.* His words at last erased the stain of Mr. Gillespie's damp clutch. *He won't want the police phoning him; it's bad for business.*

The older woman at the till told me I would find Mr. Gillespie in his small office. *What do you want?* he demanded. *My pay cheque*, I tried to say, but the words didn't come. I took a second run and got them out loud enough for him to hear. *You made a mess of things*, he said, swiveling in his chair so I was looking at his back as he rooted through a filing cabinet. I didn't know if he meant the roses and broken vases or the part about me telling my parents. He kept hold of a corner of the cheque as he passed it to me. I was careful not to rip it, waiting without looking at his face, knowing he could see mine grow red before he let go.

Father had left the car running, and when I climbed back in he said, *You know there's another flower shop across town*. I thought he was going to take me there to fill in an application so I could have a proper job again. *Why don't we go buy a bouquet of red roses?* No one but my grandfather bought flowers in our family; Mother always grew her own. *Are they for me?* I asked, barely able to speak. *For you to give to your mother*, he grinned, turning so I could see him wiggle his left ear.

During my final grade eleven exams at Central Collegiate, I woke up at four a.m. every morning to study in peace. Concentration was impossible in my shared bedroom. Downstairs at the dining table I wrestled sense out of theories on physics and chemistry, practiced geometry, algebra and trigonometry formulas, and memorized events and dates in history texts. The only subjects I didn't study for were literature and typing. Literature stayed fixed in my brain because of the pleasure I took in it, and typing was my mother's idea. She and I had struck a deal: I could take physics, *a useless subject for a sixteen-year-old girl*, if I would *do the sensible thing* and take an Office Practice course.

One morning Mother tiptoed downstairs in the pre-dawn hours to say she thought the kitchen tap was dripping. When she discovered the sound was my snapping gum, she didn't scold me but sized up the situation with a smile. *Let me see your exam timetable at dinner, okay?* she asked, eyeing the notes and my row of sharpened pencils. Each exam day, before making breakfast and driving off in her Morris Minor to her job at the legislative building, she gathered up my notes and asked me to explain them *without peeking*. It was the first time since Lynne was born I had her to myself for a whole hour.

My grades came in the mail two weeks after exams, and Mother read them to me through the bathroom door as I took my turn in the tub. *Your father and I are very proud of you*, she called. Father had not yet arrived home to know anything about my successes, but my parents often presumed to read each other's thoughts. Even a C in typing did not erase my satisfaction with a row of A's in the subjects I had studied. I regarded them as a goal to match in grade twelve when students sent off their grades with applications to university. Even though I would be the first person in the family to graduate from high school, my parents had other ideas. *If you were a boy your father might consider university*, Mother reasoned, *but it isn't practical for a homemaker.* I set the table in silence while she transferred a casserole from the oven to the stove top.

I spent that summer working at a geriatric center, delivering patients' mail, putting away files, and typing official letters. I cheered myself up by sewing pretty dresses to wear on the wards when I visited sad and lonely people who, unlike my grandma, had been sent to live with strangers. Sometimes I broke the rules and phoned neglectful relatives to coax a visit or a card.

Women who wanted to avoid office work went to Normal School for a year to become teachers, or they went into nursing, or they escaped altogether by going straight to the altar and then preparing a nursery. Even though I believed marriage and children were the ultimate accomplishments of a woman's life, I had no desire to follow Joyce into teenage motherhood. I thought of Miss Rubbertits and Miss Fester and decided nurses might be preferable to teachers. When I discovered I didn't need grade twelve to meet the entrance requirements for nursing, the idea of academic excellence lost its shimmer. *What's the point?* I asked my boyfriend, Corbett, who was going off to university. He agreed: *You can already sew as well as my mom.*

I spent spring weekends of my last year of high school sitting beside Corbett as he reshaped and outfitted his 1950 Ford with fiberglass doors that opened at the touch of a button. As he called out the name of a tool, I passed it to him. When he passed it back,

I held it until he asked for another. The hard surface of the concrete driveway never seemed to bother me as much as a persistent longing that rested like wet clay around my heart. I kept my shattered ambitions at bay and focused instead on the sacrifices I would make to become a healer.

Between graduating from high school and embarking on my new calling, I worked during the summer of 1959 as an office clerk in the Public Health Building next door to the legislature. While Mother immersed herself in accounting, I banged on an electric typewriter and stood at the filing cabinet arranging folders in alphabetical order. Over coffee I listened to a secretary complain about her husband being a *good-for-nothing* and about how the neighborhood kids drove her *nutty*. She had a sore throat from yelling and a perpetual need for sleep. Another woman expressed a fondness for her husband and their children, but she had been scolded by our office manager for making brief calls home during working hours. She was the butt of jokes when the other women watched her climb down from her husband's delivery truck every morning and back into it at the end of the day, always blowing him a kiss.

Listening to these women made me wonder what my mother talked about during her fifteen-minute breaks. *If they start complaining, I just change the topic to gardening or sewing*, she told me. When I mimicked the women in my office making fun of the mother who loved her family, my mother revealed that she too disagreed with the women in her office. *Yesterday*, she said, *I told them their coffee breaks were no place for a mother, and today they went off for coffee without me*. They were annoyed at her for taking her family more seriously than her job. I couldn't imagine anyone snubbing my mother.

What can I do? Mother asked with a sincerity that daunted me. My mother had never asked my opinion on anything about her personal life other than the snugness of her dress at the back or the length of her hair when Father argued against her having it cut. As we stood together in the kitchen, I watched the white of an egg drool into a bowl as she bounced the yolk between two ragged shells. At that moment, she stopped being simply my mother and became a woman who also felt awkward in the company of strangers. I felt an admiration for this shy person who had nonetheless stood up to her co-workers. Silence might keep others friendly, but it wouldn't make us feel good about ourselves.

As the day of my departure for nursing school grew closer, I read about Saint Teresa, a Carmelite nun who had left home in Spain in the sixteenth century on a quest to martyr herself to the needy. She had failed in her first quest because she had been forced to drag her brother along. But she had been only seven, and I was seventeen. Besides, I had no brothers to hold me back, and my sisters were indifferent. Joyce hurried between twin boys and her new baby son, and Lynne viewed me as someone who helped her with homework and finished off her meals.

On Saint Teresa's second journey she and a group of nuns had successfully sacrificed comforts for good deeds. Her acts of charity had gone down in history because she was also a passionate writer. She wrote that her love of God was so great it made her moan: *Its sweetness is supreme.* Our history teacher had told us we had to respect Saint Teresa because women seldom wrote during the seventeenth century, but I was more interested in her sleeping on a wooden pillow. Sacrifice in the name of goodness appealed to me.

Are you sure you want to be a nurse? Father asked, reminding me I had never seen anyone seriously ill. But the memory of Mother's tears in the face of Grandpa's death encouraged me to return to Misericordia Hospital in Winnipeg where I had been born seventeen years before and my grandfather had died nine years later. More important, my mother had gone back to this hospital to have a secret operation when I was sixteen. Grandma had come to cook for us and told me my mother had *a woman's problem.*

When Mother had arrived home on the train, she took in the sight of her waiting family, sank down on a bench in tears, and told us how happy she was to see us again. *It's okay, Daisy,* my father said as he sat beside her and put his arm around her shoulder. Lynne and I stared at them in embarrassment, hoping no one else noticed our parents having a private moment in a public place. *Let's get you home now*, Father had comforted. On the way, I asked my mother what a *woman's problem* was. She said, *I had a tumor the size of a grapefruit in my womb.* Later, Joyce called it *hysteria-ectomies.*

Nursing began to take on importance. I imagined removing tumors from women's bodies or helping them give birth or easing migraines like the ones my father got after driving into the sun on his way home. On headache days, we had to be quiet while he slept in a dark room and Mother pressed cool cloths to his forehead. I imagined in time I would send letters home from places farther away than the towns Father traveled to in Saskatchewan, places with African names. *Are you sure you know what you're talking about?* Mother asked when I read to her from the letter that accompanied my application. I had entitled it *For Goodness' Sake* and signed it *A future healer.*

My parents took turns reminding me I had never been in a hospital except at birth and again two years previous after a tobogganing accident. I had been too embarrassed to use a bedpan. *She's a lot more stubborn than she looks*, the nurse told my mother. *If you couldn't fill a bedpan for yourself, how will you empty one for a stranger?* Mother asked while Lynne, just out of Mother's sight, held her nose and rolled her eyes. It occurred to me my parents had not noticed how much I had grown up since then. *At least a bedpan doesn't make a flushing sound to scare you*, Mother said.

The nursing residence I'd be attending was run by a Catholic order of nuns. I hoarded a secret that shored up the idea of myself as an expert on handling nuns. Mother approved of these pious women as better nurses and teachers than women whose thoughts might possibly be muddled by young men or handsome doctors. Nuns had brought all three of her daughters from the hospital nursery to breast-feed at Misericordia. In Regina, she had hired another nun to spend Thursdays after school trying to make Lynne and me aware of musical scales played with a straight back and arms parallel to the keyboard.

When I entered the convent for my lessons, I walked down dark halls past closed rooms, where occupants were garbed in long black dresses with full skirts, faces framed by the starched white pleats of their wimples. A few faces shone like angels, but the bulky skirts prompted an unrequited desire to peek beneath the hem to see what was tucked under those layers of fabric. *They think of themselves as married to God, too holy for us regular fellas,* my father laughed. My sister saw them differently: *That penguin hit me with her ruler.* We laughed ourselves silly when we escaped the convent's solemn hush.

After one January lesson, I had been unable to find my boots at the rear entrance to the nunnery where students came and went. On a small landing, dividing the basement stairs from the first floor, students exchanged fleece-lined galoshes for indoor shoes. Frightened by the darkness after a mostly silent lesson in a room where my fingers ached with cold, I walked my hand along the alcove wall until my numb fingertips rested on a switch I was sure would light my way. When the fire alarm clanged endlessly, nuns scurried down stairs and up hallways, skirts billowing as though taking on a life of their own. Sirens emptied their cry into the darkness as fire engines sped toward the convent. I stood in the darkness realizing my imperfections.

Did you set off the alarm? asked my music teacher, appearing like an apparition in the hallway entrance. *I don't think so,* I answered, relieved she could not see my eyes. As I stepped outside the nunnery, I hoped God would forgive me and not encourage the nuns to phone my parents. My boots squeaking against the snow, I listened in my mind's ear to my father say, *Don't lie unless you want to look over your shoulder all your life.*

In the last week of August in 1959, I left Regina on my first plane ride. The Catholic nursing residence at Misericordia Hospital was four hundred miles to the east. At the airport, my grandmother gave me a dollar to buy lunch. *Your grandfather always said a good bit of food keeps a body going*, she told me. *It comes with the ticket, Grandma*, I whispered, repeating what the woman at the counter had told me. Having said good-bye to Corbett the night before, I hadn't thought much about leaving my family. When I began sniveling, Mother told me I would ruin my face. One at a time I hugged them, finally wrapping my arms around Lynne as the prairie wind caught our skirts, whipping the colorful cotton around our legs and mingling our long hair.

At the top of temporary stairs leading to what Father called *the big bird*, I turned back and waved at the familiar faces below. I slid past the knees of the woman in the aisle seat, wondering what my father would think if he saw I was sitting in row 13, an unlucky number. My neighbor seemed unhappy to be sitting in this row too, especially as I had the window seat. I thought about asking if she wanted to trade, but I feared speaking to a stranger. When the stewardess brought sandwiches with a cup of tea, I could see by the woman's lack of appetite she was still stewing over not being able to see out the window.

After lunch, the stewardess asked if I would like to go up to the cockpit. *Through the canvas curtain*, she pointed. Behind an enormous windshield two uniformed men steered the plane and read gauges. They told me the roofs far below were housetops in Brandon, halfway to Winnipeg. The pilots somehow knew the reason for my first airplane trip. *We can always use a pretty nurse*, one of them told me.

The woman beside me stared up without speaking when I returned to my seat. Her mouth hung open slightly as though she was surprised as well as sad. *Are you getting off in Winnipeg?* I asked. *No*, she answered, her voice gruff. *The old man died*. She dabbed her eyes with her cardigan sleeve. I glibly repeated Grandma's words after Grandpa had died, *God helps us face death*, and then I rummaged through my purse for one of Mother's folded Kleenexes. Without a word, she unfolded it, put the Kleenex in the cup of her two hands and rubbed her face as my grandmother did with her hot face cloth when she got up in the morning.

When the plane began its landing, the woman beside me was still weeping and taking quick breaths. She seemed unaware we were moving toward the landing strip on the outskirts of the city. The stewardess knelt down to help her with her safety belt. *It's okay to cry about important things*, I whispered, rehearsing for the role ahead.

The nursing residence looked different from the picture in the brochure. *Are you sure we're here?* I asked the taxi driver. He pointed to the arched sign over the residence: Misericordia Hospital. The building was not the snowy white edifice of the school calendar, but heavy gray stone as forbidding as the convent that housed my piano teacher. Inside, a nurse asked my name and sent me up to the second floor with Eleanor, a second-year nursing student who was to be my *big sister*. She was neither as pretty nor as sarcastic as Joyce. Eleanor was fat and jolly. She left me in front of an open door to a room I was to share with two fellow nursing students, a bedroom smaller than the one I had shared at home. *See you at lunch*, Eleanor said in her cheery voice. While I carried in my suitcase of freshly sewn outfits, my roommates sat on their beds. None of us spoke. It had never occurred to me I would have to share a bedroom with strangers. In my imagination, I had seen myself writing letters at a desk before I went into the mountains and plains of Africa armed with Band-Aids.

The clothes in the suitcase were to do me until Father sent a box of warm garments for winter. *Those all your things?* one girl asked, eyeing the clothes I put on the vacant cot. *All you need is a uniform and some pajamas.* I decided to tell Father when I phoned on Sunday not to mail the box. We each had a metal locker like those in the high school gym. I rummaged in my suitcase to show them the housecoat Mother had embroidered with an orange tiger-lily, the emblem of Saskatchewan. The girl who had not spoken giggled. A bell and a voice outside interrupted to tell us it was lunch time.

We went down to eat without exchanging another word, not even introductions, queuing up for a buffet from steaming trays. Nonetheless, we stuck together, as if old friends. My roommate's big sister came over to welcome us. Her little sister was Delia, and the other roommate, who had commented on my clothes, turned out to be Gladys.

Gladys stood as tall as my father at five feet ten inches. Her eyes bulged like a guppy's, seemingly kept in place by the supporting frames of her large glasses. I worried what would happen if she took them off. She wore her dark hair pulled tightly into a pony-tail, exposing ears with drooping lobes. I thought of African men with heavy earrings in *National Geographic Magazines*, but Gladys wore no jewelry except a large-faced watch.

Delia was round and pink, with light brown curls circling her face. Her smile was all dimples and rosy cheeks. Shy and buxom, she would sigh for no apparent reason and her bosom would heave as her face flushed. She appeared about to burst into tears or smiles, whichever got the upper hand. My roommates made me think of a starving cat stalking a plump and flustered bird.

Do we get desks? I asked, remembering the sparse furnishings in our shared room. *They're in the study room*, Delia pointed. Gladys methodically spooned lunch into her mouth. When I asked if anyone brought hot chocolate to our rooms at night, Delia looked frightened, and Gladys shrugged. Once we had finished a raisinless rice pudding, we climbed back to the second floor.

The bathroom beside our bedroom was shared by everyone in the hall. I felt relieved to be alone in there and not to worry about saying the right thing. With its claw-foot bath and high-seated toilet, the bathroom shut out the world, but no key sat in the lock. I squeezed the bath plug between the floorboard and the door, wedging it in with the toe of my shoe. The room seemed tainted by the person before me who had forgotten to flush. At first I crouched over the toilet without touching the seat as Mother had taught me to do, but then, exhausted, I collapsed onto the cold wood. The sound of my peeing seemed to fill the air for everyone to hear. In my first privacy since early morning, I struggled against tears and the lump in my throat. After I had absent-mindedly pulled the toilet chain dangling from the water box, I saw a small sign taped to the wall: *Plugged Do Not flush.* Its message, orchestrated by rattling pipes and running water, sucked back my tears.

Gladys and Delia sat in silence on their cots. *I wonder where we get our nursing uniforms?* I asked, forcing a smile. *They give them to us,* Delia giggled. Gladys shook her head, apparently dismayed. I wondered what I could do to make her like me. Her guppy eyes followed me around the room, although her head remained still, and I tried without success to resist looking back at her. Before I could impress her with my friendliness, a high-pitched voice penetrated the hall: *Toilet's overflowing!* Delia and I peered out to see water leaking from under the bathroom door. *Weren't you just in there?* Gladys asked.

On our way to afternoon class, Gladys suddenly told me she was twenty-five years old. *My parents booted me out,* she said without expression. I imagined a large boot striking her narrow hips as she rose through the air, holding onto her eyes to keep them in their sockets. *I'm seventeen,* I told her, *but I'll be eighteen in three weeks, and my parents wanted me to stay home in Regina until I married.* Delia giggled her way through telling us she was twenty-one, an only daughter of elderly parents in Gimli. She had never worked, not even as a babysitter, and she told us her brother would always be a baby even though he was born two years before she was. *Down's syndrome,* Gladys said.

In the classroom, eighteen women stood up to tell their names. My heart beat in my throat when my turn arrived. *I'm Elizabeth Anne Simpson, with an e on the Anne, but my family has called me Betty since I was nine,* I confessed. I could feel the heat rising into my hairline. Miss Calvich said, *Betty is fine,* as she nodded for me to sit down. Pointer in hand, she let us know germs scurried about on bathroom floors and hid in bedroom mattresses, too tiny to be seen but powerful enough to carry illnesses from one room to the next, strong enough to cripple the unwashed and their innocent victims. If we forgot to wash ourselves or our patients properly, we had to take responsibility for the sicknesses that moved from one bed to another, marching on to residence cots before they invaded the city at large and possibly the country.

I began using squares of toilet paper to open the bathroom door after I had scrubbed my hands, ending each day with the knowledge I had not yet been felled by germs because God was generous. I cringed to think of the times I had put my high school texts beside the school sink when I brushed my hair or had dropped my scribblers on the cloakroom floor while I stuck my arms in coat sleeves. Thinking about bathroom doorknobs I had once grasped with a bare palm made me consider my right hand with disgust. I would have to wait for Christmas holidays to bathe properly because none of us were allowed to soak in the bath unless we let the other students come and go at will. *You'll get the hang of it,* Eleanor comforted me, but she never explained how.

Do you mind? Gladys asked. *Miss Calvich says it's not ladylike.* When I looked bewildered, she accused me of whistling. Delia and I were writing letters and Gladys was reading a worn bible she kept on top of her locker. Writing home, I had been lost in thoughts of family. *Sorry.* I clamped my teeth together, just as someone called, *Lights out!* The door opened and a nun flicked off the single bulb that hung from a yellowing cord attached to the high ceiling. No one in our house except Lynne opened a closed door without tapping first. A nun's habit formed a silhouette against the hall light. *Pull the blind,* she cautioned, irritation in her voice.

Even in the dark I realized she was talking to me in my bed beside the drafty window. *Now!* she commanded; *men on the street can see right up here.* When she snapped our door closed, we could hear her in the next room. As silence descended, I lifted the blind again and looked down onto the sidewalk where a single street lamp cast its light. Just as I was about to comment on the absence of men and the nun's mistake, Gladys reached a long arm over my shoulder and shut out the night. Under my itchy gray blanket and starched sheet, I saw three days stretching out between now and Sunday's call home. I understood why people had nicknamed the hospital *The Misery*.

I'm the only Protestant in the class, Dad, I protested. *It's the same God*, he assured me. *We put needles in oranges to learn how to poke them into people's arms, and I'll have to poke real skin soon. What if I get a fat person and can't find the right spot?* Father listened but was not willing to send an airplane ticket. *You'll be here for Christmas*, he said. *We have to go to church every single day, Dad; there are so many sins around here you wouldn't believe it.* After a pause he said, *You can always find sin if you look hard enough.*

Mother put it more clearly: *You've made your bed, and now you have to lie in it; it's part of being grown up.* After she listened to my complaints, she offered a solution: *Find ways to like it.* I tried again: *One of the nuns is really pretty, Mom, but she won't be able to marry or have babies ever.* I knew no greater omission existed in my mother's mind than not being married with babies. *And there's a building next to us with girls who have to give their babies up for adoption when they're born.* I felt her disapproval across the phone line. *I know it's true, Mom, because one girl waved when I crossed the street in my uniform, and her stomach reached the curb an hour before she did.* Mother laughed, *Keep your knees crossed, dear.*

When Father couldn't hear me, I confessed my biggest worry. *I have to bath someone in a few weeks*, I told her. The phone line went silent. Finally she spoke: *It'll be just like bathing with your sister.* Surging through me was the same hopelessness I had felt when I tried to convince her to let me go to university. *It might be a man, Mom.* She passed the phone back to my father. *Make do until our next talk*, he said in a voice so soft I wondered if he too was having second thoughts. *We'll have a better picture by then.* With his familiar *Bye-bye dear*, the distance between us grew long and empty. I could hear the prairie wind, vast as night itself, hinting of winter.

Gladys was dressed and sitting in the dark when I woke up to the morning bell. Delia seldom got ready in time to eat before we crossed the street to the hospital. I had to coax her out of bed as her insecurities were compounded by an inability to fold proper bed corners. At night she visited a boyfriend in hospital. He had left her for another girl, but when he had his appendix out, the new girl disappeared. Delia figured her former beau would soon appreciate what a loving woman she was. Gladys's audible breathing let us know her opinion of Delia's hopes.

In the cold bathroom I hurried before the next girl tapped on the door, brushing my teeth in preparation for another breakfast of gummy porridge and warm milk in a cold bowl. We had to eat vitamins as well, and gossip had it we would all grow muscular and hairy from taking them. The cutlery and metal chairs had cooled in the night, making our teeth, fingers, and thighs ache. I thought how Father would be listening to the radio and saying, *Pass the tea, Daisy*, even though he could reach the pot. Mother would be serving buttered toast while Lynne fretted about the seeds in her raspberry jam or imaginary creepers in the bottom of the milk jug. Grandma would be inhaling her tea with puckered lips, deaf to the slurping sounds that drove us all mad. In the residence dining room, I used my teacup to warm my hands.

My favorite room in the hospital was the one where I had expected to feel least at home. The wooden-walled chapel where we said our early-morning prayers after breakfast was a quiet sanctuary. I learned how to make the sign of the cross, genuflecting with the other girls to make myself invisible. At meals some hands gestured toward foreheads and breasts before they reached for food, although the girls often chatted while they did this. Being close to God didn't have to be as serious as I had guessed from my music teacher in the nunnery. In the sacred silence of the chapel we could hear each other breathing. Its peace made possible the endurance of another day.

The smell of stuffy patients' rooms made me want to gag. Gathering up soiled bedding and replacing it with laundered sheets meant rolling sick people to one side of the bed and then the other. Sometimes patients didn't want to move and, worse, sometimes I was put on the men's ward. I felt awkward manipulating men's bodies while they stared with eyes full of misery or mischief. Nothing had prepared me for pushing men around. When I coaxed them from one side of the bed to the other, I heard my voice adopt an official tone. It seemed too personal, somehow, to roll a man over with soft words. With women I felt a surge of kindness rather than a sense of intrusion, but with men my small arms made a mockery of my pushing at them as though I was physically superior. When I rushed to discard old sheets and gather fresh ones, I passed Delia in the halls, her cheeks flushed as she scurried between the laundry room and beds, her plump chest heaving with sighs. When her boyfriend left the hospital and disappeared into city life, Delia's twice-broken heart shattered her faltering confidence. Gladys, meanwhile, behaved as though she had never met either of us, going about her duties without a word of complaint or a smile, her long arms rolling out patients and sheets like cookie dough, not seeming to differentiate between cotton and flesh, male and female, suffering and comfort.

We gathered in the classroom to learn that girls with swollen stomachs and absent husbands in the building next to ours were examples of their own mischief and God's wrath. Miss Calvich told us we were not to despise them, although no one had intimated feeling this way. Her tone implied they deserved as much but *for Christ's sake* we were to think kindly of them. These immoral girls had often done something *unmentionable*; they had wanted to kill the baby before it was baptized. I wasn't clear if Miss Calvich thought it was okay to kill the baby after it had been baptized, but I doubted it. The unmentionable act could not be expressed in words but it could be drawn on the blackboard.

Miss Calvich drew a pair of crossed sticks and labeled them *knitting needles*. She explained with much flailing of her pointer how girls had jammed these needles into the very place they had already violated. She tapped at the knitting needles and the diagram of a woman's reproductive system. *The needles might miss the womb and puncture a vital organ*, Miss Calvich went on to explain, and then the bedeviled girl might kill both the baby and herself with one mistaken thrust. Apparently the girl deserved to die for making a pleasure of sin, but the problem was the baby. Death before baptism was a sin greater than giving birth outside marriage. Earthly life was insignificant. The soul's destiny was a nurse's concern, and it could not go on to paradise without a priest's last rites.

The point of this lecture was *choice*. There was none. If a nurse had to choose between saving a mother's or a baby's life, she must choose the baby's because the baby could then be baptized in preparation for a life hereafter even though in its life right now it would be an orphan. *Wouldn't it be better to let the mother live?* I asked, thinking of my father having lost his mother and baby sister to the flu epidemic, leaving them with no one to wash their clothes or cook their meals while their father worked on the railroad.

I realized too late that students were expected to listen in silence. *Your point?* Calvich asked, her voice tense. *The mother could have another child while she was looking after the ones she already had*, I answered. My voice rose into the hush: *No one's going to miss a baby they haven't met.* To further the obvious, I began to explain that my father loved my mother more than a new baby. Calvich stared at a spot behind my head until she found words to break my train of thought: *Human weakness has little to do with God's plan.* My throat tightened at her reference to my father's love as a weakness. *Does the Lord decide the mother dies or do the doctors?* I asked, forgetting to raise my hand. Calvich ignored me and spoke to the class: *Good families concern themselves with eternal life and not with earthly pleasures.*

Honestly, Dad, I pleaded, *the girls poke knitting needles up their you-know-what to kill their babies.* Father's voice betrayed an awkwardness. *Your mother and I don't know anyone who's done that*, he assured me. *I figured that much, Dad, but it doesn't mean it doesn't happen.* My father agreed, impressed I had an opinion. *Maybe in New York*, he conceded. *No, Dad*, I argued. *Right here on the prairies.* I didn't have the heart to tell him Calvich thought him weak for loving Mother. *I told her you wouldn't want Mom to die for some baby we didn't know.* Father told me not to worry my head about this nonsense because Mother wouldn't be having any more babies at her age. I knew he meant I should talk to Mother about something else so as not to worry her.

I could still have had another baby if it weren't for my operation, Mother said, her voice defensive. *Miss Calvich thinks we're a bad family because we're Protestants.* Calvich had not referred to my religion, but I thought it would add to the reasons why my parents might consider me better off at home. *Well, she'll just have to meet us,* Mother answered. Father came back on to say our time was up. *Bye-bye dear,* he said, passing the phone back to Mother. *Are you still wearing your hair in braids under your cap?* Her question reminded me she and the nuns had something in common – a desire to keep my hair off my face. *I look like the woman on your Dutch Cleanser can, Mom.* She was quick to reply, *You're British dear, not Dutch.*

As September passed into October, I spent weekend afternoons with my boyfriend, who had driven from Regina to attend classes at the University of Manitoba. My eighteenth birthday had gone unnoticed except for warm gloves from Grandma and a wool cardigan from my parents and Lynne. While I poked needles into oranges, checked corners for germs, made beds around strangers, and glanced furtively at pregnant girls next door, an awareness formed that I might have to continue with classes until Christmas. After a week of giving and removing what we called *bad pans* and taking the temperatures of real patients, the first-year students were about to begin bathing patients. I was assigned my first bath on the terminal ward. The word *terminal* brought up pleasant thoughts of a place to catch a plane home.

My first bed held a girl whose chart said she was twelve years old. Since she was the same age as my sister, I felt comfortable. I had bathed with Lynne and scrubbed her back with soap, until Mother said I was too old to bath with anyone. The girl seemed happy to see me when I walked into the room with towels and a bowl of steaming water. She looked well enough to go home. *That's a big bandage on your head,* I said to her as I rolled her onto her side to untie her hospital gown and cover her discreetly. *I had something growing behind my ear and it made me dizzy,* she explained in a voice as light as a sparrow's song. Because she felt neither fear nor pain, I was not afraid. *You'll soon be as good as new,* I told her as I exchanged crisp sheets for rumpled ones.

The meaning of the word *terminal* sank in slowly. *Dad says I'm as bald as a baby's bum,* she laughed. *Do your parents come to visit every day?* I asked, suddenly fearing the answer would be *no,* and remembering we were not supposed to ask questions but to listen. *They run the grocery store in Selkirk,* the girl told me. I remembered too that we were supposed to call patients by their names, according to the chart. *Well, Marilyn,* I echoed Grandma, *there's nothing like a good bit of food to keep a body going.*

Gregory doesn't allow us to laugh and chatter with patients, Eleanor said, appearing from nowhere with a laundry cart. I realized she was supervising my first day of bathing, although no one had warned us our big sisters would be there. *Who's Gregory?* I asked. She was the mysterious Mother Superior who headed the school and whom none of the first-year students and few of the second-year students ever saw. Although she kept herself cloistered, she had the final say over the nuns who taught us and all the student nurses beneath them. *Even the doctors hop to her tune,* Eleanor told me. I hadn't yet spoken to a doctor and had almost forgotten they frequented hospitals, although I saw them asking questions at the work stations before they came onto the wards. One had winked at me in the hall.

As it turned out, happy chatter would have been wasted on my next patient. I looked down on a woman whose body was as small as a child's, but wrinkled and brown like an apple left too long on the kitchen windowsill. She appeared to be a grandmother from a neglectful family. Each time I tried to edge her over while I tackled the bottom sheet, she groaned and whimpered. I tried whispering words of comfort, but she stared from unseeing eyes. When I saw Eleanor standing beside the open door, I rolled the woman onto her side, and her mouth opened slightly to free a small stream of putrid-smelling saliva. Her moans tore into my conscience. *I can't*, I said to the pillow. *It hurts her.* Eleanor was on me like a hawk. *You have to*, she said.

I picked up the wizened yellow arms one at a time. They were skinny and puffy at the same time, as though someone had blown air between sagging skin and brittle bone. I stroked her with warm, soapy water, and she whimpered. I began singing a lullaby, *Oh little baby don't you cry.* Eleanor reminded me singing and whistling were not allowed. *She can't understand you anyway, she's Russian.* When I uncovered one of her legs, I saw that where her ankles should have been were swells of flesh reaching up to her knee. *It hurts her*, I pleaded with Eleanor. Unexpectedly, she left the room and, grateful for her absence, I covered the old woman with a blanket and whispered cooing sounds to let her know I was there but not touching her. Eleanor returned with a nun in a white robe and pleated cap. She took firm hold of my hand, lifting it off the old woman's face. *Is there a problem here?* the nun asked. *She's too sick to move*, I explained. The nurse looked astonished: *No one is too sick for a clean body and bed.* I hung my head in shame before I spoke: *It's wrong, I can't do it.*

I found myself bounding down the hallway, out the wide doors where stretchers lined the halls, and into the cold and sunny Winnipeg autumn. I ran until my heart pounded in my head. A man in a red plaid jacket had taken up pursuit. He questioned me when I stopped to grab my cap, held in place by one stubborn bobby pin that kept it from falling to the sidewalk. *Is there an accident?* I had forgotten the rule about never going onto the street in uniform. One white stocking bunched around my ankle, having freed itself from my garter belt. *Go away*, I panted. A large yellow cat brushed against my arm when I leaned on a wooden fence, and I caught its warm body in my arms. Around me I saw houses I had never seen before. *Should have a coat on*, the man said, turning away.

Delia smiled with forlorn eyes when I entered the lunch room. She passed me the remains of her meal, cleaning her spoon on her nurse's apron before handing me her cutlery too. Gladys spooned milk custard into her mouth, one measured teaspoon at a time. The other girls in our class had stopped eating to stare. *How can you eat?* I shouted, looking around at the faces of many girls I had never spoken with except to comment on food, classes, uniforms, and boyfriends. *People are dying in here*, I told them. Gladys broke the silence: *What did you expect?*

I didn't expect to be the first student to meet Mother Gregory. *You will represent the college as Freshie Princess next month.* The words sounded silly coming from the mouth of an elderly woman dressed in folds of gray cloth and sitting behind an enormous desk in a dimly lighted room. *The vote was unanimous*, she continued. Gladys had said she hadn't voted for me. The nursing college was affiliated with the University of Manitoba, and each fall a girl was chosen to represent the faculty at the Freshie Ball. The highlight of the evening was a beauty contest at which girls paraded in ball gowns in front of a panel of male judges to the whistles and hoots of the male students.

I was surprised a nun would approve of girls showing off their bodies and wardrobe. *I have freckles*, I told Mother Gregory. *God marks us in his own way*, she answered before she dealt with the real reason for my being in her office. *Nurses never wear their uniforms outside the hospital.* I wondered if anyone else had ever felt tempted to ask how she thought we crossed the street from the residence to the wards. *Yes, Mother Gregory.*

I was taken off the terminal ward and assigned to fractures and breaks. *It's a man!* I whispered to Eleanor. *Well, men break their legs too*, she said, frustrated. Reading my patient's chart, I felt annoyed that he had broken both legs. If he'd broken one leg he would have been able to hop to the bathroom to wash himself and then hop to the chair while I changed the sheets. *You don't have to look while you're scrubbing*, Eleanor whispered, passing me a pile of clean sheets. *It's not bad after the first one. They're all the same.*

As I bathed the patient, he unnerved me by getting what the nurses called *a hard on*. Even though I kept the sheet over him as instructed, revealing only bits of his body at a time, I saw the cotton rise in a pyramid of white as I soaped his thighs. I knew I wouldn't be able to tell my parents or my boyfriend about this experience. The patient's face grew as flushed as my own, and we both seemed incapable of discussing the problem. I left the room to ask Eleanor what I was supposed to do. *It'll be gone by now*, she grinned, cocking her head in a way that made me think of my mother. Eleanor was right, at least momentarily. Once my hand with its warm and soapy cloth attempted to lather anything below the patient's chest, the angle of the bed sheet changed again. My boyfriend had convinced me a hard on had everything to do with love and nothing to do with fear, but I felt unloved and fearful as I dripped soap suds on the floor. *If the doc slips on that you'll be in trouble*, Eleanor chastised me.

At a second audience with Mother Gregory, she told me, *You mustn't think of patients as men and women. Your duties as a nurse are to keep sick people comfortable and clean.* I wondered how often her arthritic hands had roamed around the private parts of a man's anatomy. *The other girls find things easy that I find hard*, I explained. Mother Gregory seemed to read my mind. *Your work will bring you closer to God. Trust in Him and remember despair is a sin.* She nodded toward her door to tell me the interview was over. *The residence is your home now.* At the thought of living with this permanent unease and my own incompetence, I picked up my apron and sobbed into it. When she didn't come around the desk to hug me, I wiped my nose on the hem. *The class will be disappointed if you ignore your role as Freshie Princess.* When our eyes met, she spoke so softly I had to strain to hear her. *When you're tempted to avoid your duties, remember you're doing the Lord's work.*

I entered the cauldron of moans and odors on the wards and reached back into my mind to Sunday dinners with my family or singing in the annual musical with my school friends or summer afternoons at the beach with Corbett. I thought too of the stories Mother had told me about her life as a teenager. My mother's dream as a farm girl, ordering her clothes through the catalogue, had been to work at Eaton's department store. Her fantasy had seemed pathetic and ridiculous to me, but it remained a fond memory to her, a wish unfulfilled until her middle age when she had phoned Eaton's one Christmas to offer her services. The manager had told her the store didn't hire women over forty. She combed her hair, dabbed lipstick on her cheeks and lips, and took a bus downtown. When she returned with a triumphant smile, she told us, *The manager said I don't look anywhere near forty*. Father took me downtown to buy Christmas wrapping and ribbon from the counter where she worked. In spite of my embarrassment, I had to admit to a certain pride when I saw her looking young and happy as she talked to customers.

Eaton's became my imaginary refuge after difficult days in the hospital wards. I gathered enough coins to phone long distance and request a job interview. I told the store manager I was moving with my parents to Regina and, having finished grade twelve, I would need a job. The manager said the store would probably need extra help over Christmas, and we agreed I could work in the men's sock department once I had been in to fill out an application form. If my work was satisfactory, he said, I would stand a chance of continuing.

I have a job at Eaton's in Regina, I told Mother on our next Sunday call. She was quick to match my determination: *You're Freshie Queen*, she reminded me, having almost finished my ball gown. *It's Freshie Princess, Mom; the winner is Queen, and that won't be me*. After a pause, she tried another tack: *You're throwing away opportunities, Betty. Just throwing them away with your silliness, spoiling your chance to have a good livelihood*. Her impatience made me hesitate.

Give it till Christmas, Father repeated, sounding sorrowful, but kind. *If you still feel the same, we'll talk then*. I could hear Mother in the background telling him, *She's going back after Christmas*, and I knew then I would have to get used to her resentment. In that moment I realized I had no intention of becoming a nurse. Instead,

I would have to pay room and board to my parents, as I had done over the summer, and share a life with them rather than making one of my own. *You may just be homesick*, my father encouraged. *I'll send your train fare if you feel the same by mid-November*, he promised. I had been demoted from the airplane to the train, a mild rebuke in comparison to being denied coming home at all.

Father sent money for the night train. I had heard Mother repeating that I was going *straight back after the holidays*, raising her voice to reach me. Without hanging up the phone, my parents had talked to each other while I waited. *I think she'll be home to stay awhile*, my father had said, his voice straining to be gentle and yet convincing. *Then she'll go straight to work the day she arrives home*, Mother had answered, her heels clicking on the linoleum floor as she left the room. *Two weeks*, my father had called after her with an authority I had never heard him use with her: *She can have two weeks to rest up in her room.*

The train took forever to arrive on the windy platform of Winnipeg's station, and even longer to leave. Corbett stood with me in the night chill. He understood my feelings of alienation. *Same as university*, he said. An hour before midnight, the engine's smoke stack filled the air with a white cloud, and I kissed him good-bye before climbing aboard to wave from the window. With each stop at a prairie town, lights twinkling over an expanse of darkness, grain elevators looming against the night sky, an unspeakable grief overcame me. I had disappointed everyone.

When dawn awakened the prairie, I hadn't slept. Frost had petrified the remnants of harvest, and a dust of snow covered the farmlands. I had no idea where Manitoba had ended and Saskatchewan had begun, but an hour before noon the landscape opened onto the recognizable outskirts of Regina. Father stood waiting outside the station. I could tell by the downward arch of his neck that his mood was solemn. Grandma stood beside him in her ankle-length muskrat coat, its oriental collar up around her ears. She seemed an aged version of myself. Left with no place to make a life, she returned now and again to stay with my parents. I understood at last what it had meant to her when she lost Grandpa to the horror of his illness in Misericordia Hospital nine years before. Who I wondered would ease the terrible and precious moments in the lives of the old and dying if nurses refused their duties as I had done?

Dad! I called out as I stepped from the train toward his smiling eyes. Our frosty breath rose and mingled in the air, marking us as family. With her absence, Mother was having her final say about the personal affront of my father's sympathy and my cowardice. I'd been gone eighty-nine days. I had left my girlhood behind and returned home a woman of eighteen years, defeated, disgraced, and grateful to my father for a second chance.

A FOREVER KIND OF LOVE

I WAS fifteen and social convener of my grade ten class when Jim asked me to the Christmas dance. Outgoing and popular, he owned his own car. One of the girls whose locker was close to mine said, unsmiling, *Some girls get all the luck*. Mother was pleased because he was student president. I liked him because he played center on our basketball team and introduced me to kissing, our closed lips soft on each other's mouths. Abandon was shortlived: I had to push his hands away when they swooped toward the front of my sweater. *Everybody else is doing it*, he complained.

Two months into our going steady, Jim came to my door with a friend. When I asked them in to say hello to my parents, the other boy came into the light. A pair of gray-blue eyes locked onto mine, eyes that made my brain numb and my stomach prickle, eyes like an owl's, large and solemn. *This is my best buddy, Corbett*, Jim called over his shoulder. Corbett swung the door shut between us to break the lock of our gaze. When he opened it again, a blush colored his cheeks and I recognized him from the tennis court where I had once caught sight of him in the distance: *You're Janet's boyfriend*.

The breadth of his shoulders made me feel fragile, as though confronted by a wall of maleness. I had to will myself to look into his face. *Same height*, Jim told me as he returned to stand beside his friend, *Six foot two, eyes not blue.* But Corbett and I were lost to him. Although I had not yet heard Corbett's voice, we had entered an unspoken pact that would map our lives. *Nope*, he finally said in the monosyllabic way I would grow accustomed to. *No what?* I asked. *No Janet*, a grin crossing his chiseled face.

Sitting together in Corbett's customized 1950 Ford on the following Tuesday, he asked me to marry him. I nodded, wondering why he hadn't known the answer already. Life's possibilities seemed endless when our gazes caught and held. My parents couldn't see it. *We're in the same grade but he's almost seventeen and he goes to Balfour Tech*, I told them. They were unimpressed. *We're older than Romeo and Juliet*, I coaxed. Mother came up with her usual logic: *Those were different times, dear. People married early because they died young.*

Jim and his buddies followed us, hanging their heads out Jim's car windows, yelling and beeping the horn while Elvis crooned "Don't Be Cruel" on the car radio. Corbett and I sighed, knowing perfect love had to go through the trials and tribulations of an imperfect world.

At home I described Jim's childish stunts. *Things change*, Father said, laughing. *Maybe Corbett will be following your next boyfriend's car some day.* Father apparently hadn't realized our relationship was as permanent as sun on prairie wheat, as splendid as soft snow on evergreens. I was stunned to discover my father's blindness. *There'll never be a next boyfriend*, I told him.

Corbett's mother and father had saved money to build a new house by living in a trailer without a bathroom. After watching Corbett's eyes glow in the telling, I was surprised to be shown a small square house with a picture window, sitting on a street with other small square houses in the east end of Regina. On the outside, the wood siding was painted pale green. On the inside there was no paint at all because the walls had not yet been put up. Insulation filled the spaces between the two-by-fours. Their telephone sat atop the phone book on an overturned barrel. Boxes took the place of cupboards for the pots, dishes, and cutlery. *We did everything but dig the basement*, Corbett boasted. *Mom'll paint the kitchen turquoise when we get the drywall up.* He seemed dazzled by all this promise. A blond Pomeranian stood at the top of the basement stairs, wagging her tail. *Trixie's not allowed in here*, Corbett told me. I thought about Boots wiggling her bum to greet us, rushing up to leap on my bed as soon as my parents left for the evening. *Maybe your mom's worried about her stepping on a nail*, I suggested. *Nope*, he replied, *she thinks Trixie'll get the floor dirty.* I looked down to see sheets of plywood.

Unlike my dad, Corbett's father seldom spoke. Unlike my mom, his mother filled the silent spaces with incessant chatter. Corbett's parents seldom spoke to one another; she told her husband what to do, and he ignored her. He could build or fix most anything. She produced endless batches of butter tarts, controlled the family's finances, and kept one eye on the neighbors' comings and goings, the other on her only child.

Corbett's mother never scolded him for his failure to finish an essay or French vocabulary lesson. She never told him to shape up as Mother told me when I fell behind. Corbett received a gold pin each year for outstanding grades in subjects other than English and French, and she blamed the teachers and his father for his weaknesses. She made certain I understood where Corbett's failing originated by revealing that his father had written home during the war to say he was sick with the *flew*. His home-room teacher told her Corbett would do better in French and English if he spent less time on his car. Mrs. Corbett scoffed at this: *I didn't figure how French would help a kid build anything, and I told her so too.* I figured they must have known something about parenting that my parents didn't know. They had produced a perfect son, whereas my parents had raised three imperfect daughters.

Every lunch hour Corbett left Balfour Tech High and sped over to the green and orderly residential area where Central Collegiate took up a city block. His lilac Ford with white leather upholstery, hand-rolled by his mother and stuffed with cotton batting, rumbled out front. Only he and I knew about the hidden button that controlled the door. *Open sesame*, I would whisper as I ran toward his car.

You shouldn't kiss your boyfriend in front of the staff lounge, my Physical Education teacher told me. *I didn't*, I blushed. *I'm just warning you*, she said. Mother told me she would pack my lunches again, as she had done in grade nine, if I would stay in school to eat them. I told her it was too stuffy to be inside all day. Running through the school corridor after lunch with Corbett, I chanted to myself words appropriate to the lavishness of my affections: *I would lie and cheat and kill for you*. Thoughts vague and dreamy interrupted the drone of teachers' voices. Emotions soared and attention wandered. The school bell startled me from my imaginary world, freeing me to slide again into the warmth of Corbett's front seat.

In the car, on the beach, or at parties, Corbett and I always sat within each other's touch. Even when we were apart we were attached by the tentacles of our feelings. We drove home from the summer beach nodding our heads to the Everly Brothers or Johnny Mathis. We sang along with "Wake Up Little Susie" or crooned to the whole notes in "Blue Velvet." Corbett's hand slid up my summer skirt and rested on my bare thigh, my head nestled on his shoulder. We believed we had always been moving toward each other. A pair of dice swung from the rear view mirror. I had knit them from black angora wool, attaching white felt circles to the six sides. Hidden inside was a penny for good luck and a secret love note, *Betty and Corbett Forever*.

Central Collegiate and Balfour Tech competed for the city's basketball championship. Jim played center for my school and Corbett played center for his. The future seemed to rest on Corbett's winning the initial leap for the ball. Surrounded by his friends, Jim argued with the referee and strategized with teammates. Corbett, solitary, gazed up at me in the gym balcony, then went on to shoot the winning basket.

His hair wet from the shower, Corbett said, *We'll have to wait till I'm twenty-one for a wedding cuz Mom'll have a fit*. I figured our secret plans to marry gave me permission to ask the question everyone had been asking. In a moment when the lilac Ford was in motion and his eyes were not fixed on mine, I looked up at his chiseled profile and understood the meaning of my grandma's expression, *heart's content*. After a deep breath, I asked, *Why are you called "Corbett"?* He shifted gears and listened for alien sounds in his motor. *It's my name*, he said, patting my knee to indicate the point was settled. *It's your last name*, I persisted; *no one calls me Simpson.* I could see from a corner of my eye he was smiling. *Who'd call anyone Simpson?* he asked, his mock baritone covering an awkward playfulness. *Mom named me after some rich guy in the States, an uncle called "Melvin,"* he said. I heard his familiar intake of breath, his response alert when asked to explain himself.

Melvin Robert Corbett's bulk and concentration made him appear slow until I grew aware that his hands and feet landed exactly where he intended them. *Slow and easy wins the race*, my father would say, and Corbett proved him true. He could turn a somersault in air with no hands and land exactly as he had begun. He could catch a buzzing fly or a floating butterfly without doing either harm. *You could use your middle name*, I suggested, thinking of the symmetry I was creating between my father and future husband. *I'm not a Robert*, Corbett shrugged. A small white spot appeared on his reddened cheek before he told me what I already knew: *Mom and Dad call me "Mel."* I didn't volunteer the opinion that shortening Melvin did nothing to erase the sissy from the sound.

Mrs. Corbett told me his grade two teacher had called him *Melvin* when she read out names on his first day of class. *He stood up and told her, "I'm Corbett,"* she grinned. *She went 'n' failed him cuz he wouldn't sit down till she agreed.* Mrs. Corbett had waited for her son's sixth birthday before putting him in kindergarten, and his failing grade two explained why he was two years older than I in the same grade. His teacher may have taught him he could wait out a woman's resistance. He was as adept at interrupting his mother's monologues with monosyllabic answers as he was at sinking the basketball.

The one thing I did keep intact was my virginity. We had time enough to discover each other in inches. *You can have lots of pleasure without getting pregnant*, Mother said, a coquettish smile on her lips. *I told your father I would get pregnant if he couldn't wait until the weekend, and that's how your younger sister was born.* I was horrified at the idea of my parents' indulgence, having never thought much beyond their frequent kissing and hugging. *You're a grandmother*, I huffed. I figured my parents hadn't realized how old they were, and I retaliated against Mother's nonchalance. *Do you have orgasms?* I asked, slouching against the deep maroon of our couch.

Having just learned the word at school, I was hoping she would ask its meaning. *Usually I do*, she said, not looking up from her sewing, *but it's not always important.* She was mending a ripped pillow slip, snaking the needle in and out along the bleached cotton seam. *Orgasm or not, I still like the closeness.* We might have been talking about chicken feathers for all she cared, and I wondered if I'd learned the wrong word for such a significant event. Possibly she knew some other momentous tidbit I had not yet discovered.

She put three pins in her mouth and then removed them to speak again. *Mother!* I cried before she could say another word. But even with my hands pressed against my ears, I could hear her ask, *Is there anything you want to tell me?* Before I could say no, she continued, apparently unstoppable, *If a woman doesn't have an orgasm, the man's not doing it right.* It occurred to me the woman married to my father must be a freak of some sort. I was certain none of my friends' mothers were crazed with lust. She seemed to think she was teaching me something common, like how to flip pancakes when the oil sizzles. *You're too young to be so serious*, she added. *You told me sex without love was wrong*, I accused her. *I haven't said anything to contradict myself*, she answered. Mother tied off the thread, snipped the needle free, and shook out the pillow case. *Time for you to set the table; your father will be home soon.* I detected a little more bounce than usual when she turned to leave the room.

No one's too young for love, my visiting grandmother added, coming in from the back garden, her apron full of green beans, cheeks flushed. For a moment I feared she too might have had an orgasm but the thought so overwhelmed me I clenched my mind against it. My heart always opened to Grandma's perpetual trust in love, her capacity for forgiveness, her willingness to share our joy. When Joyce had upset our mother by walking down the aisle pregnant, Grandma had said, *A wedding is a beautiful thing.* After talking with Mother, I could never again rid myself of the idea that perhaps even Grandma's devotion to Grandpa was suspect, that it may have had something to do with what they shared after Grandma took her long hair out of its wound-up pigtails.

My parents are really weird, I told Corbett as we drove into the countryside. He told me he'd caught his parents half undressed downstairs, *doing it against the basement wall.* We were silent awhile, uncomfortable with parents whose sex drives didn't know when to shut down. After a while we began to snigger, and our laughter grew until I held my sides and Corbett smacked the dashboard. Soon we were soaring along with the radio: *Looooooove is a many splendored thing.*

Corbett's eighteenth birthday fell on a Friday night at the end of May in grade eleven when my parents would be bowling and I would be babysitting Lynne. If I baked two chocolate cakes, piled them on top of each other with dark icing plastered between, and then smothered the whole thing with yet more chocolate before I planted eighteen candles in the top, Corbett and Lynne would be over the moon. I planned to save two huge pieces for my parents. Mother would protest, but with her delicate nibbles she'd manage to clean her plate. I planned to give Lynne an enormous slice to take to bed because it was Mother's rule that *no daughters of mine take food to their bedroom.* My sister would eat herself into a stupor and fall asleep thinking she had outsmarted our parents.

While the cake baked, I bathed with perfumed soap, toweled off, and patted my curves and crevices with talcum powder bought with babysitting money. Finally I dabbed on the Evening in Paris perfume Corbett had given Lynne for her tenth birthday. *Did you use my perfume?* she called out. *Of course not.* Corbett sniffed the air as he took off his jacket. *You smell like a perfume factory*, he said. *I told you*, Lynne piped up from where she was watching television. I went upstairs and scrubbed behind my ears and along my inner wrists before I iced the cooling cake.

· After Lynne and I sang *Happy Birthday* and finished our first pieces of cake, we dug into the remainder with soup spoons. I rescued the platter just in time to save a sliver for each of my parents and a sizable second slab for Lynne. *Just hide the plate under your bed, okay?* She loped up the stairs, cake in one hand and a glass of milk in the other. We could hear her hang a towel over the doorknob to hide the light from the keyhole. *I'm just going to tuck her in*, I said nonchalantly. Corbett thumbed through *Life* magazine, listening to Elvis on the turntable.

Upstairs I brushed my teeth until they sparkled, tiptoed into Mother's closet, ripped off all my clothes, and wrapped myself in her pink chenille housecoat. As I passed her dressing table, I covered my mouth with scarlet lipstick. The turntable arm was set to repeat the record. Elvis sang about lonely arms and tender kisses. Returning to stand before Corbett, I swayed to the music then dropped Mother's housecoat to the floor. He hadn't looked so surprised since the day the muffler fell off his car. *Happy birthday!* I whispered. The trilight and the space between us embarrassed me. Total exposure differed from the surreptitious meeting of hands and body in the dark comfort of the Ford.

You're beautiful, he said, hushing me. It was easy to keep swaying my hips to the music if I looked at the ceiling. I lost the tempo when a chunk of cake slipped from his knee to the floor and onto the magazine. He rose to his majestic height as I grabbed Mother's housecoat and sprinted off, tripping over the hem. I heard something rip as Corbett stepped on the sash that lagged behind me. *I feel sick*, Lynne whimpered when we sped past her closed door and into my parents' bedroom.

One evening's knowledge of the power in a woman's body

made me feel dangerously invincible. Elvis's voice rose and fell, slow and sensuous, from the living room below, telling me I was *so young and beautiful*. I didn't notice when Corbett took off his clothes, but in the silence of the needle returning to begin the record again, we heard the garage door bang shut and Boots scratching on the other bedroom door to get downstairs before she was caught. Footsteps at the back of the house coincided with the click of Lynne's door and Boots scrambling down the steps.

Boots has been on the table, Father said, as Corbett and I sat up in their bed, still as death. *She has chocolate cake on her leg.* We could hear the tap, tap, tap of Mother's high heels on the linoleum floor. *Are you up there, dear?* Corbett grabbed his clothes and ran into the bathroom while I stumbled over a tangle of sheet and fell into the closet. I had barely zipped my jeans and pulled my sweater over my head before the bedroom light snapped on. Corbett had dropped his underpants in the doorway, and the tip of Mother's black shoe touched them. With a quick breath, she turned, colliding with Corbett as he barreled out of the bathroom. They apologized with the polite gestures of two people who had reached for the same dinner bun. By the time I got downstairs, he was closing the front door and Father was lowering the lid of the record player. I watched him stoop to pull Boots off *Life*. She was licking chocolate from the face of Marilyn Monroe.

I returned upstairs to get my hairbrush, closing the bedroom door softly as Lynne whispered, *Were you guys having a party?* When I came down, my parents were seated and silent in their separate corners of the living room, two boxers listening to Corbett's motor rumble down Elphinstone Street. Feigning innocence, I asked Mother to brush my hair and sat on the rug in front of her, my back leaning into her knees. *Is that my housecoat tie?* she asked as we both took in a strip of pink chenille on the staircase. *I didn't do everything*, I said in my best adult voice. *Tch!* she said with disgust. Before she'd finished brushing the tangles from my hair, I heard muffled sounds that made me wish I had a Kleenex to share with her. I wondered if she would be scarred by discovering her daughter was a slut like the neighbor on our block who'd been caught making whoopee with the furnace repairman. *Fixing the heat, all right*, my father had said.

As I rummaged in my pockets, my mother's small muffled sounds rose to a breathless soprano. When I turned, I saw her eyes were brimming with laughter. She clenched a hand over her mouth to contain her merriment, her small diamond twinkling among the tears as they rolled onto her cheeks. Pushing herself away from me, she held her sides as though fearing she would topple over. Father's face dissolved into a ridiculous grin before he began laughing along with her, holding onto the television to support himself. When they'd finished making fools of themselves, my father asked me what perfume I'd *poured over my head*. That set them off again, and they bobbed around the room like a couple of chickens, raising and lowering their heads, clutching their sides. *You'd better tidy up our room*, Mother told me, attempting to be stern. *What's going on?* Lynne called, padding down the stairs, encouraging Boots to come out of her corner.

Are your parents still mad? Corbett asked when he phoned on Saturday to ask if I had his underwear. I told him I had assured my mother we hadn't gone all the way. He didn't seem comfortable with my having shared our secret. At movies, skating parties or sports events, couples denied doing anything in private they didn't do in public. Corbett would neither confirm nor deny. He seldom spoke beyond monosyllables unless he was talking one-on-one, and then his topics focused on tools or muscles or mathematics. He was like a solid tree trunk amid fragile leaves; others rustled and fluttered around him.

Instead, Corbett spoke with his large and dexterous hands. He built his own bedroom suite: a set of drawers with crafted knobs, a night table, and a hope chest for me. Never idle, his hands moved from furniture to car to boat to basketball to flesh. On weekends, when he wiped grease from his fingers and climbed out of his overalls, we danced the polka at barn dances. Fiddlers sat their hats on empty chairs, as sweat rolled off their faces and ours. At school dances, we waltzed through the reflection of the mirror ball while a student crooned hopefully into a microphone.

Once Corbett drank too much beer and threw up on my shoes. His mother frowned, fearful he would go *right into the gutter* like his uncle had. My father worried instead about *telephone poles and cars coming the other way*. Chocolate milkshakes were my favorite drink, even at Christmas when my parents urged me to try a bit of wine. *Just a glass can be nice*, Grandma said. *Were you ever drunk?* I asked my father. *Once*, he admitted, before telling me not to be too hard on Corbett, *as long as he doesn't drink too often*. I reminded him of his motto about a person getting *two chances and then to hell with them*. Father smiled when I quoted him.

For Sunday dinners at Corbett's house, Mrs. Corbett cooked up sugared parsnips, mashed potatoes, and roast beef, ending the meal with her heavenly butter tarts and tea made milky from the Carnation can. She always agreed when Corbett asked if I could join them; having me there meant he would stay home. Corbett and his father cleaned their plates before Mrs. Corbett had filled hers, and I would remember my father's admonishment, *Your mother's not here yet, so don't start*. I learned to eat in two shifts – the right half of the plate with Corbett and his father, the left half with his mother.

My teenage album bulged with pictures of Corbett. In one I'm reaching up and failing to circle his biceps with my two hands as we pose by Wascana Lake. In another he's on the basketball court, arms rippled in the moment of releasing the ball on its way through the hoop. Physical strength was often the topic at his dinner table; Corbett's father believed might was right. My lack of brawn and height, like my love of reading books, was a sign of endearing inferiority. My role was to appreciate Corbett's superiority, and his role was to protect me while I did so.

I realized something essential rested on my being small boned, thin, and from a family of girls. Since he was big and all-knowing and I was small and ignorant, his needs seemed more important than mine to both of us. Because I imagined he protected me from the threats of the outside world, I felt safe in the closet of my femininity.

The only thing Corbett seemed to fear was the moment my focus on him wavered. *Don't wear those things*, he complained, pulling my sunglasses off my face. *I can't see you*. When I explained it was hard to read in the bright sun without them, he said, *Why read that stuff?* Reading anything other than directions was a waste of time in Corbett's house, although his mother read the obituaries in the newspaper every day. *You just never know*, she said.

Corbett and I plotted our weekend escapes from parents by driving into the surrounding farm land and out to the prairie lakes. My parents had always shooed me and my sisters from the house because my father didn't want us *moping about when the sun's shining*. Corbett's mother had never grown accustomed to her son's independence: *Remember, you're all I've got*, she'd call after him. A generation earlier, her own in-laws had asked when she would have a second child, and she had scolded them for minding her business. The year after she told me this story, she asked Corbett if he'd like a baby brother. *Sometimes my mother's crazy*, he said, shaking his head. *It would be fun to have a brother*, I told him, remembering how Mother had wanted five children, recalling Grandma's story of my uncle's loneliness when her first-born died of smallpox. Corbett cut into my thoughts: *We'll have the kids, not my mother*, he said. *Ten, for our own basketball team*.

I took Mother to Corbett's grade eleven workshop open house where we pretended to be interested in tools, work benches, and motors. We met Corbett's father on the school steps. I introduced them, and each parent grew self-conscious. Mother forgot to speak, looking flustered and blushing. She had always told me she had trouble *thinking up things to say*, but I had never seen an example of this at home. Corbett's father went young and soft around the forehead as he took off his hat and nodded. He brushed his raven hair back with an awkward hand before he stuck it out to shake hers.

I had always been proud of my mother's porcelain skin, her big breasts and coltish legs, but at that moment I understood men's feelings for her were more awkward than my own. I wanted to tell her she was too old to blush, but I felt a little sorry for her. Mr. Corbett moved furniture when he wasn't building their house or fixing his car, and his long body had the supple muscles of a young man. *My goodness he's handsome*, Mother said, astonished. *You blushed*, I accused her. Just to make certain she knew where her heart belonged, I told her about the time he put a cricket in the bottom of my purse and didn't tell me until I touched it and screamed. *Dad would never do anything that mean.*

The men in Corbett's family were silent and brawny whereas the women were bossy and chatted up a storm. In late summer Corbett's aunts, uncles, and cousins would organize picnics at the beach. The women packed up food and the men gassed up their cars and brought their fishing gear. We ate sandwiches stuffed with roast beef, forked up homemade fruit pies, and washed dishes under an outdoor pump. These were happy times when his parents and relatives reminisced, forgiving each other for past feuds. The mood was contagious, inspiring Corbett to chase his mother with a garter snake until she peed her pants.

After Corbett and his father had built a boat, his parents spent summer Sundays at the beach. His mother would roll her mending into a bag and sit on the shore while his father fished in the middle of the lake. They were prairie folk who had built their world with their own hands. Sometimes Corbett and I would go with them to ride in the boat and cook fresh trout over a campfire. When we stayed for a weekend, Mrs. Corbett put my sleeping bag on one side of the tent and Corbett's on the other. His father snored in the middle. Father was watching from the window when Corbett dropped me off. *You looked just like my own mother when you turned toward the house*, he said. Mother's voice trailed off to a whisper when I arrived home too late to join them for Sunday dinner: *Your father and I will have to wait for you to get over your infatuation with Corbett's parents.*

Mother raised canaries as a hobby, sucking sound from her tongue as the birds fluttered in the light after she removed their night cloth.

She anticipated the moments when newborns cracked their shells and popped out beak first, changing from wet balls with stick legs to fluffy chicks. Recently, though, she had begun to worry because her female was laying unfertilized eggs. *Does that mean the male's not doing it right?* I asked. *Oh no*, she was quick to reply. *He's doing his job, there's something wrong with her.* I asked her how she knew it was the female's fault. *Oh, it's always the female*, she said. *Our apparatus is more complicated than theirs.*

She bought a new female and put it in with the infertile one where the male could get access to both. Soon the new female was building a nest. On Saturday morning while I was pouring milk over my cereal, I caught Mother lamenting over the cage. She refused to allow me to peek over her shoulder, whispering from a tight mouth, *It's okay.* By the time I had vacuumed my bedroom and carried my sheets to the basement laundry, I saw the new female alone in her cage and the male in an adjoining one. Mother told me that during the night the pregnant bird had pecked the feathers off the infertile one, killing her. *It's the way birds make strong families*, Mother assured me. Images of a torn and dying bird troubled my dreams that night, my face reflected in the pleading eye of the doomed canary. When I told my mother about seeing my face in the bird's eye, she grew impatient. *Don't be silly, dear. She's buried in the garden.*

In summer I worked as a nanny for a Jewish couple with two children. The wife spent weekdays at the lake with the children and me, and the father joined us on weekends when Corbett packed up his tent and came to the beach as well. The five-year-old copied me by brushing her hair with her head bent down to her knees. *One hundred strokes for dark shiny hair*, I would tell her, and we would brush until she grew tired. *Come on, let's get a move on then*, she would say to her cat, just as I had said to her, just as my mother had said to me. Locking herself in the bathroom while she dressed, she would call out her need for *some privacy*, mimicking my request of an hour before. Moments later she wandered out naked. *Where's my bathing suit?* she asked.

Reading to them in their twin beds and tucking them under their quilts, I imagined my own babies, five open faces above five pretty quilts, eyes as big as Corbett's and skin of porcelain like my mother's. I read the children stories with colorful pictures of talking farm animals and we created animated wooden toys by attaching puppet strings. The three-year-old boy hung onto my arm when I read about monsters, ghosts, and pirates, certain that any minute they would climb out of the pages. I could never understand why he wanted to hear the same story over and over again, especially when, as his mother said, *it frightens him half to death.*

Meals became more organized and the cottage tidier the hour before their father arrived from Regina. He would press thumbtacks into envelopes on the bedroom door, each with a child's name and a quarter inside. If the children left their parents sleeping in the morning, they could put their coins in their piggy banks. If they banged on their parents' door or yelled over walls that did not reach the ceiling, they had to leave their coins untouched. The boy was heartbroken every time he banged on the door and had to open his palm where his coin sat sweaty and warm, allowing his father to put it back in the envelope. The mother would protest, *Oh let him have it this time*, but the father would say, *He'll never learn the lay of the land that way.*

One summer Sunday I swam out to an island while Corbett listened for knocking noises no one else could detect in his engine. After I'd been swimming awhile and grown breathless, I seemed no closer to the island and rolled onto my back, sun warming my face. As I had learned in a lifeguard course at the community pool, I brought my knees up frog-like and my hands above my head before I drew them down and shot forward in one smooth motion, my body a canoe and my limbs the paddles. When I had pulled myself shaking and exhausted onto the island, I imagined being stuck there while Corbett worked on his camshaft, oblivious until darkness fell.

My anxiety was interrupted by the sight of a pair of arms that rose and fell in a rhythmic crawl toward the island. *Howdee*, the swimmer called as he rose from the water. *Jeff*, he said, catching his breath. *Betty*, I smiled back. After he'd warmed away his goose bumps, we swam back together, stroke on stroke. I thought of Mother's description of her early evening turns around the skating rink with Father: *I just keep falling when I don't hang onto his arm.* The resentment I'd harbored over her apparent helplessness floated away as I crawled through the water to a stranger's rhythm.

Corbett's head was under the hood when I took my swimming friend over to introduce him. *I almost drowned*, I said, waiting for Corbett's exclamation of relief. *Hi there!* Jeff greeted him when Corbett turned his expressionless face toward us. Straightening up to his imposing height, he nodded before he stuck his head back under the hood. *Were you showing off?* he asked, annoyed. I stood beside the open car door toweling myself and wondering if a man's impatience was the price a woman had to pay for being loved. *Just filling time*, I said. *Stick around*, he told me. I knew his idea of ownership extended to me, as well as his car. He reached over and enclosed my small hand in his large one to keep me nearby.

Driving back to the city, Corbett pulled off when he saw a small car at the side of the road with a skinny man bent over the open hood. A young boy, pale and frightened, came over to where I sat with the window down. I asked him to sit with me while Corbett went over to peer under the stranger's hood, but the boy shook his head and ran back to sit with his mother. *We're giving them a ride home*, Corbett said when he returned to the car. I watched the woman get out of the front seat, a baby in her arms. Tubes attached to a small tank were clamped to the baby's nose, his stick-like arms still. They squeezed in beside me while the boy climbed into the back seat with his father. Their accents made it difficult to follow their story except to know the man was looking for work and the baby hovered between life and death. We dropped them off at their rented house on the corner of a busy street. Corbett's charity to a fellow motorist in distress lifted the chill of his earlier encounter with Jeff.

Corbett had a summer job delivering milk. On his first morning, he helped the others load their trucks. When he reached his own truck, he discovered the men had driven off and left him to load his crates one by one. The next day he filled his truck and waited idly by for the others to load before he could drive his truck from the back of the garage. By four o'clock he was short fourteen dollars and aware that his scholarship in mathematics didn't prevent people from shortchanging him.

He moved to a job at the local pool where he met an articulate boy with a crippled body. Between them they took on the world: one with disabled limbs and a flexible vocabulary, the other with arms built for safety and a penchant for silence. Joey's mother said no one had ever been able to make her son relax during water therapy. After school began and into the winter, Corbett encouraged the boy to float away from his frailty each Thursday evening at the pool. They returned from these swims with rosy cheeks and bright eyes. In March of the following year the boy's chest collapsed with coughing. Mother recalled that my paternal grandfather had lost his life to a coughing disease after his wife and their baby had died. I knew better than to mention this to Father; his silence about his parents' deaths was impenetrable. *Joey died*, Corbett said, voice cracking, hands in his pockets.

Corbett planned to study engineering at the University of Saskatchewan, a three-hour drive from Regina. Disappointed by my parents' refusal to allow me to go to university, I concentrated on Corbett's future instead. I told his parents over Sunday dinner what I'd heard about Engineering students who drank themselves silly and stole girls' panties from residence. At the round chrome table in the family kitchen, his mother stopped talking, and I saw my chance: *Architecture would be perfect, and there's a school at the University of Manitoba.*

Built a house already, his father agreed, realizing he had prepared his son for a profession. *He can build libraries and hospitals too*, I encouraged. *You could live with your aunt and uncle in Winnipeg*, his mother joined in, although we all knew she was wondering how her son would survive the distance. *His father thinks*

Corbett will find another girlfriend at university, Mrs. Corbett told me while we washed and dried dishes. She often used her husband as an excuse to say what had never come into his mind.

I had sewn a new dress from fine black wool and worn it to Father's year-end banquet and ball at the Hotel Saskatchewan. Mother was recovering from her hysterectomy, and not yet able to dance. Having made Father proud that night with my high heels and upsweep, I slipped the dress on again for Corbett, watching him flush with appreciation when I changed from a freckled teenager into a woman with strap shoes and red lipstick. The flow of hormones hit Mrs. Corbett like a monsoon when we dropped by. *Nice dress*, Corbett said to her, his eyes on me, his voice asking for his mother's approval. *She sewed it herself*. His mother examined my seams and darts. *Take it off*, she said. *I'll fix the zipper*. I stripped down to my underwear and sat on the edge of her bed in a borrowed housecoat.

If you ask me, I think you should have your first time in my bed, not in the back of a car, Corbett's mother announced later in the kitchen after I had zipped up the dress. As she spoke, she examined her sink. *Who asked you?* Corbett shot back, his shaggy blond hair hanging over his eyes as he lowered his head. *Where's Dad gone?* Corbett asked before his mother's tears could rebuke him. She pointed toward the garage: *If you're wanting a smoke, he's down to his last one*. Then turning toward me as though we were conspirators, she said to him, *Betty and I will get some when we buy groceries*.

I hobbled around the grocery store, my feet burning from the high heels, while Mrs. Corbett filled her cart and ticked off each item on her list. When we reached the cash register, Corbett's mother commanded the attention of the line-up by pointing to a red package of cigarettes behind the counter: *du Mauriers*, she said, *for my son's girlfriend here*. She nodded in my direction, although she had never seen me with a cigarette. My mother had said she *wouldn't stand for it* when Joyce had tried smoking, and I knew her opinion hadn't

changed for me and Lynne. Even Grandma thought it was a habit
of *fast women.*

Corbett and I were separated for the first time when I flew off to
Misericordia Hospital. Two weeks later he drove to the University
of Manitoba to begin his five-year course in Architecture. In
Winnipeg he moved in with his father's brother and his aunt, who
was nine years older than the uncle. Taking a younger husband was
a difficult choice to understand until I met Corbett's stunning aunt.
When Corbett and I returned to their house unexpectedly one
evening, we noticed lipstick on his uncle's forehead. They told us
they were hoping to have a baby and were considering adoption as
the months passed into years. We wondered what was wrong with
Corbett's aunt, but we were too shy to ask.

Corbett came home to Regina over the Christmas break, a
month after I had quit nursing, and when he returned to Winnipeg,
he moved into residence. Away from everything familiar, he ignored
assignments, skipped classes, and watched television in the common
room. His only pleasure seemed to be the company of a law student
who shot off one-liners that made Corbett laugh. During this time,
the postman brought letters from Winnipeg, the envelopes adorned
with elaborate drawings surrounding my name and address. The
crayoned picture of ribbons twisted into a bow suggested a present
was hidden inside. I tore open the flap to find nothing, a sign of
Corbett's trust in my knowing without words how he felt.

Father was impressed by the next envelope, which bore an ink
drawing of a shopping mall with a wooden bench and shoppers
strolling in the foreground. We all laughed when one arrived decorated with a cave man, his red hair fanning out from his massive
head. He wore a loin cloth over his private parts, a club dangling
from his long arms and resting on a bulbous knee. Before spring,
an envelope carrying a delicate leaf came, its many veins fanning
out from the center. It was followed by an abstract painting, angular
lines in red, yellow, and blue. Mother liked best the one with a

three-layered cake on it, candles burning in blue ink to celebrate our third anniversary.

During Corbett's mid-term break, I flew to Winnipeg on money saved from my new secretarial job. Corbett had been waiting in the arrivals section for three hours. He seemed withdrawn from the world around him, anxious for the term to end. Three weeks before his twentieth birthday in late May, he returned to Regina, saying he had quit university and wasn't going anywhere again. By then I had completed a night course in shorthand and typing and had acquired the single most helpful skill I could offer him. My high school friends were away at university and, with nothing else to do at night, I had studied hard. The other students called me *the brain*, sarcasm in their voices.

Corbett turned twenty-one in the spring of 1961 and we married on June 24. I was nineteen years old and had lost my virginity in my mother's Morris Minor a few months before. Corbett had phoned the next morning. *You sick or something?* he asked. I was surprised he should wonder. *Must've hurt you or something to make you bleed*, he worried. I remembered reading about a culture in which townspeople checked the bed sheets to verify the bride's virginity. *What are you smiling about?* Mother asked as I hung up the phone.

In 1961 people planning to marry had to be tested for syphilis. I underwent a physical examination, comforted that the doctor was an old man like my father, who had reached fifty. His wife and two sons beamed at me from a picture on his desk. While I lay with my feet in stirrups, he said, *It must be painful to be marrying such a big guy.* He had met Corbett the previous week when we had our blood tests. *Painful?* I asked. *Having sex*, he continued. *You're just a bit of a thing and he's built like a bull.* He washed his hands at the sink. *We're a perfect match*, I bragged.

The friend from work who blew her husband kisses as he drove off in his delivery truck organized one of my five bridal showers, and I had a trousseau party to show off the matching housecoats and satin nightie I had made for our honeymoon night. A woman whose husband had died of multiple sclerosis made my dress of white cotton eyelet. We talked of her widowhood as she tucked and pinned the material around me. *Do you miss him?* I asked. *His dying took a long time,* she told me, then abruptly changed the subject: *Your waist size is the same as your age, nineteen inches.* This measurement seemed less important than my weight. *I'm one hundred and seven pounds,* I told her. *Seven is a lucky number and it's the time of our wedding ceremony.* Although I didn't need more luck, it seemed to follow Corbett and me.

I tucked my arm through Father's and followed Lynne and a girlfriend down the aisle. Joyce was pregnant with her fourth child, and the size of her belly disqualified her from being a bridesmaid. The minister whose children I had babysat for years stood at the altar with Corbett and his school buddy. When the minister asked, *Who gives this bride to be married to this man?* my father responded, *I do.* My body trembled in anticipation of exchanging rings with Corbett, but suddenly the ceremony was over and the tenor was singing "Because God Made You Mine."

Corbett's father surprised us by crying over his sandwiches at the gathering afterward. When he brushed his tears away with the sleeve of his new suit, I understood why Corbett loved him. After four and a half years of courtship, we waved good-bye, now wife and husband, trailing cans and paper flowers behind our car. That night Corbett gave me a silver locket in the shape of a heart. Its tiny hinges opened onto a space for two miniature pictures. Our photos would kiss each other when I closed the locket. With the top down on our 1959 Volkswagen convertible, we drove west to see the ocean for the first time. Our vows had freed us to have uninterrupted sex every night for the rest of our lives.

During our honeymoon I read that Ernest Hemingway had committed suicide; I assumed his despair had been caused by his unhappy marriages. In contrast, Corbett and I awoke each morning in our attic apartment happier than ever. We loped downstairs to the bathroom we shared with tenants on the second floor and later brushed our teeth at the kitchen sink. They made jokes about our bathing together, and we were sorry they had to bathe alone. I put on the silver wedding locket every day when I slipped my engagement ring over my finger. Like Grandmother and Mother, I never removed my wedding band.

During our first month of marriage, Corbett and I made three firm resolutions. We would save money for Corbett's return to architecture using no more than three squares of toilet paper at a time and picking the toothpaste tube empty with a toothpick. We would travel to Europe after Corbett graduated and while my first pregnancy unfolded. And finally we would avoid all the errors our parents had made in raising their children. Corbett, a thriving and highly respected architect by then, would support all of us. *Our daughters will go to university too*, I told him. *Daughters?* he asked, grinning.

As an only child, Corbett considered his ambition to have ten children a reasonable one. We were young, healthy, and destined for success as architect and mother. No child of his would ever be as lonely over school breaks as he had been. However, I thought my mother's ideal of five children was more appropriate. I had discovered my own powers of persuasion in his appetite for love, and I was sure he would see my point of view once he understood how many children five actually were. Ten children was more like a Sunday school class than a family.

Everyone except Corbett accepted my decision to change *Betty* back to *Elizabeth*. I admitted my birth name was a bit formal for a twenty-year-old and modified it to *Liz*. *You can hear how wrong Betty Corbett sounds with all that "etting,"* I explained. *You're Betty to me*, Corbett said. *Listen to "Bett Corbett,"* I said, exaggerating the parallel *ett's* to defend my point. *Sounds right*, Corbett nodded: *It rhymes*.

Corbett and I walked to and from our jobs with the provincial government. He worked as a draftsman in City Planning, and I was secretary to the Deputy Attorney General. When this eccentric and amiable bureaucrat went into hospital for minor surgery, I sent a card to the *Deviation Ward*. From that day on, he considered me a woman with a brilliant wit. I never confessed I had no idea what the word meant, and had simply heard incorrectly when I asked someone's assistance in addressing the envelope.

Our office in the Legislative Building was shared with two other women assigned to answer telephones and deal with visitors. The receptionist, a woman of twenty-six, complained her husband hurt her when they had sex. Tears rolled off her face as she confessed how she detested the moment when, without warning, he climbed on top of her in the darkness. The other woman was a middle-aged mother whose vitriolic criticism of her husband embarrassed me. In response to my asking if she'd ever been happy, she described a Sunday morning when her husband bet he could put her big toe through one of the vents in the storm window at the end of their bed. *Who won?* I asked. *He did!* she shrieked, her cheeks reddening with a joy I couldn't understand.

I took coffee breaks with a woman in her forties from across the hall. Margaret had embarrassed me by offering congratulations on my wedding and telling me she had just been married too – for the fifth time. Other women called her *the queen bee* behind her back, a referral I thought had to do with her beehive hairdo. I agreed she was scandalous for her lack of commitment, but her multiple marriages intrigued me. To make the contrast between us clear, I told her I was *a lifer*, that Corbett and I had a forever kind of love. Father said I should think twice before I judged others. But from my position as Corbett's wife, I knew Margaret was a lesser person than I was.

Margaret had been eighteen when she married Cyril. Within weeks he'd gone off to war. *Blown to bits*, she said through tight lips. *Didn't even have a body to bury or a baby to hug.* I couldn't understand how a woman could love a soldier who wore a uniform like a milkman or a postal worker. It surprised me too that an immoral woman like her had planned to have children. Margaret didn't realize that a woman was better off with widowhood than leapfrogging from one man to another. The woman whose toe had been pushed into the window vent called Margaret a *nymphomaniac*. I looked up the word, and kept to myself the opinion that it was normal for a woman in love to have a *persistent desire for sex* when she was married.

I told Margaret I planned to help my husband through university: *I'm taking an English literature course at Regina College right now to prepare myself.* Margaret was quieter than usual and appeared to have tears in her eyes when we stepped from the elevator. She confessed her second marriage had been to a Russian-born geographer who was the love of her life: *Nikov did his Master's degree as a mature student, and even with the language difference he did well.* She mimicked his accent when she said *luff* for *love.* She told me she had typed his thesis on an old manual typewriter with keys that had to be *pushed down to Hades.* I asked her why she hadn't stayed with him, and she pulled her sweater around her shoulders and shuddered.

After the weekend, Margaret told her story over coffee: *Nikov complained about his back when we got home from our September canoe trip in the lakes up north.* Her hands fluttered nervously toward her lower back. *Damn doctors couldn't find the problem even after all their fancy tests, and it was almost Christmas before they found a tumor in his stomach, his stomach of all places.* Nikov had reacted to his terminal diagnosis by returning to Russia where he could lie down in his boyhood bedroom and be nursed by his old mother before being buried in an ancestral plot. Margaret had learned of Nikov's death four months later when his cousin had written about the burial and the sadness of his Russian wife. *His wife!* Margaret snorted. Shortly afterward, Margaret's son Nicky had been born. He was sixteen now, and I'd seen him pick her up from work once in a while. *I was his real wife*, Margaret said, *I've never doubted it.*

On Friday, as usual, Corbett and I visited my parents for deep-fried halibut, French fries, and soft ice cream from the corner shop. These weekly binges were my family's escape from my mother's frozen garden vegetables and canned preserves and our time to tell each other stories about the week. While dipping our fries into ketchup, I talked about Margaret. *Why didn't she go back to the Old Country with him?* Father asked. *I think he had another wife over there,* I told them in a hushed voice. He shook his head in sympathy. Mother piped in to say, *I bet he didn't ask her because she was only married in her imagination,* her tone reminding me she was suspicious of all things Russian. *Tea for everybody?* she smiled across the room. I figured Margaret must have known from the look in Nikov's eyes whether he was lying or not when he said he loved her. *Do you think he loved her?* I asked Corbett on our way home. *Maybe he loved them both,* he shrugged. *We only have one heart,* I reminded him.

After a little wine at the Christmas office party, Margaret's cheeks grew rosy and she confessed that her third husband, Ron, a realtor, had emptied her bank account to spend money on another woman. I couldn't imagine how a woman would be blind to a husband's betrayals. If she had thrown herself under a train, I could have forgiven her, but once she had found out that he loved not only her but also several other women around town, she had packed her bags and found a new life. *Some men are just led around by their you-know-what's,* Margaret said, laughing with the other women from the steno pool. *Men are like trains,* one of them joined in. *If you stand in the station long enough another one arrives to pick you up.*

Margaret must know how to make a man feel good, Mother said, spreading melted butter on our toasted buns. *How can a man feel good about a woman who's been doing it with everyone?* I asked. *It depends what he's looking for and what he's got to offer.* Mother barely concealed a snort of self-satisfaction, as I went back to reading the *Leader Post*. I knew Corbett would never fall for a woman who had slept with another man. I thought too that if a woman married a weak man she should learn how to keep him in line. When Margaret had tired of being alone and nabbed herself a man she didn't have to support, he had bounced his car off a concrete divider. *It's a good thing she wasn't killed with a young son to look after,* Mother said, later. They'd been married less than two years. Two of the secretaries remembered the crash, and one said she was lucky to have survived because her husband had been *dead drunk.*

When we next gathered for coffee, Margaret popped open the top button on her blouse to show me where the shattered windshield had ripped her shoulder. I couldn't help but wonder what her current husband must think when he saw her naked body tattooed by a former husband's careless driving. In the washroom later, I told my office partner whose toe had somehow connected her to happiness, that nothing seemed to break Margaret's heart. She paused to watch me scrub Gestetner ink off my fingers. *You seem like such a child*, she said: *Life has its ups and downs once you're on the far side of forty.*

In the same season that I had dressed up in my white cotton percale wedding dress, Margaret had slipped into a dark green suit and black heels to join her latest man for a fifth set of *I do's* at City Hall. There was something vulgar about her ability to survive her disasters. I wondered if Margaret realized she deserved her tragedies, just as Corbett and I deserved each other. We'd seen the movie *Spartacus* in which the heroine, hugging her baby, shows the child to her husband as he is dying on a cross by the roadside. At school I had learned these men were hung upside down, but for the purpose of their last conversation, Kirk Douglas was crucified with his head above his feet when Jean Simmons came to say good-bye. As tears dripped down my cheeks, Corbett put his arm around me. *Maybe she found somebody later on*, he suggested. *Of course she didn't,* I snapped.

I never saw Margaret again, but I thought of her when I was visiting Joyce and my three nephews to say good-bye before Corbett and I left Regina. Joyce's widowed mother-in-law had dropped by, and when Joyce asked if we'd heard about Marilyn Monroe's suicide, her mother-in-law was quick to answer. *It's about time*, she quipped. It occurred to me that widowhood, however unhappy the marriage might have been, shielded women from criticism tossed at divorcees and women who remarried. Hollywood was like literature; it allowed us to keep private our own lives while we peeked into the souls of those in despair, like Marilyn Monroe. Corbett was working under the car when I asked his opinion of the suicide: *Get me the big wrench, will you?* he asked. *Can't loosen this nut.*

At the University of Manitoba I took two jobs – secretary for Zoology in the morning, secretary for Botany in the afternoon. I typed up papers for eleven men who read over my shoulder, puffing on their cigarettes, and pleading that their papers would be published by some prominent scientific journal if I could get them done by mail time. They danced around one another's egos as my fingers flew over the keys. How foolish these men looked next to Corbett. His future was my reason for sitting under a cloud of cigarette smoke and daily pressure. Pain concentrated itself in the small of my back by three o'clock in the afternoon. To ease it, I slept an hour each evening, after I'd done dinner dishes and before my major work began. At eight o'clock I would begin writing Corbett's essays after reading aloud his assigned literature. If he had no essays due, I turned to sewing our clothes or preparing for the single night class I took each year for a degree that would take fifteen years to complete.

Doreen, the secretary in Microbiology, was only nineteen to my twenty-one. Her husband had proposed after she had agreed to have a shadow of down removed from her upper lip. She seemed to consider her almost invisible peach fuzz a small price to pay for the man she loved. Her smooth upper lip always spoke to me of the sacrifices a woman will make to nest with a particular man. I confessed to Doreen about shaving off all my pubic hair after a girl-friend told me her husband was driven crazy with desire by her hairless body. I confided too how grumpy Corbett had been to see me looking like a schoolgirl when he had married a grown-up woman. *A porcupine*, he complained after a week had passed.

We returned to Regina for the summer, and Mrs. Corbett bought us a television set after I told her we couldn't have one because Corbett's studies would suffer. The small black box created the first serious disagreement between mother and daughter-in-law.

Corbett compromised by returning the television before we went back to Winnipeg. At Christmas we traveled back again to Regina, snowflakes swirling on the highway, creating the sensation of riding into a funnel. His mother gave him a down sleeping bag of Egyptian cotton, one not designed to zip together with mine as our honeymoon bags did. With the money his mother had put in his stocking, Corbett bought me a new sleeping bag to zip onto his. At New Year's, he topped up her teetotaling orange juice with vodka. Without a slur or a stumble, she continued her evening as usual. In the years that followed, Mrs. Corbett commanded the attentions of her undemonstrative husband and son by wrestling five heart attacks to the ground. The one belief we two women held sacrosanct together was our faith in Corbett. If anyone criticized him, their judgment was seriously flawed.

News of the Cuban missile crisis came on our car radio in Winnipeg as we drove to campus in the fall of 1962. Kissing each other good-bye, we worried that the world would blow up before we met again. As we turned to wave, I saw his corduroys had shrunk in the wash, exposing his ankles. It occurred to me he could be vulnerable too. We were winding our way to the outskirts of Winnipeg in November of 1963 when Jacqueline Kennedy became a widow. Speculation about her husband's assassination and gossip about his rendezvous with women less gracious than she competed for our attention with the Beatles' latest recordings.

Unhappiness struck our family in the winter following my father's fifty-third birthday. Always happy to see me when I visited, Father remained in his chair, staring into space. *Why the long face?* I asked Mother. *He hasn't slept for a week*, she said, pouring batter into a greased muffin tin. After she had popped the tray into the oven and taken off her apron, she left the kitchen as though she had an errand in mind. Father sat in the living room like a man looking at something none of us could see. *You'll have to tell the kids, Bob, or I'll tell them if you want me to.* Mother rested her hands on his unresponsive shoulders.

They've let us all go. His words seemed to struggle free from the clench of his throat. *Even Edgar,* he said. The name sounded familiar, and I looked to Mother with raised eyebrows. *The family with bad hearts,* she prompted. *He fell over on the job,* Father reminded us, *and went right back as soon as he was out of hospital.* My mother translated for me. *Edgar's wife has had a bad heart for years, but Edgar had the heart attack, and he went back to work too soon.* I wasn't sure whether she was making a joke when she added, *He'll have a good rest now.*

Almost thirty-seven years, Father said into the space between himself and the front hall. The tremor in his voice was almost worse than his silence. We couldn't imagine his *not* going off to work in the morning. He had always worked at the General Steel Wares Company, never missing time except when, as a fifteen-year-old delivery boy, he had mangled his leg after a car hit his bicycle. *Maybe there's some mistake. What about Bermuda?* I asked.

I was reminding Father of the sales prize, the fact that his life had seemed to play out the rewards of loyalty – orphaned delivery boy in the streets of Winnipeg promoted to limping file clerk at a desk in the office, advanced to a managerial clerk with people working under him, and then sent off to Saskatchewan as Western Manager responsible for appliance sales across the province. He had won the Bermuda trip because he had sold more fridges and stoves than any other employee. A picture album records my parents dancing together in a hotel ballroom, my father in a yellow checkered shirt with the collar open and my mother in a blue dress with its full skirt caught mid-twirl as they move their limbs to the music. People watch them from a distance.

Once, perhaps for lack of anyone else to tell, Father showed me the $1,500 commission he had made on top of his salary in July 1953. I was twelve years old, my dog had just given birth to puppies, my bangs swept down over one eye, and I wore a long white shirt hanging over the top of my pedal-pushers. *It's just money,* I said. When he turned toward the garden shed, I saw his shoulders droop, and I wanted to call out to him about how proud

I was to have such a successful father. After eleven years in Regina, Father had asked to move back to Winnipeg where he could come home each night for dinner. Never having accustomed themselves to being separated, my parents had looked forward to waking up together again each morning and had settled into a house by the river on a crescent where the neighbors had manicured lawns and private gardens.

Father explained that all the men out of work had been hired shortly after he joined the firm. Together they had built General Steel Wares Company in Western Canada. These men were within sight of their pensions after decades of loyal service to the firm. Just before the dismissals, two men in their early thirties had taken over the company. In Toronto, they had set about to rid themselves of aging employees who would drain the company's pension plan. A dozen men who had been working with the company when the new owners were born had been sacked.

I'll write them a letter, Father said a week later, after he'd finished mowing the lawn. When he didn't receive an answer within two weeks, he changed his tactic: *I'll have to talk to them eye to eye.* It seemed almost normal for him to be kissing Mother good-bye and for her to be telling him to *drive carefully* and to *stop for tea* if he was tired. He made a U-turn at Sudbury when he decided my mother was right: instead of leaving him in Winnipeg, his employers would offer him a job down east, where the cities were crowded and the lots too small for gardens.

If your mother was surprised to see me, she didn't let on, Father told me. *She just took another plate from the cupboard and nipped some food off her own plate and some off your sister's. That's when I knew I was home.* A letter offering Father his job back had been waiting on his return. *How can I do it?* he asked, shaking his head. *They're not going to give the other guys their jobs back.* The offer caused my parents to switch positions. *We have to take care of our own kind*, Mother said.

Damn it, Daisy, my father reasoned, *it can't be right. They helped me, I helped them.* Mother responded with the same foreboding silence she used when any of us mustered a reasonable argument she couldn't ignore. But Father must have had his own means of persuasion because, in the end, he won her support, refusing to return to an office emptied of its loyal employees. When Father took out the garbage, Mother explained his decision as though she had thought of it herself: *They've all worked alongside each other for years.*

Father had never been a man of means but he was always a man of substance, and he had a chance to prove his worth when he filled out an employment company's forms and wrote exams for the first time since leaving school at thirteen. The employment company phoned to tell him his exam scores were the highest they'd seen in years and asked permission to tout his accomplishment in a newspaper story to encourage other men past their youth to take heart. I couldn't understand his upset when I read words praising his performance. His intelligent face peered back at me from the page. *It's his age*, Mother explained. I reread the number. *Fifty-three, isn't that your age?* I asked. His sigh was audible. Mother popped her head around the corner: *It's a secret when you're over forty.* She was smiling as though the family had begun to revolve around its own sun again.

After our second year in Winnipeg, Corbett and I took a summer break, driving our Volkswagen convertible around the United States – winding along the ocean roads of Oregon, sweltering in the desert of New Mexico, admiring the weeping willows and mansions in Georgia and the Carolinas. At Daytona Beach I fell asleep in the sun, and the motel owner's wife ran a vinegar bath to soothe my burn, cooing to me as my red skin touched the cool water. When we searched out the carriage houses of New Orleans, we saw our first stripper dancing on a bar in front of a massive mirror. *Look at the men's faces*, Corbett said. In Tennessee a white truck driver sat beside us in an air-conditioned restaurant and left a black man to wait in the hot cab. *Can we take him a Coke?* I asked. *You all mind your business*, the driver said without smiling. The incident cleared up a sign Corbett and I had puzzled over on a campsite pump in Florida: *Whites Only.*

As Corbett drove to the edge of the Grand Canyon, I memorized the names of the states in alphabetical order. He would never let me take the wheel, not just because he was smarter but because women didn't drive if their men were in the car. His grandmother had fought the government for lower bus prices for pensioners and won, but she always sat in the passenger's seat while his grandfather picked up speeding tickets. *Mom points right at oncoming cars,* Corbett laughed as though his mother's driving had something to do with mine. My mother had insisted on getting her driver's licence when I got my learner's. Thinking Mother's lessons were essential but nerve-racking, Father had said, *Your mother does the damnedest things behind the wheel.* Corbett's father regarded women drivers as a strike against manhood.

Each night when Corbett put up our tent in another scarcely populated campground, we slept in a haven of green canvas. In our transient homes away, we carried everything in the luggage compartment of our Volkswagen. While I cooked, Corbett took the motor apart, putting bolts and odd bits of metal on a blanket beside his toolbox. After an hour or two, he would return each polished piece to its place in the cavity behind the back seat. My incessant back ache disappeared after a few days on the road, and the car always purred after he closed the hood.

I was official map reader of the back roads we preferred to travel, often singing my father's car songs. Corbett never expected more of me than cooking, cuddling, chatting, and singing, as long as I didn't shut him out by reading, falling asleep, or wearing my sunglasses. *Your mouth fell open,* he told me after I nodded off. *Sorry,* I blushed. It was bad enough he patted my bangs down over my forehead each morning as I was waking up; I didn't want him to close my mouth as well. *Next thing you'll be snoring,* he grinned.

In our second year at the university, I was promoted to executive secretary for the Associate Dean of Science and enjoyed a lighter workload. Alone in a spacious office, I prepared a welcome for a distinguished nuclear physicist who was joining the department and was expected any day from Oxford. While I waited, I typed the associate dean's letters and studied for my night class.

Paul here, a young man said to me, his brown tweed jacket flying out behind him as he came up to my desk. *Here to see O'Connor.* I thought him a bit cheeky, a man in his late teens bounding into the office and forgetting to put the Dr. in front of my boss's name. *Do you have an appointment?* I asked. *Barker's the name,* he said, dropping his briefcase to the floor. The respected physicist was twenty-five, homesick, and waiting for the arrival of his girlfriend. After she joined him, we became a foursome for movies, skiing, and dinners together. *We're an odd couple of ducks,* Paul would say to me, laughing.

When Dr. O'Connor hired an assistant, we three moved into a new office designed by Corbett. I had a skylight over my desk and a great wooden door that slid along a track, rather as I imagined a castle door would do. To help explain his work to us, the dean took the new assistant and me into the bowels of the building to see the nuclear physics laboratory. We moved through concrete doors that normally barred outsiders from this charged world. Even with bright lights and white walls, the windowless subterranean space was claustrophobic. I sensed the ominous force of radiation.

The assistant told me he was saving pennies in a piggy bank to buy some new *boobs* for his wife. He also said he wished she had a figure like mine. *Can you believe it?* I asked Corbett, sounding indignant, feeling desirable. Corbett lowered his voice, making me strain to hear him: *What's he talking about your tits for?* Our vocabulary had not included the word *tits* before. *Tell him to bugger off,* Corbett said, turning up the radio.

At a party, I told this story to Corbett's closest friend in architecture. *You wouldn't say "fuck" if your ass depended on it,* he responded. I kept my eyes on his to make my point that *anyone can swear, but it takes imagination to say something meaningful.* I'd read this sentiment somewhere and when Corbett's friend smirked, I added a bit of my father's wisdom to it: *Maybe people should swear less and think more.* He turned away, laughing. *You're full of shit,* he said. *Fuck you,* I called after him.

In our top-floor apartment, Corbett sat at his drafting table when he wasn't eating or sleeping. He was seldom sick, but during a week when he had the flu, I put together one of his assignments. For this task, asking students for what was called *a design plate* on the concept of space, I had pasted a boy with his hand in the air. Far above I pasted a ball. The space between hand and ball caught the eye. It came back with *Commended Retain* on the bottom, the highest mark, and Corbett was beside himself with affection for me. Other nights I sat against a cushion at the foot of his table, reading aloud the books from his English class or mine. He listened attentively, roaming across sheets of paper with his sharpened pencils as we progressed through the short stories of John Steinbeck, confused by *The Red Pony*, saddened by *Of Mice and Men*, and shocked by *Cannery Row.* When I read Ayn Rand's *The Fountainhead*, I wondered how other students could be so drawn to its selfish heroine. Corbett and I never discussed these works, assuming we each saw the same scenes, heard the same dialogue, and recognized the same thoughts. He said talking was a waste of time because *everybody wants to hear themselves.* The scientists who tried to persuade the dean to raise their budgets seemed to prove his opinion.

We ended our evenings with long walks, occasionally stopping at a local restaurant, The Salisbury House. Tired and hungry, I hoisted myself onto a stool while Corbett ordered hamburgers. *Give me some of that burger of yours?* a man said to Corbett one night. *Nope,* Corbett said, not looking up. The muscular stranger grabbed Corbett by the jacket and, bouncing like a boxer, pounded Corbett's chest and arms. The waitress dialed for the police as I scrambled over the counter to grab a fork from the cutlery tray. While the men's fists collided, I leaped onto the stranger's back and clung there like a squirrel, trying to jab his eyes. He flicked his head, bellowed, and swung his fists against Corbett until sirens wailed. *Sorry 'bout that,* he said, stopping abruptly. Corbett took his extended hand of apology and, as he did, the stranger's fist came up for one last blow. Corbett ducked and smashed his fist into the man's belly. Onlookers cheered. *Some big guys see other big guys as a challenge*, the police officer told us when two uniformed men dragged the bully into the back of their van. Holding his chest with one arm and me with the other, Corbett limped home. *My little tiger*, he grinned, licking blood off his bottom lip.

The next day Doreen and I swam in the campus pool as we often did over the noon hour. She called me later in tears and asked me to meet her in the bathroom. *I'm pregnant and bleeding*, she said, her voice frightened. When I got there, her eyes had narrowed as though wincing from pain. I called her doctor while she lay on the secretary's couch. *Elevate her feet, and keep her still*, he advised while we waited for the campus intern.

My doctor thought by your voice you were a middle-aged woman, she told me. *He said to thank you for keeping your head.* I was thrilled to know my voice belied my freckles and said so, but Doreen could not be humored. She had lost the baby. *I'll never get pregnant again*, she mourned. It was to be the first of six pregnancies and the only one that miscarried, but her girlhood was gone forever. *Why don't you get pregnant?* Doreen asked, three months into her second pregnancy. *I intend to*, I told her, *the day Corbett graduates.* I didn't tell her I had no need to hurry, that no one in our family had ever miscarried. Although Grandma had birthed two stillborn babies and lost her five-year-old first-born, that was two generations ago when doctors didn't know much.

The wife of another architecture student began to forge a sweet and awkward friendship with me. Frances, or *Frane* as we called her, worked as a secretary on campus to support her husband, Francis. On paper, his *i* and her *e* separated their identities; in bed, his inability to love her often separated their flesh. Roman Catholic and refusing birth control, Frane gave birth to a son before their second year on campus ended. The baby had slipped into the arms of a nurse as the taxi door opened at the hospital. On a frosty afternoon just before Sunday dinner when our husbands were in third year, she collided with a bus on her way home from buying milk. The ambulance driver told me she had tried to save dinner as she lost consciousness. *Turn off the oven or the roast will burn*, she had called up to the blue winter sky. At parties, Frane would grow maudlin with drinking, wrapping her slim body around anyone willing to fill the space her husband left behind when he chatted up other women. *Thought I might as well marry a rich girl as a poor one*, Francis told us, laughing. The only daughter of generous parents, Frane was momentarily steadied by their frequent visits.

At the beginning of fourth-year architecture, the class left on a field trip to Chicago. Corbett asked me to drive him to the station and then follow the bus to the edge of town. After he had climbed aboard, he pushed his way to the back where he could flatten his nose against the glass and make silly faces. I tucked the Volkswagen behind the bus until it reached the outskirts of town, where I waved good-bye and made a U-turn. My energy quickened with an unfamiliar appetite. Corbett and I had never been separated in four years of marriage, and I didn't know what a woman was supposed to do in her man's absence. It was a time of sweet loneliness and abundant reading. Corbett's intense eyes came in and out of my imagination, and I would hold the image before I let it fade, keeping comfort and freedom in balance. I read under warm blankets, lingering over certain passages without hurrying to switch off the light. Afterward, when I looked back on those seven days, they seemed the gold dust of memory.

We all slept around in Chicago, except Corbett, a student told me a week after the bus had returned. Her short curly hair stippled her face like chocolate icing. She called down to me from where she had draped herself over a seven-foot partition that separated two art exhibitions, her head, arm and leg dangling above my head. *I asked him what kept him faithful, and he said he loved his wife.* She laughed as if his sentiments were ridiculous. *I've parked the car to pick Corbett up*, I said, reaching for a toehold in our conversation, *but he seems to have driven off without me while I was in the washroom.* I phoned home. *Thought you'd left the car for me and taken the bus,* he said; *told my friends I had you well trained.* When I passed the partition again on my way toward the bus stop, the interior design student was still dangling from her post. *He would be an architect even if you didn't help him,* she called out as she swung down to the floor. *He'd just have to work as hard as the rest of us.*

Shut your eyes, Corbett ordered me over the Christmas holiday. I thought he would kiss me; instead he steered me to a space between the kitchen and front hall in our newly rented house where there was an opening to the attic. *Okay,* he allowed, smiling when I exclaimed at wooden skis in the rafters of the crawl space. His gifts were always thoughtful, but mostly we were frugal. I responded by sewing him a pair of gray woolen pants with burgundy silk lining to keep the itchy wool away from his skin. Neither of us asked for much, saving our money for our trip to Europe when he graduated and I became pregnant.

But at the end of fourth year, the Volkswagen began to make noises Corbett couldn't fix and he bought a new Mustang with leather upholstery. When I took a turn at the wheel, he slipped his hand alongside mine and pressed his foot on an imaginary brake. *I've driven since I was sixteen,* I said. *You're still a woman,* he told me. In his presence, I had begun to feel as though I was wearing my old felt hat. It had blown off my head when we stepped from a ferry in Northern California. Although it dried in the sun, its fit had changed. From the outside it looked the same, but once it was on my head, I had the sensation my brain was being gently squeezed by a large pair of hands.

For those women who reached adulthood on the Canadian prairies before the 1960s, career success in a female hinted at an unattractive woman who couldn't find a man. By the time the feminist revolution made news in the middle of the decade, re-evaluating the six years I had devoted to Corbett's career was too exhausting to consider. He graduated in the spring of 1966 and our future was fixed. We had even named the beach cottage we intended to build: *Corbett's Corner.* My reward waited in the five children who would fill its bedrooms, the walls reaching short of the ceiling so we could listen in on each other's happiness.

The hope of one day being a full-time student had been lost with time. I was a quarter-century old now, and Corbett would never agreeably support me in something independent of him. *You can catch more flies with honey than with vinegar, dear*, my mother advised me. After ten years of knowing each other, our habits determined the impossibility of love and independence co-existing. The *honey* of Mother's theory created a sweet stronghold for me in one place only – the bedroom. There I could hold Corbett's attentions even when his career flourished. Whatever shadows came into our daily lives they faded in the glow of the night.

I thought of myself as a gift, often offering myself up to Corbett by dancing, distracting him when he needed a break, removing my clothes a piece at a time and tossing them about the room. I knew he was only pretending to concentrate on his drafting board. At some point in the twist of my bare feet on the wooden floor, he would carry me off to bed. I had no thought of ever being ignored or of being jealous of other women. I was married to the only man who inspired my sexual appetite, and our hours of love drove back the uncertainties that crept in while I typed for deans and professors, none of them women. Mother had told me, *Sex clears away the cobwebs*. I would have used the word *differences* instead of *cobwebs* if I had thought to contradict her. Corbett and I never rested long enough for boredom.

One night in the autumn of Corbett's final year at university, he saved a young boy's dog from a drunken father by bringing her home. Although I argued against keeping her because our year in Europe was only months away, the three-month-old blond border collie had won my heart by morning. We named her Fred. My yearning for a dog had been waiting to be satisfied since the loss of Boots under the wheels of a car a decade before. Fred fit easily into our lives, creating a trio for evening walks, remaining nearby while we worked at home, and sleeping in a basket next to my side of the bed. Although we rented our house to gentle friends who readily agreed to puppy-sit during our absence, my saying good-bye to her was almost too difficult.

I also said good-bye to Frane, whose marriage was steadily crumbling. Her husband had spent the week in Chicago keeping his bed warm with an interior design student, yet he complained Frane's second baby, due at summer's end, was not his. Innocent of consequences and desperate for solace, she had apparently wept on some man's shoulder and found herself pregnant. Holding close to her Catholicism, she refused an abortion. Francis left her crouched and sobbing in a corner of the airport, her belly swollen with child. He had a degree and a plane ticket and no longer needed her financial support.

We also said farewell to the associate dean and his wife when they took Corbett and me to dinner. I sewed a winter-white dress that showed a little cleavage and made Corbett's eyes light up. When the waiter asked for our drink orders, I ordered rum and Coke. *You have to be twenty-one to drink on the premises*, he said, turning to our host. *I'm twenty-five*, I said to his shoulder. *I believe she's over twenty-one*, the dean said. *I'll get the manager*, the waiter argued. *She's twenty-five*, Corbett said, rising from the table to tower over the boy. *She's twenty-five*, the associate dean assured people at surrounding tables. *Have to have a birth certificate*, the waiter insisted. My birth certificate sat at home with my passport, ready for Europe. *Are you sure?* the manager asked when he came to our table. I wondered how many years would pass before I could take credit for being a woman: *If it's too much bother, I'll have milk*. Corbett stood up again and proved the value of a university education. *She'll have a bottle of wine – the kind that comes in a basket*.

I discarded my diaphragm the morning we gave away our house keys, patted Fred, who had grown suspicious about our bags, and climbed into a professor's car to catch a ride down the Trans-Canada Highway to Expo 67 in Montreal. On the road, Corbett and I kept to ourselves the momentous nature of our journey. No tourist attraction compared to the event taking place in my body. I checked for signs of life, stroking my tummy, knowing it was too soon to tell but unable to resist talking to the future. Before the *Empress of Canada* sailed into the St. Lawrence, I expected to be pregnant.

Instead I sat in the stainless steel sink, the only drain in our stateroom. It caught the flow of my blood and delivered it into the cold Atlantic. Sleeping together on the top bunk and piling our clothes on the bottom one, I clung to Corbett. We hardly talked about the anticlimactic end to six years of expectation or the towels I stacked under my bottom, except to dismiss it: *It's probably all the rich food we've eaten or being anxious about Fred.* When Corbett remained crestfallen, I grew defensive: *I've never bled this much before.* Our meal partners were childless too. The woman, weighing over two hundred pounds, never let her girth interfere with her appetite or cheerfulness. Her husband, a diminutive and silent man, pulled out her chair as she wriggled in.

It never occurred to me to see the ship's doctor over the inconvenience of my unwelcome period, even though I could barely contain it with sanitary napkins. Late in the afternoon each day, we escaped into the fantasy of the movie theater. On the final night everyone was expected to attend a costume ball. Corbett dressed up as the first cave man, wearing his fur vest and bathing trunks and carrying a baseball bat covered with brown paper. I went as the first Playboy bunny in my one-piece ski underwear with a Kleenex tail pinned to my behind and cardboard ears in my hair. Corbett chased me around the ballroom, and I slipped into a bathroom before he could catch me. After dark, blankets around our shoulders, we circled the deck, looking up at the stars and down to where the prow spread white froth along the hull. It curled its arms up as though beckoning me into its icy depths.

Blood followed me from Liverpool to Chester, where we stayed in the home of Paul Barker's parents. They missed their son since he had left Oxford for Canada. At Stratford we saw *The Taming of the Shrew.* It convinced Corbett that Shakespeare had something to say. In London, we bought ourselves an old truck that had once delivered bread, and I sat on a folded towel as we drove from Dover to Calais. Corbett told me to cover my eyes as we entered Paris on a starry night. *Okay, you can look now*, he said. I opened my eyes to see the Eiffel Tower soaring into the night.

In Spain I became well again, and my spirits lifted. Our love mended too while we played on the beaches of Barcelona. But Corbett's irritability and my guilt were always close to eruption, finding excuses in small things like our search for a gas station or a bank. We seemed uncertain how to relax, having accustomed ourselves to the intense labor that gave us a feeling of control. I sent a letter asking for advice from my bridesmaid, a nurse and mother now, married to a doctor in Toronto. When I wrote my parents, I kept our disappointment secret. Back home, they pressed colored pins into a map on their wall, searching out the unfamiliar names of villages on my postcards.

I learned to enjoy wine as we traveled the Mediterranean shore. *Drink it slowly*, Corbett cautioned. Our moods rose and fell with the weather, intermittent disappointments interrupted by sunny adventures. Corbett had a certain confidence in his own dark moods that made me try harder to lighten the atmosphere. He was gruff when I cried in Valencia after a toreador speared a confused bull. I knew what it was like to have determination surprised by blood.

We climbed through the Pyrenees and floated on the current in the Rhone before we headed north. After drinking from a campsite well in Frankfurt, Corbett lay moaning in the back of our van. Dysentery kept him horizontal while I maneuvered the British right-side steering wheel on the right-hand side of the German autobahn. It had no apparent speed limit and I had no way of seeing cars behind me. Weary and frightened, I drove to Copenhagen, where I found an affordable hotel and a landlady who spoke English. She thought I was underage and refused me a room, relenting only when I dug out my passport to prove I was legally married and then opened the back of the van to reveal a man with a matching wedding band who was as sick as I had claimed.

Corbett's introduction to frailty softened him, and our worry about the future slowly dissipated in favor of the moment. We opened up to the experiences we had once imagined when we first said the word *Europe*. By falling in love with the days, we fell in love with each other again, driving back to the French Riviera and into Italy, where Corbett scuba-dived while I swam in the salt water we had never known as children. Together we discovered the mysteries of the Roman forum and the massive cathedrals with their coffins, bells, and domes. Hand in hand, we walked through Florence, watching Corbett's volumes on *The History of Art* come to life.

At night we pitched our tent along the Arno, listening to the music of Florence across the water. In Rome we drove beside the Tiber and into the bustle of the city where we slept in the van and woke to discover our watches had been stolen. The policemen laughed when I told them we had left them on our camp table with our dishes and stove. *It's a crime to steal in Canada*, I said to the officials. When they shrugged us off, I tried to shame them: *All those churches and no one's reading the Ten Commandments.*

In Venice we stood on a small bridge reading a letter that began, *Here's to Fred.* Our house sitters wrote about the kitten they had bought to keep the dog company during the day. I didn't dwell on the hollow in my gut when I thought of Fred sleeping in her basket beside them. Whenever Corbett and I felt homesick, we moved on. In early September, a cargo boat took us across the Adriatic from Brindisi to Greece. For a cheap ticket, we drove into the bowels of the boat under cover of night by way of shaky planks, and looked forward to sleeping on deck.

The romance of warm night air and bright stars disappeared when a wind roared over the water and tossed us off our feet. We slipped around in our own vomit, trying to edge away from the waves. *God help us*, I moaned into the wet wind from where I lay shivering in stained clothes. Once in a while a sailor would pass, clutching hand over hand onto the railing, spitting out indecipher-able words. Corbett hunched into himself, silent and soiled. Finally I attempted to say the word *doctor* in French, Italian, and Greek. The sailors grinned and pointed toward the tavern floor where other passengers had wrapped themselves around metal posts holding up small round tables.

At dawn I woke to silver light. The ship moved through mist and calm waters, giving me the impression of our being alone in a silent world. *Corfu*, a sailor said, pointing into the distance. Corbett lay near me, his hair glued to his face as he raised his head. Over a glassy sea the early sun streaked the mist that separated us from a distant island. *Corfu*, I called over the wind to Corbett. *Corfu*, he growled back, grinning.

After the boat docked in the Peloponnesus, we traveled through orchards hung with nets to catch falling olives, climbed up to windy ruins, and walked along hot beaches. We grew languorous under perfect skies, eating squid in Sparta, walking hand in hand down the famous track in Olympia, rolling out our tent among the goats. Greek children laughed at us in their shy and curious way as we climbed up to share our water with a braying donkey. The owner motioned for us to peek into his stone shed where the sun caught the soft down of a baby donkey.

In Athens we returned again and again to the old city, the Plaka, where swarthy men served us retsina, fried octopus, and oil for dipping bread. Then we drove into the green of northern Greece. I washed our laundry on rocks in a river bed and hung them on branches to dry. In Thessalonika we hid under our clean sheets to escape a cloud of gnats in an otherwise perfect country.

On my twenty-sixth birthday, I saw a bear tied to a stake outside Belgrade. The bear looked bewildered and dusty, far from the Yugoslavian forest. Its owner held out his upturned hand, covered by a dirty cloth on which some coins lay. The bear sat down suddenly as though it had given up. *Let's give the man some money for the bear's dinner*, I coaxed. *He's not buying bear food with his money*, Corbett said, pressing the accelerator. The bear reminded me of a loss I couldn't quite name.

In Switzerland, a letter waited from my bridesmaid. She told me women often don't get pregnant while traveling in foreign countries with strange food and water. As Corbett and I wandered through pristine shops in the Swiss countryside, the surface of my gypsy life quarreled with a tight throat and fluttering belly. A shop-keeper gasped before I noticed I had dropped an egg on her polished wooden floor. Its yolk had a streak of blood stretching out like a fine thread. In a Swiss meadow, we woke up to an old woman standing near our open van where we slept with our heads in the fresh air. She pointed to the nearby gravestone, marveling at our having slept beside her husband and reminding me of my grandmother. I wondered if she too mourned for the past. *I want to go home now*, I said. *After Vienna*, Corbett promised, and he drove toward the loveliness of the Danube with its weeping willows and its gracious Austrian men who tipped their hats.

We flew home to all the fertility tests available in Winnipeg in 1967. My tests came back one after another suggesting we had simply not given ourselves enough time. *Six months is not much of a trial*, my doctor suggested. *A year is more reasonable. Rest is helpful. Get your husband checked.* While I stayed home for a year, Corbett worked for a prominent architectural firm. As days dragged, months flashed by. I hid loose dresses at the back of my closet and watched people move up and down the street, wondering where they were going. One Monday, mid-morning, I answered the phone in the downstairs hall. A corner of my mouth pressed against the pins I was using to hem a skirt. *Mr. Corbett*, a male voice demanded. *He won't be home until 5:30*, I apologized. *It's Mrs. Corbett, then?* his voice brightened. *Your husband's tests indicate a low motility level*, the doctor told me. *How will you fix it?* I asked. He hesitated: *There's not much we can do.*

My face looked the same in the bathroom mirror even though a new woman had muscled under my skin. The oak banister with its one large wooden sphere felt warm at the bottom of the steps. I stood on the landing where a floor-to-ceiling window let in the morning sun, pressing my cheek against the wood's warmth. Neither sadness nor thought trespassed on my stillness; I simply stood there for the rest of the day, the collie's head on my foot.

My spine straightened with the sound of Corbett's car turning into the lane. *He can't do anything*, I told him from the porch door. *Who can't?* Corbett asked, turning away to shut the gate. *The doctor*, I explained. A look of slow recognition passed over Corbett's face as he walked past me and up the stairs. For the first time we lay in bed without touching. When I moved closer, he turned his back. In the weeks that followed, my doctor tried to persuade me that Corbett's lack of desire was insignificant. *A week or two of no sex is not unusual for two people in their seventh year of marriage.* I felt a traitor to Corbett for speaking of our private life. *It happened only once*, I corrected him.

The missing knives finally prompted me to make an appointment. One minute I would be slicing a tomato or a loaf of bread and the next minute the knife would disappear. I found them later under the kitchen sink in the garbage can. *You should never have been left to tell your husband. Do you understand he feels he has disappointed you?* the psychiatrist asked. *What can I do to fix things like before?* The psychiatrist thought a moment before answering. *Have you thought of getting away, going to Europe?*

Where's the car? Corbett asked when he came in from work. We found it in Eaton's parking lot, behind the steel mesh of the night gate. *What's the matter with you?* He sounded cross. *What's the matter, dear?* Mother asked when I visited alone. *You've barely spoken for weeks; your father and I are worried.* Her voice was soft. *Why don't I make you a banana and peanut butter sandwich?* The thought of moving banana and peanut butter over the lump in my throat made me weep. *You've lost weight, dear.*

Corbett and I walked Fred around the block before we went to bed. She trotted beside us, scampering away when Corbett broke the silence by pounding on a tree trunk until his fist bled. *Do you want to adopt?* I asked. *An eight-year-old Native kid*, he said. I thought of the curled hands of my younger sister when Mother had brought her home from the hospital. *I want a new baby.* Corbett shook his head. The phone was ringing when we came in from our walk. *Your mother and I want you to know we're thinking of you,*

Father said. I washed Corbett's hand, smoothing the broken skin on his knuckles.

You could go to the Massachusetts Institute of Technology and get a Master's degree in Architecture. I was thinking of the meaningful days we had spent together as student and wife and of the Harvard Medical Clinic in Cambridge. *I don't know*, Corbett shrugged. He turned back to his drafting desk. I sent for an application, filled in the blanks, and stood over him as he signed it. When he was accepted, he applied for a scholarship to cover the tuition. An elderly man from New York had lost his only son and had set up a perpetual fund for a promising student of architecture. I wrote a thank you letter to the scholarship committee for choosing Corbett. *We'll take Fred with us*, Corbett told me. *I want her to have puppies before we have her spayed*, I reminded him. *Who's stopping you?* he asked, almost smiling.

Are you in love with someone else? I asked on our way home from a midsummer party before we were to leave for Cambridge. The question surprised even me because I would have said I took Corbett's faithfulness for granted, like my beating heart. He put his forehead against the steering wheel. *I love both of you*, he said, as though he spoke of a dilemma like choosing between two cars. *If you love someone else, you should be with her.* I closed the car door softly behind me. He spoke through the open window. *I just said that, but I didn't mean it. I never loved Terri except for about fifteen minutes. Just, you know.* His voice dwindled off as he followed me into the house. *Terri Williams?* I gasped while Fred circled our confusion.

Terri had given birth to a son while her husband was in third-year Architecture. He had been in school a long time and showed no signs of graduating. She worked at Eaton's and neither of them had wanted children. Their child spent most of his time in a corner, making small sounds, patting their black poodle or banging toys on the blanketed floor. Terri had told me I was crazy when I confessed I saw children as a gift; she protested that motherhood was a twenty-four-hour job without holidays. Together we had taken the pushcart down the steps, the boy's blue eyes squinting in the prairie sun as we set it down. *Have you got a hat for him?* I had asked. *He'll just pull it off*, she said.

Terri? I repeated, as Corbett followed me back outside and we sat down on the curb. *She made me nervous*, he explained. I thought about her olive skin and sultry blue eyes. *Did you know she was having another affair with someone from her office?* He hunched his shoulders. *We're not having an affair*, he said, raising his voice. I remembered Terri's thin body stretched out in a red bikini on her beach towel. *Did she sit in our car?* I asked. Corbett thought awhile. *Once*, he said. *Sell it*, I shouted, slamming the porch door in his face. When he came in, I had an afterthought. *She didn't even finish grade twelve.*

Oh god! Terri said when she saw me standing on the other side of her screen door. *Why did you do it?* I asked. *Don't fret about a one-time thing*, she advised: *You're still number one, but he thinks you might leave him, and he just doesn't want to be alone.* In my family *number one* was an expression we used for peeing. Terri and I sat at an angle, our hands on her kitchen table, eyes straight ahead, missing each other's faces. *It's the baby thing*, she said. *Why is that a problem?* I asked, assuming our fertility issue was private. *No one will ever know how much I loved him*, she told me as I got up to leave. *How could you tell her about us?* I asked Corbett in bed. He rolled away from me.

My parents considered people responsible for their failings. I hesitated to tell them about Corbett's and mine. *There'll always be the poor and the lame*, Mother had said, as though that freed the comfortable and able from responsibility. I couldn't think how to tell her I might never experience the mothering she had praised as the core of womanhood, the reason for love. I feared she would no longer love me if I didn't prove myself normal by having children for Corbett and grandchildren for her. *We might separate*, I told her.

You can't just leave him after putting him through five years of school, Mother said, her mouth pinched. *What's going on?* Father asked in a frightened voice. We sat around their chrome table, none of us touching our tea for fear of a shaky hand. *Has he become a Communist?* Mother asked; *it's all university students talk about these days.* She had never been to campus. *Your father and I don't want you moving to Russia.* Her voice became tense. *It's bad enough he voted for Tommy Douglas and the C.C.F. in the last election. He'll miss you when he realizes what hooligans they are over there*, she continued, breathless, one hand comforting the other. *Nobody's moving to Russia, Daisy*, my father assured her.

When I told my parents of our attempts to have a family and his dalliance with Terri, Father said nothing. Mother listened intensely and spoke through pursed lips: *Who'd have thought, such a big boy?* she whispered. *Do you think we should adopt, Dad?* I asked because his sisters had been adopted after his parents' deaths. *It's a matter of personalities*, he told me. *One of my sisters ran away from her new home every chance she got, even though they were good people; the other still thinks her adopted parents are the best thing that ever happened to her.* When I waited for him to tell me something more, he said, *I guess it's not much different from the stork's visits.*

I found my own apartment and painted it white while Patsy Cline sang *I fall to pieces* on the neighbor's radio. I rollered the walls in time to the music, covering stains, keeping upright. *Want some help?* the landlord asked me, having entered without knocking. *No thanks*, I told him, repeating myself until he finally left me alone. When I had finished, I cleaned the floor and windows and loaded the car with empty cans. After Fred's welcome, I climbed into bed beside Corbett and fell asleep with my hand dangling over the edge on the dog's warm head. In the morning I phoned the landlord to tell him I had changed my mind and he could rent out the newly painted rooms. The exercise and the solitude had been good for me.

When Fred came into heat, the male dogs of the neighborhood fought on our steps as they waited. When she escaped, I imagined she was enjoying herself running up and down the lane in her various liaisons. *That's enough*, Corbett yelled when one excited male was unable to detach himself. It yelped when Corbett hit him and took our whimpering collie inside. *She's crying for him*, I complained. *She's hurting*, Corbett snapped. When he arrived late from work the next day, he drove up in a white MGB GT, a sports car with a hard top. *It's not new, but it's got leather upholstery*, he told me. *Did you tell the salesman about giving Terri a ride in the Mustang?* I asked. *What about it?* He opened the door to show me the black leather seats. *I think people should know what they're buying*, I explained. *We don't know what we've bought*, he argued. *Fred'll be having puppie*s, I reminded him, looking at the cramped space. *Not before we get to Cambridge*, he said, counting out the nine-week gestation. We packed the MG two days later and moved onto the highway.

Fred had seven puppies one night in early autumn while the Vietnam war raged and students in Cambridge worried about their numbers coming up. We lived in the midst of squealing puppies and boisterous students, the commotion echoing traffic on Massachusetts Avenue. In a grove of trees, our apartment sat midway between MIT and Harvard. Fridays we went to the Harvard Theater to see its double features for two dollars. I lost myself in film – shocked by a woman drowning herself for betrayal in *Le Bonheur*, weeping to see Anthony Quinn crumble at the sound of a song in *La Strada*, astounded to think lost love can be forgotten in *Hiroshima, mon amour*. Across the square at the Brattle Theater, I felt ennobled by Ingrid Bergman when she chose her lawfully wedded husband over Humphrey Bogart in *Casablanca*.

The Personnel Officer told me I had scored the highest mark in the history of MIT on my typing test. *Others have matched your speed, but not your combination of speed and accuracy.* I canceled my appointment for an interview at Harvard, telling them I would come later if my husband did a Ph.D. The next week I was given my own typist and receptionist when I became executive secretary for the dean of Engineering, a perfectionist who threw a letter at me when I misspelled a Spanish word. His five pages of scrawl in Spanish – a language I had never studied – and a Spanish dictionary were all I had to help me through two pages of single-spaced typing. The pages floated to the floor where I picked them up and began again in my familiar place, a secretarial chair.

The German psychiatrist available to faculty and staff at MIT encouraged me with her warmth and patience. In a hushed voice, I told her about the fertility tests, Corbett's despondency, and my inability to put things right. *You don't owe anyone your life*, she responded. I grew confident over the hour with her, confessing that sometimes I felt like moving out. She considered this reasonable. *Who will look after him if I leave?* I asked, weeping. *He has to take responsibility for himself*, she said. As her words sank in, the purpose of my life seemed to evaporate. *You're both adults now.* I wasn't sure what she meant since we had been adults for six years. *How can any man cook and clean and work at the same time?* I asked her. *The same way you do*, she answered out of the blue.

On my second visit, I told her I had begun with a perfect marriage and had ruined it, and how sometimes I felt unhappy with my husband, *even though he's smarter and better looking than I am.* She told me I didn't have to leave forever, *just long enough to clear your mind.* The thought of proposing this idea to Corbett was daunting. It wore me out more than the memory of putting him through school. I recalled a classmate's wife in Cambridge who had slipped out of their apartment after an argument and driven into the next state, then called home when she ran out of gas. It seemed to me she feared going forward and then came to a standstill, while covered from both ends. I didn't return to the psychiatrist for a third time, even though she welcomed me to come. Being responsible for others seemed less onerous than having to be responsible for myself.

MIT's psychiatrist wasn't the only extraordinary woman on campus. Maggie, known from her television show as *The Magnificent Machine*, had been close to death as a sickly child. Early in her marriage, she had spent two years in a wheelchair after a car accident.

Now, slim and fit, she told us, *Never give up*. Obedient, we swiveled our hips and pumped our arms, inspired by her example. *Don't complain about those chubby thighs, get rid of them*, she commanded as we bounced toward beauty. An older secretary commented on her reflection after showering. *It's the neck that goes first*, she complained. *Maggie promised us anything is possible*, I reminded her, and for an hour each day it was true.

Side by side in our two-room apartment, Corbett at his drafting table and I at my portable Singer, we gradually regained a sense of purpose. He had given me the sewing machine as an engagement gift. Small as it was, I could sew dresses and jackets, terry-towel housecoats for Christmas gifts, and curtains for privacy. Fred's seven puppies wrestled and slept in a pyramid of breathing flesh while Corbett drew and I stitched. I admired Fred's discipline when she snapped at them if they pestered her, whereas I never tired of their trying to catch my right foot as I pressed up and down on the pedal. *We'll keep them all*, Corbett broke the silence. *Where would we live with eight big dogs?* I asked. *In a house with a big yard*, he said, drawing the blankets over me as I sank down beside him on a bed without legs.

In March we drove into the mountains of New Hampshire where friends had renovated a chauffeur's house with four garages on a century-old estate. They had turned two garages into studios, hers for sculpting and his for drafting. I took Fred and the one puppy we kept for a walk in the crisp and sunny air, losing all sense of time while sharing forest trails with two happy dogs. Later, I sat in an old green rocking chair by an open fire toasting my toes and drinking warm tea. Spring snow covered mountain peaks, narrow steeples rose from wooden churches, and large farmhouses dotted hilly properties. On Monday morning we found the same rocking chair on our second-floor balcony with a note: *Rock awhile*.

The Harvard Medical Clinic was easy to find when I finally looked for it in the phone book. I made an appointment with a fertility doctor and visited him alone. Disinterested in any previous diagnoses, he asked me about venereal diseases, abortions, miscarriages, and infertility in my family. I shook my head and answered *no* to each question, feeling as always that my body was a vacant lot. I thought of a woman whose story had made the news, a blackout alcoholic with venereal disease who gave birth to ten children before social workers discovered one son living under an outdoor staircase with his skates on, the only footwear he possessed. When the doctor flipped shut my file, he invited me into a second visiting room to meet a mother who, though once barren, now held twins in her arms. *I would like that to happen to me*, I told him. *I'll see what I can do*, he said, booking a series of tests.

Some of these tests were painful. I had dizzy spells walking home after my first visit, and I took the bus next time. Getting off I tripped on the bottom step, my legs exhausted from the tension of the doctor's prodding and poking. *Your pelvis is small*, he'd said, making me feel deformed. *I don't always weigh less than a hundred pounds*, I defended myself. *Bones are bones*, he answered. I locked myself in the bathroom after the last tests because I couldn't catch my breath in the presence of the interns he had brought in to watch the basement-room procedure. *Are you okay?* he called through the door. *Yes, thank you*, I told him and stepped into the path of a bicycle as I left the bus.

Corbett visited the clinic after my series of exams. The doctor had refused to take me on unless I assured him my husband would be tested again. *It takes two to make a baby*, he said, and then paused: *Three sometimes*. Male patients had to take a small vial into a private room furnished with magazines of naked women. The receptionist didn't thank Corbett when he returned with the bottle in a brown bag; she wrote our return date on a card: *Once the tests are in, the doctor will talk with you again*.

You're as fertile as a young colt, the doctor told me. Corbett and I sat staring at him across the desk, looking for a future, wondering if he realized a colt is too young to fertilize anything but grass. He shared some statistics with Corbett: *You have only a one in ten thousand chance of having a child. Did you have childhood mumps?* Corbett left without answering. He walked home with our car keys in his pocket. The doctor didn't mince words after Corbett left: *You'll need a different man or artificial insemination.*

Yes, he had mumps, his mother told me when I phoned: *One side went right down,* she continued. *Why do you ask?* Corbett, an only child, had considered marriage to be all about children, just as I had considered it to be all about romantic love. With reluctance he had agreed to part with five of the ten children he had dreamed of having, but nothing had prepared us for giving up the remaining five of our imagined offspring. We had thought fertility and virility were inextricably connected. *How do we know he'll use my sperm?* Corbett wondered. I asked the doctor if the power of love could energize my husband's sperm. He examined the backs of his hands.

Mother took a plane to Ottawa where her sister lived and then a bus to Cambridge. What could I say to this woman who put such priority on babies, the creation of family that preoccupied her whether it was in her own nest or a robin's? How could I warm to her generosity when I knew I would disappoint her if I left or stayed with Corbett? She would feel responsible no matter which route of failure I chose.

In the streets of Cambridge, the sweet smell of marijuana offered a powerful aphrodisiac to youthful rebellion, political protest, and, in our case, infertility. I admitted to not understanding the politics of Vietnam, except for its remote connection to my mother's evaluation of campus communism, but I never accepted that my man might be incapable of getting me pregnant. When the topic of single motherhood came up at social gatherings, I thought of my father and shook my head. Marijuana allowed Corbett and me to escape our unhappiness and to regain our eroticism, but it was as temporary as promises of peace. After the wonder of music and sex, I was still not pregnant.

Fred and her puppy, Cleopatra, crowded into the rear of our MG as we made our way back to the prairies, leaving behind five pups with new families and a sixth, the alpha dog, who had been killed on Massachusetts Avenue. His owner, a warm-hearted secretary at Harvard, had returned to my apartment to weep and apologize. Our two dogs, happy to overlap in crowded quarters, kept us from wondering about the point of dreams and hard work. In a three-day trip from Boston to Winnipeg, Corbett drove into the night, stopping as seldom as possible. He had arranged seven months in Winnipeg on work study before returning to Cambridge for his final term.

As the miles passed in silence, I remembered Corbett's mother talking to herself in the kitchen for lack of anyone who would respond. I thought of my own father coming home with more stories than my mother could handle as she stirred the gravy and sliced the roast for hot beef sandwiches. She had once told me our kitchen was a madhouse when Father arrived home for lunch at the same time as Joyce and I came in from school and Lynne was on the breast. I told Corbett that I wished we could talk more. After a moment, he said, *Okay, talk*.

I told him my dream: *I'd like to be a day student*. He considered this without looking at me. *What for?* he asked. *I'd like to study literature*. He raised my hopes by nodding. *Why do you want to study that stuff? None of it's true. Can't eat a poem*, he laughed. *Stories are true*, I argued, quoting my English professor in Regina: *They're full of universal truths*. Corbett patted my knee. *You can be an architect and work with me*, he said. *I've spent seven years working toward your architecture degrees*, I pleaded. Even the dogs seemed to listen. *What's better about different?* Corbett asked.

When we returned to Cambridge after Christmas 1969, I was struck by the dissimilar expectations of women in Massachusetts and those on the Canadian prairies. Only a few prairie women acted or reacted without a consciousness of male approval. In Cambridge, the word *feminist* fueled quiet independence or angry defiance. Women paid less attention to husband-hunting and more to their careers. Even so, it was easier for me to fold my sunglasses or to close my book than it was to beat against the immovable force of Corbett. The price of victory would be a deafening sullenness.

Looking for approval away from home, I modeled petite clothes in a fashion show and make-up for an advertisement. In the *before* I looked like me and in the *after* I had a face of orange plastic that looked surprisingly good in pictures. My photograph ran on the third page of a Cambridge paper, and I sent a copy home to my family. I auditioned for the Harvard Choir, but quit after two rehearsals. Hitting the high notes and carrying a tune were enough to get me in but not enough to sustain me alongside others who knew Latin and musical theory.

My interest in Katherine Hepburn, Gloria Steinem, and Simone de Beauvoir grew to a fascination. Hepburn's lengthy affair with Spencer Tracy had a dignity to it. Steinem's feminist rejection of matrimony and motherhood spoke of a naughty freedom. De Beauvoir's dogged resistance to women being categorized as less capable of thought and flirtation than men brought democracy into the home. Not only did these three women remain detached from the legalities of marriage, but they insisted on being happy about it and on remaining friends with their ex-lovers – better to be a woman with a history than a woman in neutral. But this would mean sleeping with someone other than a husband, and I had never been attracted to any man the way I was to Corbett.

At twenty-seven, my inner thighs unexpectedly responded to a geologist at MIT. Tom and I worked together on the seventh floor of the geological sciences tower across the Charles River from Boston. He studied wave action and earthquakes and gave me a picture of himself with John Glenn, Neil Armstrong, and Alan Shepherd during a time when Tom thought he too would walk on the moon. *Why didn't you do it?* I asked when we were able to look at each other. *When they phoned to tell me I was the last guy not chosen, I didn't believe it. I told them they had to be kidding.*

He said this two days before he left me a message. My fingers were hanging over the typewriter waiting for his dictation when a love song came through the earphones. Pounding the *off* button, I knocked the tape deck to the floor. The director opened his office, saw what had fallen, and banged the door shut. The campus psychiatrist told me I was not responsible for Tom's fantasies or his way of dealing with them. When Tom's wife visited from their home in Maine, she lay her nine-month-old girl on the couch in the director's office to change her diaper. Their four-year-old boy stood near his mother. He had been featured in the Boston paper for his precocious skills on the computer.

Corbett took me to Cape Cod on a Sunday in May to fly kites. Neither of us wanted to bring them down after our picnic on the sand dunes. Instead we tied them to logs and left them bobbing with the tide, two orange and yellow triangles moving against a blue-gray background. When we returned to the car, we cranked up the radio to keep our mood upbeat. As I joined Paul Simon in singing about bridging troubled waters and shoring up despair, Corbett drove back to our apartment. Music filled the space between our initial dreams and the hovering sorrow.

When the term ended, Corbett returned to Winnipeg with Fred and Cleo while I took the subway to the airport. I had a round-trip ticket from Boston to Copenhagen, bought from the Harvard Co-op for $99. I was on my way to visit Lynne in Germany. When the airplane's landing gear jammed over Denmark, I reasoned I was about to get my just deserts for taking a holiday away from my husband. On the train to Heidelberg, I met a man and his young daughter who kept me company, helping me through language barriers and showing me where to disembark.

The train arrived shortly before midnight and, after waving my new friends good-bye, I was intercepted by another man who introduced himself as Lynne's landlord. He told me he was an American who worked at the same army base as my sister. He had come to meet me because he wanted to surprise my sister, who was unaware of my arrival because he had purposely given her the wrong train schedule. Alone on the platform, it didn't occur to me to be afraid. This journey had been so much easier and more rewarding than the one I had traveled in search of motherhood.

Lynne's joy in our reunion was childlike. We knit together

quickly as we traveled into wondrous summer days. After visiting Paul Barker in Switzerland, we climbed aboard the Orient Express and then onto a train through Yugoslavia. Armed guards took our passports, and I woke up to find a crowd of men talking about my wedding band, one clutching my left hand in his. I struggled to make him let go, shocked he would think two women traveling without men were up for grabs. This was the first time I had been free of both father and husband, and I soon adapted to the liberty of my sister's company.

The summer of 1969 lasted as long as a child's summer does – every day as important as the one before. The Plaka in Athens had changed to a gathering place for young travelers. I had made a friend of Dimitri in Cambridge, before he and Corbett had graduated. Dimitri's parents had sent an open invitation, eager to meet the woman who had translated their only son's thesis into passable English. *Most women would type with their toes if they got to work with Dimitri,* Lynne told me after meeting him. An Adonis of twenty-four, he came from one of the richest families in Greece. *We have to behave ourselves,* I coaxed. *Virtue is its own punishment,* Lynne admonished me.

Even though we had bathed after the dusty train ride and stored our knapsacks and guitars under our hotel cots, Dimitri's mother, sister, and aunt were not pleased. They expected us to wear nylons and make-up in the suffocating heat. Instead, we wore matching cotton dresses. They clung to our bodies like soft winds. Dimitri's mother thought they were nightgowns. Our scrubbed feet peeked out from our sandals, scandalizing the servants. When I thanked the chauffeur, Dimitri told me I was supposed to pretend he was invisible.

Dimitri's father, a cosmopolitan engineer, asked us about our adventures. When Lynne flirted with Dimitri, his father joined in. He showed us how to swallow raw oysters with one gulp of Greek wine and laughed at his son when it became apparent Dimitri had temporarily abandoned all thoughts of his fiancée. Lynne and I talked and sang and sampled all the food. Dimitri's mother and sister stared unsmiling at two apparently ill-bred North Americans.

A shopkeeper gave us sheer mini-dresses, Lynne's lavender and mine turquoise, a fashion new to Greece. The palace guards moved their rigid necks to follow us with their eyes as we smiled back at them. When a widow grabbed at our crotches, Lynne whispered, *Maybe her husband dropped dead having sex with a tourist.* We protested the attention, all the while loving it. Learning enough Greek to get by, we turned our thoughts to song lyrics and how far a taxi would take us for one American dollar. A guitarist spat on us when we stole his audience on the ferry to Santorini.

Outside a waterfront café in Mikonos, we argued about the muscular young men escorting elderly ladies with jewels and bleached hair. These reversals of May-September strolled by, arm in arm, old women giggling, young men looking over their shoulders at passing girls or each other. *It's awful*, I groaned. *They're all over twenty-one and getting what they want*, Lynne argued. The contract seemed a form of mutual robbery – nubile male bodies squirming into fading females' bank accounts.

I arrived in Denmark two hours late for my charter home, perhaps hoping I could simply put down roots far away from anything that reminded me of the uncertain future. The plane had been delayed for repairs, and I was just in time to climb into my seat. Before it landed in Boston, I had made a new friend. Joel, a psychology student at MIT, had stored his motorcycle in the belly of the airplane with enough gas to get home. *Ride?* he asked, but I shook my head.

Two days later I caught a plane to Winnipeg. In Arrivals the wall was covered with the mural Corbett had worked on three summers before, a time when we expected our lives to follow our imaginings as a work of art follows inspiration. The escalator swept me down into Corbett's arms, and I made coffee for us in the morning as I had for most of my adult life. Alone in the day, I sent a handful of stones from a volcanic beach to Tom at MIT, never speaking to Corbett or our friends of my time away. Instead, I walked for miles in the summer heat, listened to the crunch of autumn leaves underfoot, and finally watched snow fall. I found companionship in the pages of books.

Late one evening on a week night, a young woman knocked on our door. I barely saw her face before Corbett came between us. *My wife's home*, he said, and she hurried away. He followed me into the living room, but suddenly pivoted back to the door: *I have to talk to her*. When he returned minutes later, he told me she was a waitress who had kept him company during a lonely night or two. *Couldn't just slam the door in her face*, he said, his voice defeated. Feeling distant and lonely, I visited with another architect's wife, a confident model with one son and a fetus uncurling in her womb. She invited us for Friday dinner.

By the light of a candle stuck in an empty wine bottle, we drank after-dinner coffees. I watched my friend move through the room with grace, resting her hands on the table napkin that stretched over the globe of her stomach. Her smock covered her body like gift wrapping and I was entranced by the simple knot in her hair, the way her eyes expressed contentment, the blossom of breasts and belly. I imagined the baby forming a permanent connection between this woman and her man. The conversation flowed but no sound reached me.

I was standing across the room when I felt Corbett's hands grip my shoulders. I had no memory of our leaving the table, nor could I explain why our hosts stared at me, clinging to each other as Corbett clung to me. *What's the matter?* he was asking. My hearing returned as suddenly as it had disappeared. *You were moaning and rocking, making sounds like an animal*, he told me. I had apparently keened on and on, rising from my chair, walking slowly toward the door. *Sorry*, I said. We got up next morning as if nothing had happened. On Monday I bought a single ticket to Boston.

When I returned alone to MIT, an engineer I worked with surprised me one Monday morning by telling me he and his wife would like to send me to Harvard to study. He spoke thoughtfully, telling me how his children had all the education they needed. He had talked it over with his wife, who was in full support of the idea. His tone of voice suggested he hadn't considered my refusing, my need to move along awhile in a cocoon. When I couldn't think what to say, he told me I could speak to him on Sunday when I joined them for dinner. I phoned at noon to excuse myself, never telling anyone about the offer, not even my friends, Nora and Bob, whose couch I slept on and whose coffee cups I washed each morning. Pushing the boundaries was one thing, acquiring new obligations was another. I feared the loss of parents who might turn their prairie hearts away from me. I feared for Corbett's feelings. I feared exposing my limitations.

I wore these thoughts like blinkers when Joel caught me at the entrance to MIT. *Remember me? Airplane? Motorcycle?* he asked. The next night he called my friends' apartment. *Good for you*, Nora said when I put the receiver down. At twenty-three, Joel was the quintessential American psychology student of the late sixties – bright, rich, and looking to share secrets. Known for his talent on the dance floor, he swept women out of their sandals and into his word play. Father and Corbett had set up an expectation about keeping emotional dilemmas private. I could feel their eyes commanding me to silence even as I clung to Joel's black leather jacket as we careered into the mountains of New Hampshire. *He's pretty smooth*, Nora cautioned. *People get killed on motorcycles*, Bob interrupted.

Inside MIT's massive entrance hall, I also met up with David, a shy and handsome recluse who generated conversation among admiring secretaries but seldom spoke. We knew each other from the geology department where he had been finishing his doctoral degree under Tom. *Are you back?* he asked. *For a while*, I faltered. He grew outgoing with my hesitation: *How about an afternoon walk on Sunday in Beacon Hill Commons?* David's number had come up for Vietnam, and he planned to go to jail as a pacifist. *What will happen to your degree?* I asked, imagining him behind prison bars. *It'll wait for me.* David, like me, was confined to choices he didn't want. As Corbett had proven, scholastic excellence was no protection against lost dreams.

By the time we had developed our Sunday photographs, a riot

had broken out on Massachusetts Avenue. David and I watched from the laundromat as police cars passed, German shepherds behind wire mesh in the back seats. It was the first time I'd seen guns up close. Young men yelled from wheelchairs, their hard bodies and tender eyes showing how recent their wounds were. We watched an agile student climb into a clothes dryer to escape the chaos. *Will he run out of air in there?* I asked. David's hand came to rest on my shoulder. *Nora and Bob are expecting me back*, I said.

Why didn't you invite him in? Nora asked. *I have a husband in Winnipeg*, I reminded her, realizing my contradiction even as I spoke. *You've lived with an ego the size of an ostrich egg*, Bob told me, barely looking up from where he was writing. *I always thought how easy it would be to go through life if I had my talents in Corbett's body*, he continued. I'd never heard Corbett criticized before, and it seemed wrong to leave him undefended, but on Bob's turf I resisted argument, grateful for a corner to rest.

One day it was Tom's face I saw coming toward me in the crush of students. He took my shoulders in his hands and turned me as the sun turns a plant, pivoting me out a side door and onto the grass. We sat under a tree as if we had planned our meeting all along. Each day we met by the Charles River, dawdling between work schedules. *I didn't come to hear about Corbett*, he quietened me, ensuring my past would be excluded from our time together. A month later, we went to Cape Cod for a meeting of geologists. In his Volvo on the way there, he said, *I told my wife about us.*

Rain bounced off the windshield, making the countryside forlorn. *Why are you crying?* Tom asked. *It's Halloween; children will be ringing her doorbell and they won't know how she feels.* He had a ready answer: *Well, it was either you or her.* Over dinner, I softened with his energetic chatter. Afterward, I realized Tom and I were strangers to one another, my body belonging with Corbett even though my spirit yearned for change. In the morning I took an excursion on the water, pressing my face into the wind while a guide described the surroundings. Driving home, Tom was euphoric, as sure of himself as I was uncertain.

You'll never find happiness by hurting a mother with two young children. Mother spoke in hushed tones. *Corbett collapsed and hit his head on a sink in the new building,* she continued. I thought of his sculptured head, heavy with blond hair, falling against white porcelain in the theater he was designing. *Oh no,* I moaned. *"Oh no" is not going to help him,* Mother said, separating one word from another in clipped syllables. *Your father's furious with me because I told Corbett it was your birthday when he last visited, and he left in tears.* I couldn't imagine Father's fury at her or Corbett's public tears. She paused for me to absorb the enormity of it all. *Left without a word,* she went on. *Your father thinks he knew all along it was your birthday and that's why he came over.*

At Logan Airport in the fall of 1970 Tom and I refused to let go of each other. Officials rolled the stairs back into place after I decided to ignore his pleas and to climb into the plane. The people in uniform seemed to take it in their stride when I turned around at the top stair and descended to where Tom was still standing. I looked up to see passengers on the plane crowded toward the windows, sun glinting off silver. People appeared to be taking sides about whether I should leave or stay.

Send for me if you're ever on your own, I whispered, turning to the stairs again. I crawled over another passenger to get to my window seat. *Can I help?* he asked, passing me a handkerchief. When I looked up people were kneeling to stare, swiveling between the windows that looked out on Tom and the seat where I blew my nose and closed my eyes against indecision. Once home, I sent a letter to Tom's wife, telling her the most important events of her husband's life had been her gift to him of a son and a daughter.

Corbett took me to the official opening of the new Manitoba Theater Center. During intermission an acquaintance asked if I had heard about Frane going through the windshield of her car: *Drunk in the middle of the night and speeding on an icy road in Alberta.* I waited for the woman to tell me she was joking, trying to make me feel badly for having lost touch. *Oh god*, I whispered, disbelief and shame colliding. The woman leaned against a counter, a glass of wine in hand. I found Corbett talking to another architect. *Francis gets everything*, I reported; *the respect of being a widower, even their boy.* Corbett looked shocked, but volunteered nothing. *Why couldn't he accept her unfaithfulness if she had to accept his?* Corbett answered without a pause: *Woman have babies*, he said. Like my mother's arguments, his logic was indisputable.

Once in a while Joel or Tom would phone. Their voices entered the silence of the house, pointless reminders of a life I wasn't able to accept in a place I would never live in again. Corbett and I began to spend time with new friends, a landscape architect and his bride. In his mid-twenties, Stephen had gone to the United States to study and returned with a stunning go-go dancer in her late teens. He spent his days in the same firm as Corbett and she spent hers making cinnamon buns and chatting to her miniature poodle, Too Too. Her toenails were always brightly colored, further alienating her in-laws who were distraught to discover their only son had married a gentile. Stephen was certain his wife would settle down, and his parents would forgive him when he and Cindy had provided grand-children to frequent the synagogue.

Why don't you have kids? Cindy asked me after the four of us had stopped for lunch on our way to a nearby lake. *Hasn't happened yet*, I shrugged. She confessed Stephen wanted her to get pregnant right away. Our waitress interrupted to order Too Too outside. *Put Too Too with Fred; she'll look after him*, I offered. Cindy frowned: *Your dogs are mongrels.* I looked through the window to see our border collie-cross and her puppy waiting untethered outside, their eyes focused on the door.

Corbett and I divulged a little of our own history to Stephen and Cindy when they arrived one night to share theirs. Stephen's insubstantial fertility tests had shocked them. *I know they're mistaken*, Cindy said, rigid in her chair with Too Too on her knee. But when we saw her two months later she had a glow about her. *I was pregnant all the time!* she exclaimed. *You're really lucky*, I told her, my heart constricting at further proof of a world moving on without me. Each time she served us cinnamon buns and coffee, Too Too wore a new bow to match Cindy's latest maternity smock.

Corbett and I ran into Stephen one Saturday morning in Eaton's hardware department. Usually his dress was impeccable, but on this morning he wandered the aisles unshaven, his eyes as crumpled as his clothes. *It was hysterical*, he said, dispensing with hello's. We thought he was referring to something funny, although his bloodshot eyes and dry lips belied humor. *A hysterical pregnancy*, he explained. *She was full of air.* When Cindy's tummy had suddenly flattened, she put on stiletto heels and stepped into the arms of a curly-haired artist in his late teens. When she gave birth to twins, I thought of the chaos when Joyce's boys had been born. By the time Stephen had married a young widow with two small children, Cindy's new man had disappeared.

Did you two ever think of staying together? the lawyer who signed our separation agreement asked. He told us we were much fonder of each other than he and his wife or most of his friends were. I wasn't sure how lovers sipped on the nectar of *fond*. When Corbett offered me lifetime alimony, I thought of Kipling's poem *If* that had hung on the wall of every house my parents had bought. It talked of beginning again *with worn-out tools* after seeing your life's work *broken*. I didn't feel my tools had been worn down or my life's work yet discovered. *Help me for three years until I get a Master's degree*, I suggested. *Think carefully*, the lawyer advised. *Why would I need support after I have an education?* I asked him. He raised his eyebrows. Corbett gave me a necklace hung with silver dice. I wasn't sure if he had chosen this present in memory of the angora dice I had made for his lilac Ford, or whether he was commenting on the risk I was taking in leaving our life behind.

In the summer of 1970 a three-year separation was legal grounds for divorce. People no longer hired detectives to take pictures of their mates in the arms of someone else. Divorce became a way for me to define my freedom, to make decisions, to buy a car without a husband's signature. We agreed we would either remain single or renew our vows. We never talked about the complications of getting from here to there and back again. We vowed to keep the *us* together in spirit. Back at the house, I sat on the couch Corbett had built, reminded of his talent and beauty as he lay stretched on the floor with his hands behind his head.

Mid-August I moved into my own apartment, a home almost unbearably quiet without dogs by the bed or visitors at the door. After a week I was awakened by barking. From my window I could see Fred looking up toward my third-story bedroom. *How did she know where I was?* I asked Corbett on the phone. *Dogs know things*, he answered. Realizing my budget would restrict me to apartments and feeling guilty about having left home, I hadn't asked to share the dogs. I had registered at the University of Winnipeg to finish my Bachelor's degree and Corbett was offered a job in Alberta setting up a Department of Environmental Design. He left me a note in red ink telling me he would forever love me in some way: *I will always feel that.*

With the two dogs in the back seat of his Alfa Romeo, he came to say good-bye. *I'm sorry I can't come with you*, I said. *Who asked you?* he replied, looking into the distance. In the passenger's seat in front of the two panting collies sat a stuffed owl I'd given him for his twenty-fifth birthday. The owl looked to the future, keeping company with a man who was heading into a life on his own.

I intended to be celibate, an academic on a journey to intellectual fulfillment. Instead I began to think of mortars without pestles, useless vessels tucked away in dark corners of people's basements or out of reach on high kitchen shelves. During my fragmented life, a photographer came to my apartment door in Winnipeg. We had met at a party the year before. He stood on the threshold without speaking until I let him in. We moved between his apartment and mine for eleven months while I studied and he printed photographs of me, always in black and white, always capturing the wistfulness I thought hidden. Often he would flick the shutter as I sat reading.

Our canoe trips, motorcycle rides, winter camping, and art projects balanced my spirit while Janis Joplin sang about freedom and having nothing left to lose.

I was taking a rest from love. My parents would have called the time *a lapse*. Mother phoned the photographer's apartment one night just before midnight. *What are you doing there at this hour?* she asked. *Mother, why are you calling here?* I didn't have to remind her I was thirty years old; she had baked my birthday cake and watched me blow out the candles. *Who is this man anyway, dear? Why don't you bring him home?* When I didn't answer, she restrained herself: *Well, I hope you know what you're doing.* When the snow got too deep to cycle to my parents' house for Sunday dinner, Father picked me up and counseled me in the privacy of his car: *You don't have to tell your mother everything. She's had a different life from yours, and she'd only be hurt.*

I was enrolled on the campus where Margaret Laurence had studied. The ghost of her student days made the halls sacred to me, and I wrote an essay that caused the professor to stutter out her delight by giving me an A+++ on a study of *The Stone Angel*. Being alone with my books seemed easier than being with other students until a skinny woman leaned over from the desk next to mine. *Restoration or Romantics?* she asked. Arlene filled our conversations with lines from the poetry I could never quite memorize and with contrary views on who was really the spice of our Victorian novels. *She's just a goody-two-shoes*, Arlene said of Amelia when we read Thackeray's *Vanity Fair*. *Becky keeps things going.* I began to think about how little I knew and how clichéd my interpretations were. *Maybe you should do pottery instead of poetry*, she suggested when I confused the poems of Byron and Shelley: *It's like confusing sardines and swallows.*

When I fell in love with the conclusion of *Middlemarch*, Arlene read George Eliot's final lines with exaggerated pathos: *For the growing good of the world is partly dependent on unhistoric acts; and that things are not so ill with you and me as they might have been, is half owing to the number who lived faithfully a hidden life, and rest in unvisited tombs.* Laughing over the heroine's unmourned death, Arlene asked if I thought I would meet a man who stood in *a belly of sunlight* like the heroine's new lover had. *I doubt it,* I answered, wondering how someone so smart could avoid having a lump in her throat when she read about the heroine having mistaken her first husband for a man wiser than Solomon.

I applied the same affection to the aging Hagar after we read *The Stone Angel.* When I told my parents about the story, Father suggested, *Old people don't get wiser, they just get more like they were in the first place.* I thought Hagar proved his point when she died in her nineties as stubborn as my grandmother was flexible. Grades came easily to me in courses I liked, but I got bored memorizing biology notes for my required science option. When I told Corbett by phone about my poor grade in the science elective, he told me to get a reread: *They must have made a mistake.* I feared they had simply found me out. Harder still was making sense of picking true from false in psychology. *Why think about what's false?* Arlene asked. *You're okay if you know what's true.* Her shoulders hunched as we moved through the hall, her legs taking two steps to my three. I wondered why my brain stuck like pudding while Arlene's slipped like oil.

Mother brought her favorite canaries, a male and what she called *his pregnant female,* to my apartment. She needed a birdsitter so she and Father could spend time with Joyce and her four sons in Calgary. The female bird was about to lay eggs, and Mother explained in detail how to care for the chicks. *I can do it,* I promised, looking forward to the familiar cheeping of birds, worrying she didn't trust me because I had an empty nest.

The two mating birds lived temporarily in one cage, an empty cage attached to it and waiting to house the male when the chicks were born. Within days, three eggs appeared and the female fluffed herself down on them. I moved the male to his own cage where he could feed her through the bars. Three wet chicks peeped from under the arc of their mother's wing while the father fed the mother and she in turn fed her featherless babies. I remembered my father tucking me and Lynne into our beds, saying, *I don't want to hear another peep out of you two* and of Lynne calling out just as he closed the door: *Peep, peep*. At night I took away the soiled cage lining, and rolled out a clean sheet of white paper. Each day the chicks were bigger and noisier, filling my apartment with their neediness.

On the fifth day, I took the cover from their cage and found the mother fluttering on the top bar where the four of them slept. Only two of her chicks perched with her while the third scuffled about on the floor among bird droppings. Mother responded quickly when I phoned: *That's how they keep a strong line*, she explained. *The mother rejects the weakest. Just let nature take its course, dear. It won't take long, you'll see.*

The first open drugstore I found sold me an eye-dropper and some Pablum. I fed the fallen chick warm cereal, clucking to it as I filled the feeder with seed for the others. They seemed oblivious to my interference. I named the chick *Scrawny* as I squeezed warm mush into her beak. I was not surprised when a literature professor taught us that birds represent the poetic spirit.

Pablum? Mother asked when she arrived home. *I've never fed a canary Pablum*. We looked into the cage. *Well, he's certainly plump*, she agreed. *It's a female, Mom*. During the week, Mother called daily to report on Scrawny's progress. Before she could sell her chicks, a prairie storm broke open all the windows of her sunroom. The cages swung on their hooks until the wind worked them free and sent them rolling onto the floor. Mother never knew whether the birds died from cold or impact or fear. She only knew that Scrawny was chirping at dawn when the others had been silenced.

Mid-winter Lynne returned to Winnipeg after honeymooning in Greece and Turkey with her new husband. I went with my parents to meet them at the airport. When Lynne drove off with the luggage and our parents, I was left to chauffeur my new brother-in-law, Ken, and their two pairs of skis. Temporarily lost in a snow-storm, we established what would prove an enduring friendship. My elder sister came to visit too. She knocked on my door, but refused to enter the apartment or hug me. *I noticed, dear*, Father said, shaking his head. It was Joyce's way of making a statement about family values, the ones I desecrated by living on my own.

After the fall, winter, spring, and summer semesters, I completed my Bachelor's degree. And in the simple accident of finding my life between the covers of books, I began to replace childlessness with forward-looking hopes. When I applied to UBC for graduate studies, a letter of acceptance came almost immediately. But I would have to work for a year to afford the tuition I had thought I could cover with Corbett's monthly cheques for food and rent. I sent a letter back asking to delay my acceptance for a year while I saved money. They wrote again offering me a teaching assistantship so I could come immediately.

After my final class at the University of Winnipeg, Corbett came from Calgary to sit in the balcony with my parents during my graduation ceremony. They formed a trio of weepers, sorry about something my parents discussed in euphemisms. *He seems a bit lost*, Father said, hands in his pockets. *He had more on his mind than her degree*, Mother agreed, making certain I could hear her. Father helped me pack my brass bed and bicycle. He roped up boxes and built a crate for the electric typewriter Mother had bought second-hand. She wondered how long they would have to wait before I came to my *senses*. But I knew Vancouver had become the second chance my father had taught was each person's due.

Lynne had moved to White Rock, a seaside city near Vancouver. She helped me find an apartment in Vancouver in an old house with windows opening onto a weeping willow. It was a block from Kitsilano Beach, and I shared the bathroom with seven male musicians who slept together in one room and who got up about the time I was rinsing lunch dishes. In my kitchen, both taps ran cold. I had heard of cold-water flats in London, so I splashed my face and felt grateful for a warm shower among the wet and dirty towels of neighboring tenants. The landlord laughed, telling me the element in the hot water tank had simply worn out.

Where's your stuff? he asked when he caught me sitting on my sleeping bag on the floor of an empty room. I had lived off graham crackers for four days, afraid to go out in case I missed the delivery truck, thinking I had misunderstood the shipper's promises in Winnipeg. Confused and impatient I finally wept into the phone, and someone at the depot responded by finding my typewriter under a fallen refrigerator. *Never seen that happen*, the man who fixed the bent roller told me. No one could explain why the bicycle, bed, and boxes had spent four days traveling back and forth between the prairies and the coast.

When I entered graduate school at UBC, I abandoned the abbreviation to my name and became again the subdued *Elizabeth* I had been in grade one. I lived in terror of being asked a question by students or professors, cracked open and exposed when called upon to speak. On weekdays, I studied in my L-shaped room, the French window open to the sound of fog horns in the bay. The friendliest of the musicians knocked on my door one Friday evening and passed me a small bottle with the name *Cointreau* on it. I glanced at the label, thanked him for the *Coin Tree*, and returned to my studies. After two hours of sipping and reading, the future seemed less formidable.

On weekends I skied Mount Baker in Washington where Lynne and Ken had rented a chalet built from an old train station. Warming up around the fireplace, I regained my balance. They gave me a place to belong while I became acclimatized to a daunting city. Among the group at the ski chalet was a middle-aged widow and widower who had fallen in love. Their discovery of each other suggested endless possibilities, a defiance of time. *Love at fifty!* Lynne called across the snow, and we skied down the hill laughing about something we could barely imagine.

Ken and Lynne drove me through the old-growth forest to Tofino to see the open ocean, hiking through Cathedral Grove on the way. They invited me to sail with them on Sunday afternoons and sometimes the three of us would share a single cigarette, thinking ourselves outrageous for smoking it, or share one toothbrush to prove our nonchalance. In their company I slept as deeply as I had before I had left my marriage. They enabled me to jump into life attached to the safety lines of family.

Weekdays before seminars, I awoke again to moths fluttering in my belly, nibbling away whatever comfort the weekend had granted. My hands began to shake as my weight dipped again to a hundred pounds. The knot in my throat separated me from others at the seminar table where students chattered easily about the treasures shelved in the great university library I had not yet learned to maneuver. I had come to graduate school to learn what everyone else appeared to know already. I wanted to say, *Teach me*, but I was expected to say, *Listen*.

I took up smoking three cigarettes a day until I realized the smoke made me dizzy and nauseated. I dreaded anyone finding out I had a husband in my untidy past, and in one day I managed to tell everyone I met in order to avoid their finding out some other way. When one of my professors asked me to join him for dinner at the Faculty Club, I realized I wasn't invisible. He bounded into our crowded classroom, hands in his pockets, camel leather jacket flying open. His words flowed without prompt cards. I imagined the Faculty Club to be a place where men in leather chairs read British newspapers, lost in a fog of cigar smoke, dressed in nineteenth-century clothes. Instead I found tables draped in white linen and held in place by silver, china, and flowers.

Over dinner with another couple and in response to my saying how lovely the campus was, the professor asked what I liked most about the university. *The rose garden*s, I told him, thinking how my mother would thrill to the sight of early spring roses when snow still covered the ground at home. He laughed with his friends at my response, confessing to them how much he enjoyed my *sense of humor*, repeating my words as we passed another table of his colleagues on the way out: *She's here for the roses*. Realizing I had been expected to say something about literature, I nonetheless turned back, gathered the roses from the vases on empty tables, and wrapped them in a napkin. They too needed nurturing.

In my study carrel, I sat next to a Master's student who had started on his degree the year before. We exchanged ideas about the American literature seminar we shared. Rampton showed a respect for English literature I had never considered possible in a man. Our conversations were hesitant at first, but as he realized my eagerness to learn, he suggested how I might support my interpretations at the seminar table. When our discussions evolved into infatuation, I never considered our ages. But after two months I learned my being thirty-one and his being twenty-two meant something to a man who intended to settle down and raise a family. I missed Rampton's endless hunger for the precise expression, the way our conversations explored variations of meaning. When I glimpsed him across campus with his future bride, a student who was twenty and beautiful, I felt erased by her too answering to the name *Elizabeth*.

Hi there, Corbett would say in his gruff voice when he phoned, firming the ground beneath my feet, encouraging me to chatter. On his first visit we drove to Mount Baker for a Sunday afternoon. On the next, we took a ferry to Victoria to browse through Native art galleries. Our friendship grew as our marriage receded. Arlene came to Vancouver too, following a year of exchanged letters. We celebrated by taking the ferry from West Vancouver to Vancouver Island. When it docked, we hid in the washroom to make the trip back undetected. *What birds are those?* Arlene asked. *Sea gulls,* I told her. When guests left, I was aware how big the city, how few the friends.

Three women helped me survive my loneliness and intimidation. Susanna with her British accent and reputation for brilliance invited me for dinner and, over time, showed me by example how a woman could juggle a husband, children, friends, and Ph.D. studies. *You're the only person I know who wants to hold a screaming baby,* she laughed, unaware she was teaching me the possibility of my being a career woman too. Carole shared the Thomas Hardy seminar with me and Susanna. With her lush red hair and her Master's degree in Canadian literature, she too encouraged me: *Your work is on par with the class,* she told me; *don't be too hard on yourself.* Working on her Ph.D., Carole suggested I move at the end of term to the apartment she and her husband were vacating for a larger one in the same building. It was about five minutes away from my current place. I would still be close to the water but able to wander through three rooms and sit out in my own small garden before I soaked in a private bathtub undisturbed. *We want someone quiet next door to us,* she said.

Diana was the third woman who befriended me after we met in our American literature and linguistic classes. She invited me to her cottage overlooking the sea in White Rock, where we studied in her quaint kitchen, an alarm clock on the table to remind us when to quit for tea. After driving the highway to visit Diana or Lynne, I began to arrive home with a sense of being settled at last. Carole introduced me to a relative from Argentina, an architect who was the only son of an established family. Clever, handsome, and athletic, Ricardo thought women had been put on earth to admire him. In our time together, he refinished an oak rocking chair that architect friends from Winnipeg had given to me as a house-warming gift after they had moved to Vancouver. Unlike the rocker I had once been given in Cambridge, this one was an armless nursing rocker to use when I had a baby.

Corbett came to visit with the two dogs. *This is my ex-husband, Corbett,* I said to Carole, happy to be bringing my two lives into one. As soon as we were alone again, he folded my small hand in his large one in the all-encompassing hold of our former days. *Ex?* he said, as though I was going through a temporary petulance. His being there reminded me how much I had begun to revolve around the axis of my own life. When he opened the trunk of his car, he pointed to his books on design and construction: *These are my friends.* I knew he would never consider my literature books as friends.

Knowing Corbett's long hours drafting in his studio, I asked if I could have Fred for companionship. I didn't think about his having salvaged the collie's life over my initial objections seven years before or of Cleo's dependence on Fred for company. The two dogs had been separated for only one day since Cleo had been born. *I'd feel safer at night if I had Fred*, I told Corbett. Without a word, he pressed the dog's head to his knee, left the screen door swinging, and climbed into his Alfa Romeo.

Fred pushed the door open and loped after him just as he pressed his foot to the accelerator. When I reached the road, I could see her back legs pumping, but Corbett never looked back. I found her panting by the roadside. She refused to look at me as I carried her home. *I see you had a visitor*, Carole called through my screen door. *I hope the landlord likes collies*, I called back.

In time Fred forgave me, but her affection for Corbett never diminished – her tail sweeping to and fro when he visited, her howls protesting his leaving again. Perhaps she embodied the love Corbett and I had once held sacred. I like to think that in her canine memory, she kept unspoiled the early years when she had padded along with us as we moved about in the boundless security of our young love.

MOON GLOW

I BEGAN to come home to my own skin that summer in Kitsilano. In mid-July two new tenants came to the house next door, their music filling the air as they carried in tables and mattresses. Gossip spread: The men were bachelors working in the film industry and *crying the blues* about past relationships and funding cuts. Walking Fred, I saw them moving between their van and the front steps, a man with dark hair concentrating on the path and another with light brown curls looking about, talking all the while. If the gods had signaled this day as a turning point in my life, I would have mistaken its meaning.

The curly-haired neighbor tossed a smile my way as he passed my kitchen window in the morning, his head golden in the morning sun. By the end of the week he had grown cocky, raising an eyebrow as he smiled. I began to anticipate this blur of lanky manhood that set my senses vibrating. He often turned back to catch me looking up from my books, a slight swagger affecting his walk. A thinning pate told me he was older than his youthful face suggested. I resisted waving as he glanced over the top of his red Volvo before sliding behind the wheel. His energy was deafening.

Two weeks later, I saw him at his car with a statuesque beauty, her luxurious hair swaying as she listened. He arched his left eyebrow as he emphasized a point with his hands, looking over her shoulder and into my apartment window. Nervy as an alley cat, he spread a heat that beckoned me from cloistered readings.

I had decided to write the Master's Comprehensive exam after my first summer to make up for being older than many students. To cover the requisite five hundred years of literature, I began studying with my morning coffee at six and closed my books when Vancouver's ship whistle alerted the city to lunch hour. In the warmth of summer, I took my books outside to sit with Fred in the shade of the small garden. It linked me to the neighbor's larger yard by a walkway to the garbage bins at the back and to the side street where we parked our cars. On my second day of sitting outside, the new tenant came home for lunch. He stopped near my table, struck a match with his thumbnail, cupped his match and cigarette with his hands, and kissed a smoke ring into the air. It floated over my table as he sauntered by. I felt baptized in sin.

Suspecting I needed to spend less time with books, I invited my study partner, Diana, and her boyfriend for dinner the following Friday night. While I peeled vegetables, I tried to put out of mind seeing the tenant looking over his girlfriend's shoulder yet again, apparently eyeing my floor-to-ceiling bookshelves. I felt edgy at his ability to unleash disorder in my tidy life, but my own eyes responded, especially in the speed I looked down whenever he caught me looking up. As the slanted light of evening shaded Kitsilano, my guests arrived to rescue me from idle fantasies.

Over dinner in the garden, Diana and I disagreed congenially about the American authors she preferred to the lengthy Victorian novels I treasured. During coffee I told them about a movie producer who had asked to use my apartment for a film based on a true story about a young single mother dying of cancer and her insensitive boyfriend. *She's recording her life story for her daughter to read when she grows up*, the director told me. I was paid one hundred dollars a day to let movie stars enact anxious love scenes on my doorstep. Crowds of people lined the streets, some women wearing broad-brimmed hats and bikinis in the hope of winning a role.

Talking with my friends, I looked up to see my neighbor. *Mind if I join you?* he asked, appearing from nowhere, standing under the August moon. In one hand he held an opened container of yogurt and in the other a spoon. *Spears*, he said, entering my movie plot about misplaced love, terminal cancer, and a future orphan. *This seat taken?* He sat down on a stool I had used as a side table. *I'm the kid next door*, he told my friends. I disliked him immediately for using the word *kid*, but my guests were charmed. At the end of the evening, Spears made no attempt to leave. He simply stood beside me while I waved good night to my guests.

How about taking in Ike and Tina Turner? His voice came from behind me. *Who are they?* I asked, turning. He raised his eyebrow in mock surprise. *She's got a mouth that threatens to swallow the mike.* I tried to imagine this in the positive light he seemed to see it. Spears wore the lopsided grin I had seen when he talked to the statuesque mystery woman, his face expressing awkwardness and bravado in the same instant. *They're coming to a Vancouver nightclub this fall.* I wasn't sure if he was flattering or mocking the singer, but something made my saliva disappear.

Into some popcorn? he asked before I could respond to his first invitation. I thought he was inviting me to a late-night movie, but instead we wandered along English Bay, sharing popcorn from a vendor. *He's a regular in the street circus along the Bay*, Spears told me between mouthfuls. He talked about Dylan's music, and foreign movies, especially Fellini and Chaplin. He spoke as though too few hours existed to enjoy waiting pleasures.

How old are you? Spears asked when he came by the next morning. *Thirty-one*, I told him and waited for him to express surprise. *Thought so*, he said; *I'm thirty-two in January.* He told me he was an Aquarian and then asked about my sign. When I told him late September, he laughed. *Libra*, he said; *scales of justice.* He raised an eyebrow before asking, *How about tennis?* I liked being connected to Spears by the alternating swings of our rackets as the ball journeyed back and forth, keeping us a comfortable distance apart, keeping us attached. When he missed the ball, he raged against his misfortune, tossing his racket into the mesh fence.

Where's your old man? Spears asked. I held up the plastic holder while he dropped three balls into it. *In Winnipeg with my mother.* Spears chuckled: *Your lover, husband – you know, that guy.* My lips dried as I answered, feeling a sense of disloyalty I had never felt before. *Calgary,* I told him. Spears diminished with a laugh the importance of everyone who came before him. His green eyes were seldom idle and his body was as animated as his words, anticipating welcome and friendliness with every turn. No dead air lingered around us.

How about the beach? Spears suggested when I told him it was time to walk my collie. Fred loped along the sand with us as he revealed that years ago he'd quit work on his Master's degree in History at UBC. *Spent the year makin' my own history in England.* While we walked away from the beach, he asked about the evening: *How about some din-dins and a film party tonight?* Before going out, I braided my hair, using small white elastics to match my summer blouse.

At an Italian restaurant, Spears twirled his noodles around his fork with the same finesse he had used to kiss smoke rings across our table. When I tried to mimic him, the noodles slipped down my chin. Jerking my chin over the plate, I dipped both braids into the tomato sauce. Jerking back, I sent each braid toward a breast. Both his eyebrows went up as he stared at the bull's-eyes on my blouse. *I guess I'll have to go home before the film,* I said. *Here.* He rose from his chair and circled my shoulders with his jacket. I went home with sleeves that hung down to my knees, wondering how women navigate the treacherous channels of dating after thirty.

Bring him to our party Friday night, my sister suggested, her tone naughty. When Spears arrived home the following Wednesday, I bounced out to his car, face scrubbed and hair brushed. *Smell this,* he said, pushing his lapel toward my face. Pinned on it was a paper apple advertising fresh juice from the Okanagan Valley where he had been to a two-day conference. I stood on tiptoes sniffing the paper apple, blushing at our proximity. *My sister wondered if you wanted to come to her party*, I wavered. *You're on*, he grinned.

A floor-length red T-shirt is perfect! Lynne encouraged me. *You don't think I'll look too eager?* I worried. *Be eager*, she said. Spears bewildered me when he didn't appear at the agreed time. He answered his door with half his face covered with shaving cream. *She looks good enough to eat*, he said to his housemate, arching an eyebrow. The housemate blushed as Spears went off to finish his face. On the highway, he told me I was *a match for the cruise-mobile*, and he patted the dashboard of his red Volvo. In White Rock we sat on the front steps of Lynne and Ken's home while the party carried on inside. Spears and I careened through several hours of conversation before we drove back to my apartment and tore each other's clothes off.

He was staring at the ceiling when I woke up. Looking at him was rather like catching something in my binoculars, a long-legged bird contemplating the quiet in its search for morning sustenance. Carole's voice broke the silence. She was tapping on the unlocked door and calling as she opened it. Our clothes were strewn from living room to bedroom. *Don't come in . . . please*, I called back, clutching the covers. My housecoat stared back at me from a hook across the room. Carole uttered a tentative *Oh* as she closed the door.

Spears hadn't moved. *What are you thinking about?* I asked him. *Linda*, he answered, stretching and staring at the ceiling. *I thought you'd broken off with her*, I wavered, thinking of the statuesque brunette and noticing the golden brown hair on Spears' chest. *Not that Linda*, he said. *The one expecting my kid at Christmas, somewhere down east, around Toronto.* He spoke as though I should have known there were two Lindas in his life. Alarmed, I decided to back away by spending time elsewhere.

The following week I met Lynne and Ken for a drink at the Sylvia Hotel on English Bay. Spears had found his way there as well, and he sat at a table with two women, one of them Linda of the luxurious hair, the other a stranger. *Isn't that him?* Lynne asked, and I made an effort to shrug indifferently. *Hello there*, Spears called, coming over to the table alone. *How about a ride home?* he asked, pulling my chair back as I got up. *Nightie-night*, Lynne waved, reminding me of our childhood when bedroom arrangements had seemed less complicated.

Where's your car? I asked. Discovering we had both been driven to the hotel, we got a taxi home. I retrieved my key from under the staircase while Spears explained his evening. *Linda asked me if we could get it on one last time*, he explained, *but the old mojo won't wake up for her anymore.* He reached for me as I realized his meaning: *You went to bed with her to find out?* I asked. He lifted his eyebrows in mock innocence. *All yours, baby.* I shut the door in his face and stared into the darkness, wondering why he didn't knock. By morning he had developed selective amnesia. *Marine-View Coffee Shop on fisherman's Wharf, enough food for anyone, how about lunch?* He didn't wait for my answer. *Bus it down to my office for one o'clock.*

It was odd to see Spears in an office, to hear him tell his secretary he was taking me out for lunch. In my imagination he lived outside office spaces and routines. The restaurant, its door at the top of long rickety stairs, perched over the water beside a muddle of old boats. Surrounded by dock workers, I ate prawns for the first time. A man in a dirty apron served us. Spears told me about interviewing his secretary with his feet on the desk. *Leaned back too far, and went ass over teakettle before I gave her the job.* Nothing was too embarrassing to make a good story. All his verbs were active ones.

When we returned to my apartment, I locked myself in my bathroom and cried. *Come on, luv*, I heard him say as he waited for me on the bed. *Love* was a word my family used sparingly, and I had not yet distinguished it from British slang. *It's only me, baby*, he said through the door. I knew I was not supposed to like being called names idly applied to all women, but something in me rose to the bait, something about the promised easy come-and-go of it all.

I need birth control pills, I told my doctor. *I'm having sex with a fertile man.* I had meant it as a joke, but the doctor looked away. Spears' story about his first Linda's pregnancy made me cautious. I walked to the pharmacy feeling like a modern woman about to order up the pills Corbett had always opposed as experimental. When I returned to the apartment, Spears was in my kitchen. He had taken the key from its hiding place under my steps and used it so he could move his stereo, records, and clothes into my sanctuary. I noted the size of the speakers and thought of Carole having chosen me because I was quiet. *We can figure out where to put the rest of the stuff later,* he said, passing me a glass of wine. The table held three birthday presents. Draping its edges was a fringed shawl woven in blue wool, held there by a blossoming zebra plant. Beside it, he'd propped a book called *Indoor Plants.* It explained the process of fertilizing and tending nature's gifts.

I wrote the Master's comprehensive exam the next week, the morning after an exhilarating night. Gossip went from carrel to carrel that only a third of the candidates had passed. In October, after teaching my one class of students, an envelope appeared in my campus mailbox. I hid in the stairway to open it before running down seven flights of stairs to reach the grass and call out to two gardeners: *I passed the exam!* They both hooted and called back: *Good for you!* Rampton asked if he could borrow my notes for the next exam sitting. His asking was almost as rewarding as my having passed. He returned the notes on a day that Lynne, her tummy round with child, was sitting in on my class. Rampton, the knight who had been won over by another Elizabeth, bent down on one knee in front of my students and sister to thank me.

That winter, Spears picked up his mail from a postbox downtown. A card had arrived from Linda in Ontario with news of the birth of their baby girl. She had hitchhiked pregnant and alone across the country, finally giving birth in a communal farmhouse and naming the child Melon Iris. *Melon?* I asked. Spears shook his head. *Probably chewing melon seeds and communing with an ashram dropout when she came up with that one.*

What if she came back? I asked. *She ain't gonna forgive me for telling her to get rid of it*, he assured me; *I done her wrong and she stuck it to me.* His blend of anger and laughter came easily, especially when he drank. *What if she came back?* I repeated. *Ended badly*, he admitted. *She gave her first kid away*, he went on, as though this explained everything. I tried not to register my jealousy at these babies blessing random sex. *Yours?* I asked, my throat dry. *Not responsible*, he said, holding up his palms. He showed me a picture of Linda turning a cartwheel in an Okanagan meadow and told me she would *stand on her head and fart god-save-the-queen for a little sympathy.*

Everything between me and Spears seemed to generate sunlight until he talked of his past. I attempted to work out the complex tangle of women but eventually grew adept at storing things beyond the access of sense and soul. *Look, luv, I've had a life*, Spears told me. *Got my high school girlfriend pregnant and listened to her yelping her way through a back-room abortion.* His voice implied her suffering was an imposition. *Got my university girlfriend pregnant.* Suddenly he cheered up with a new thought. *Saw her again just recently; a stewardess now and into make-up in a big way. I visited her between the two Lindas but couldn't get past the painted face.* I asked what had happened to the stewardess's baby. *Had to choose between her and Nan*, he said. *That was then and this is now.*

Who's Nan? I asked. *The old wife*, he explained. *She's expecting a kid right now with a chemist from SFU.* Spears gave me his gosh-shucks-darn look, as though women on the highway of his life were driving around out of control. *She left me after a couple of years to pay me back for my two and a half years with the stewardess when we were at university.* He shoved back his chair and sidled over to me. *Didn't tell Nan about the woman in England during my year there; missed her when I got back here.* He sobered at the thought of his loneliness. *She made Linda buzz when she came back for a couple of months. How about you?* He spoke as though we were giving school reports on how we had spent our adult summers. *You lived with Linda and Nan at the same time?* I asked. *Alternate times, you might say. How about some music?* He turned away to put a Rolling Stones album on the stereo and I glimpsed the soft curls that rested on his shirt collar.

Spears could knead a loaf of bread until it floated out of the hot oven on its own. Many of his dishes were original creations of exotic cheeses and endless spice. He loved the taste and smell of vegetables and fruits, picking them with care from grocery bins. Often he bought flowers from a street stall to decorate the space between our pots of steaming food. Mother had told us about my grandfather's cooking, how he had made Sunday dinners during her childhood and bought roses for Grandma's birthdays. I had considered Grandpa's time in the kitchen odd, his beer drinking sinful, and his hours at the racetrack disrespectful. Neither my father nor Corbett cooked while a woman shared their lives. But in our Kitsilano kitchen, coaxed by the music, I began to appreciate my grandmother's taste for her man. Spears and I tapped our toes on the linoleum, chopping carrots, whipping batter, and discovering the alchemy of heat.

We laughed when our eyes caught across the room or we saw each other coming down the street. Voluptuous hours enclosed us between Spears' random disappearances. Each time I thought I had come to know him, he surprised me. *Who's the letter from?* I asked, as we sauntered out of the post office after an intimate lunch. Spears read the address with the soft-shoe number he used to dance away from discomfort. It was from a married woman he had introduced me to when she had visited Vancouver with her husband. She was offering to meet Spears in Mexico where we planned to holiday. *How did she know when we'd be in Puerto Vallarta?* I asked. *Oh, she's just a little desperate up there in the boonies,* he explained, his voice casual. *She's ridiculous!* I blurted. *Great tits, though,* Spears grinned. After he fell asleep that night, I sent her letter back up north, addressed to her husband. *Win some, lose some,* Spears philosophized when I confessed.

In the hours alone, I pondered Spears' life. He had got three women pregnant, none of them his wife. Somewhere on the other side of the prairies a baby girl was carrying Spears' genes into the future. I began putting Spears' cup or plate in my left hand as I passed it to him, ensuring he would not be my right-hand man as Corbett had been. When I passed him his left-handed coffee, Spears was in good spirits, distracting me with a story of his childhood cat. *I used to put my cat in a pillowcase and spin it until she yowled. Then I'd dump her on the floor and watch her stagger off. Don't know why I did it.* He shook his head as though sorry and surprised at himself. I imagined the cat stumbling into my arms where I could soothe its confusion.

The sound of Spears' voice, the persistence of his cravings, and the explosive nature of his anger held me captive, drawing me away from the contemplation that led to despair. Still, I was never blinded to his easy eye contact with women, his tongue slippery with gossip, his hand reaching for a beer or a toke long after the party was over. I knew what I had to do but I also knew I wanted to postpone it awhile. Being with him was like spinning on a merry-go-round, a dizzying existence. Our appetite for each other had become palpable, and friends either envied us or suggested sex did not make a lasting connection. I retaliated with the example of my parents and grandparents, though I recognized the difference. Disciplined studies and undisciplined sex swept me forward until the habit of being with Spears was as strong as the desire.

On Christmas Eve, Spears' father asked why we didn't marry. I bowed my head and smiled. He had lost his voice box to cancer, making speech difficult but possible with patience and mid-sentence intakes of breath. Over dinner, his mother filled our plates until we begged for mercy. When we exchanged gifts, I discovered a bottle of Grand Marnier in green tissue paper. It was from his parents. I opened it to sniff in something sweet and beckoning. The first sip went down like fire, making everyone laugh at my watering eyes before it left a warm afterglow. Each further sip allowed me to discover the suppleness of my tongue and the fun to be had around a table bereft of my own mother's rules. I considered taking my parents a bottle on my next visit.

When the room began to spin and I excused myself, I heard Spears' father: *My gawd, she's gone through a good chunk of booze.* I pressed my face against the cool of the bathroom linoleum and stretched my body along the soft pink bath mat on his mother's spotless floor. The room swirled into a dark vortex. Spears banged at the door and raised his voice: *You've been in there for a bloody hour; it's the only toilet in the house.* When I stumbled back to the kitchen, Spears' father winked at me.

A couple of months later, I left my hard-won freedom behind by trooping across the lawn with Spears to the much larger apartment he had shared with his former housemate. Fred padded back and forth with us as we carried books, dishes, and clothes. The day I agreed to exchange addresses marked the loss of my independence, but acquiring a fireplace, a narrow view of the bay, and my own study seemed worth it. I could write my thesis and lecture notes in private while living in chaos. Weeks later, carrying in groceries, I saw Fred standing at the study window waiting for me. She watched for me exactly as she had once done in the house I shared with Corbett in Winnipeg. A sense of continuity swept over me.

When Spears' mother celebrated her sixtieth birthday, I joined the family. Literate and high strung, she talked of music, books, surgeries, and certain death in one articulate paragraph. I was astonished, trained by my parents never to mention death or family problems, especially at the table. Spears had developed a passion for opera while his mother ironed and sang arias. When she wasn't singing for joy or weeping over the hardships of marrying an alcoholic, she shared her fascination with literature and her talent for cooking. She loved her two sons unconditionally but never denied the difficulties of raising a child. She even talked about Nan, Spears' first wife, calling her a *Barbie doll*, meaning it as a compliment, expressing her disappointment when he *robbed the cradle by bringing that other woman home.* I didn't ask which other woman. *He was born with a horseshoe up his ass*, she laughed. *Oh yes, that's how he ended up with you.*

In late winter, when Spears went up north to work for two weeks, I re-covered the couch and chair, painted the dining room walls, hung curtains, and invited my class home for a spring break party. Spears was struck dumb by the change. He found his voice when we moved from the bedroom to the refrigerator to start dinner: *Come on baby, we make great music together. Let's get married.* Something gnawed at my giving in, something about Spears I was certain I would understand someday if I could just put my mind to it. In the meantime, I had found a place empty of either past or future. I knew one day I would have to examine the contradiction between what Spears said and what he did, between my girlhood dreams and this grown-up chaos. In the meantime, my answer was *no*.

Days sped by as I wrote my graduate thesis and taught freshman students. Nights spun around Spears' perpetual search for entertainment and escapade. *Don't you have anything better to do?* he would say when I asked him why he had kept me waiting an hour or two. *I have lots to do, but you choose our meeting time*, I argued. *So what're you going to do now*, he would ask, *ruin the rest of the day?* At these times, I counted on my university life to restore a sense of worthiness.

As my teaching load increased, so too did the time I spent talking with Jane, my colleague. Known for her photographic memory, she enriched my knowledge with her ability to extract depths of meaning in the dialogue she quoted. Jane lacked the cynicism of many academics, and together we commiserated over students' needs and our pleasureful but exhausting responsibilities.

In my academic hours, I would have agreed the unexamined life was not worth living, shaken my head in pity for those who were not enlightened. I would have questioned the wisdom of befriending anyone dishonest. At home I counted myself fortunate for having a man who could hum opera melodies, absorb levels of meaning in a novel, and converse with stuffy academics or learned bartenders with equal ease. I never asked myself why Spears continued to arouse and satisfy my passions. I just knew that his storytelling eyes praised or scorned the world in a glance. Physically energetic and morally lazy, Spears moved between affection and disloyalty, kindness and disrespect, like an actor with many roles to play.

Spears put women at ease before knocking them off balance, attracting a woman's attention and then watching a second woman over the shoulder of the first, turning the blame back on the accuser when caught. On holiday in Sausalito, he walked behind me through a row of shops. I saw in the reflection of a floor-length mirror Spears' eyebrows shoot up to give the salesgirl the look I thought reserved for me when I was climbing into his arms. *Why did you do that?* I asked, amazed. He gave me his oh-so-bored look before saying, *You have no bloody sense of humor.*

In the back of my mind, escape was as close as the moving companies in the Yellow Pages. Spears' mother warned me, *You've taken on a lot of problems with him.* Ignoring her, I concentrated on his having acquired his mother's charm and cultured sensibilities. It never occurred to me a woman could be contaminated by soiled spirits just as easily as by dirty water. Neither had I learned there is an odd strength in those who are self-serving, those who see power in another's weakness.

Suddenly and without apparent thought for the future, Spears quit his career in the film industry. When his colleagues suggested a leave of absence, he refused. Instead, he became manager of a Keg and Cleaver restaurant in North Vancouver. Surrounded by loud music, energetic students working for slave wages, and young women in slinky dresses, he seemed rejuvenated. Although I had difficulty adjusting to Spears' wandering eye, I believed a woman could tell by her husband's loss of desire for her if he was having affairs. I felt safe in the arms of his frequent arousal, especially as he always had a reason ready when he arrived home late.

You won't believe it, he told me, *but I dropped your car key in the Garburator.* At three in the morning, I refused to take a taxi across town with a second key. A month later he woke me to say he had been *held up at closing time*. He enjoyed these events as fodder. *I could see the cartridges in the bloody gun when the guy told us to sit still and put our hands on the table*. When he went to the station to look at the line-up and identify the thieves, he had to sit where suspects could see him. *They wore nylon stockings over their faces and toques, so how could I recognize them?*

My friends were more accepting of him than his friends were of me. His buddies complained when I tacked a *do not disturb* sign on the door, intending to grade papers or work on my thesis. I hated the idea of being a pit stop for people who wanted to smoke a joint or use the phone. They considered me inflexible. Although my campus friends appeared to enjoy Spears' company, he considered them narrowly ambitious and strait-laced. Living within two frames of reference was like having two lovers. The scope was broader but depth and significance diminished.

I learned to divide the days into study hours and party time. My abilities on campus seemed to increase in direct proportion to my happiness at home, even though the two spheres appeared incompatible. Unlike Spears, I was not practiced in the art of lasting out an evening of debauchery, often falling asleep just as others were revving up. He rubbed his hands together when he discovered I had never tried LSD. I noticed a quote from Ann Landers about LSD and saved it. Next time the topic came up, I read it to Spears and his friends in our kitchen nook. They listened quietly before they turned her theory on the destruction of brain cells into satire. I giggled at their cleverness, but was not convinced the drug was harmless. It was enough that I had recently joined the countless women who took birth control pills and even the odd Aspirin after grading for too many hours. *I'm just not equipped to become a druggie*, I told Spears. *There's nothing wrong with your equipment, my sweet*, he grinned.

I seemed unable to articulate my frustrations in a way Spears would understand. *Some day your prince will come*, he'd say over his shoulder when I asked where he was going. My home life had become attached to his and simultaneously disconnected from the world I understood. *The problem with you is you think too much*, Spears complained. Corbett had uttered those same words. I tried to articulate my loneliness to a girlfriend in the attic apartment above us. *Not much difference between his addictions and the way you wolf down a loaf of bread when there's peanut butter and bananas around*, she told me. *Do your own thing when he's doing his*, she advised, as though a woman could refrain from being influenced by a partner. I figured Spears must be doing something right: He had never been depressed enough to miss a movie, whereas I had missed a year of my life when Corbett and I discovered our infertility.

Fred loved Spears' liveliness. Never a jealous dog, she responded to his homecomings as I did – waiting on scraps. Hers were from the steaks left on plates at the Keg and Cleaver, mine from the relief of knowing I could fall asleep without worry. In his absence I lost myself in the complications of the Victorian Age, writing my thesis on George Eliot's books, loving her for her insights about women miscast by unexpected twists in their destinies.

When the restaurant held its annual Christmas party in December, I went reluctantly, knowing I had to get up in the morning to teach an early class. Refusing alcohol, I sat at a table with the juice punch and tried to make conversation over wall-rocking drums and screaming guitar strings. Three people I had never met shouted back and forth with me. My throat scraped against the cigarette smoke and the smells of sizzling meat. I reached for a glass beside the punch bowl marked *non-alcoholic*, filled it, and drank until the itch in my throat relaxed.

The heat in the room rippled in visible waves and the music slowed to a waltz. Stained glass lampshades melted into lava flows, smiles glazed faces everywhere, and a stranger talked of his windshield having melted when he tried to drive away. *Someone's laced the punch*, Spears told me and suggested we go home to bed. Instead I persuaded him to go to Lighthouse Park and sit on a hill overlooking the water. There I talked about long-hidden secrets. As I spoke, two green horns sprouted from his soft curls. I watched them bend toward me, pointing. When he asked why I looked frightened, I couldn't find words to explain. My fear had something to do with facades within facades and with disillusionment made manifest, awesome – and desirable.

Before dawn I had divulged all the carefully guarded secrets Corbett and I shared. Spears rose up from the grass fully aware of my vulnerability – the heartbreak of infertility, the brief unfaithfulness, the sorrow of parting. When the sun rose I was still wide awake and full of asexual energy. Suddenly I was in front of my class, having forgotten how I'd got there, but feeling a surge of hope for the youth of our country. Instead of my lecture notes, I pulled a steak from the dinner table out of my briefcase. During our discussion of Coleridge, my heart swelled with the knowledge that my students were flowers of the universe, my intellectual offspring. I could send them into the world equipped to seek goodwill and loving kindness. No one reported me when I announced the wonders of LSD and pontificated for over an hour about life's hidden riches. They sat mesmerized until I drove home to sleep from late afternoon until dawn.

That next evening, exhausted and weepy, I stood in a movie line-up with Spears and his friends, wondering why we had to go out every evening. It seemed people in crowds should bathe more frequently and talk less. *I couldn't have kids either*, our female companion said in a loud voice. Only my dearest friends in Vancouver were aware I had wanted children, but now everyone waiting to see *O Lucky Man!* knew not only that I was separated from my husband but that we had suffered the tragedy of childlessness. *My ex-husband couldn't handle our divorce either*, she said. On the movie screen, someone ripped the cover off a hospital patient and exposed the body of a pig attached to the head of a man. I left the theater and stood on East Hastings with the hookers.

The knot in my stomach didn't ease, even with Spears' concern. His massaging my hands and feet couldn't warm them or stop my shivering. *I didn't mean to hurt you, baby, honestly.* He vowed he would never mention our conversation at Lighthouse Park again: *I didn't know it was such a big deal.* He wore the same look he had when he told me about the treacheries he had performed as a youth with a pillowcase and his trapped cat.

In the morning Spears talked of inviting his parents for Tuesday night dinner. I knew mothers loved their sons better than their sons' women, and this was a love I envied, especially as my mother seemed capable of loving her sons-in-law at least as well as if not better than her daughters. I made it clear to Spears I would help him put dinner together but that it was his week for doing dishes and buying groceries. His parents arrived to discover me at my desk, an empty fridge, and a sink full of dishes. Spears came home with a bag of wine shortly after. I tried not to apologize to his parents or to laugh when Spears did his chicken imitation in response to the messy counters, knocking his lanky legs together and flapping his bent arms while he crowed at the ceiling. I served wine and talked with his folks, and Spears put on a pair of rubber gloves and splashed about until each dish and fork sparkled on the sideboard. We were all *into our cups*, as he called it, by the time Spears put an elaborate egg dish on the table.

Spears eventually told me he had been unfaithful to all my predecessors. *Learned my lesson,* he said before he again suggested we marry. The more I thought about the children our marriage would foster, the more I relied on his promise to be faithful. His self-preservation would calm him, a sense of purpose would come with age, perseverance would further my cause. My rationalizing had something to do with the way Spears could spin my words around to his convenience until I'd forgotten what I'd thought in the first place. He knew more adjectives than any Victorian writer, created more images than American poets, and confused my truths with his selective amnesia. Once Spears had taught me to see my life as a series of tales, we began to compete for air space. I exchanged my jeans for long flowered skirts and tossed my bra in a bottom drawer. On good days I felt Spears had freed me from my past. On bad days I despaired that he had separated me from my roots.

When Corbett came to visit, I worried Spears' cynicism would aggravate him, and my first love's fist might land on my second love's jaw. But the two of them sat in our kitchen nook and talked, seemingly indifferent to my presence. I took Fred for a walk along the ocean's edge. Spears had left for work when I returned. *How did you get on?* I asked Corbett. *A bit superficial, isn't he?* His tone suggested I might reflect on my present life.

Mother phoned just after Corbett left to say she was coming to visit. Having been diagnosed with kidney cancer, she had been persuaded by her doctors to visit her daughters and see Lynne's baby before surgery. The likelihood of her survival would remain unknown until later, when the doctors moved her ribs aside and clipped out a kidney. The odds were not in her favor. I was frantic with apprehension when Spears and I drove to the airport where we would meet up with Lynne, Ken, and baby Jordan, and welcome Mother together. I dreaded to think how I would look in comparison to her other daughters – a woman in her thirties, living outside marriage with a stranger and still going to school.

When Mother came into arrivals, Spears was his charming best, talking and listening with perfect timing, making certain Mother was comfortable over tea while we waited for her luggage. I watched him make this prim woman in her sixties feel young and beautiful again. His boyish demeanor, his love of good food, and his knowledge of music, allowed her to forget the cancer that lurked behind our small talk. Before I had a chance to explain how I had come to share a bedroom with a man I had refused to marry, Mother offered her own opinion: *I'm so happy you're not alone anymore, dear. I won't have to worry about you all the time.* She smiled when she whispered, *He may want to marry you eventually, dear.*

In spring a pianist loaned me her cottage by the sea, an hour's drive from Vancouver, while she gave a music workshop in Japan. There I escaped into the silence of conjugating the same French verbs I had learned in high school, studying for my language qualification for my Master's degree. When I returned to Kitsilano, a letter from Tom was waiting in my English Department mail slot.

He no longer taught in Cambridge, having been stricken by stomach cancer the year before. He had moved to the countryside with his wife and children to chop wood and shovel snow, mending in the company of nature. *The tumor was the weight and size of the pain I felt when we separated.* Tucked in the envelope was a photograph – Tom tanned and smiling.

The difference between a first and a second relationship, I was discovering, is that the second comes with two previous histories. Spears seldom commented on my earlier life, simply talking over and around it. He had gone to see Linda and baby Melon when they came to Vancouver briefly to visit her family. *Who does the baby look like?* I asked. *Winston Churchill,* Spears said. *Was it comfortable being with them?* I prodded. *Not much. She was nursing it, nipples the size of grapes, those big-bunioned feet of hers in moccasins.* I tried to imagine the woman others had told me was doe-eyed and beautiful. *I can understand you wanting to see the baby,* I admitted, *but I'd just like to know what's happening.*

Grandma Blore died in her sleep in February 1975 at the age of ninety-two, having never returned to England since her arrival in this country in 1907. The following summer my parents drove out from the prairies, Mother having recovered from further surgery to remove her spleen. I ran out to greet them when their Chevy pulled up, forgetting my family's disapproval of public emotion, throwing my arms around my father's neck. *It would be worth all those miles on the highway to have just one more of those hugs,* he told me, and I hugged him again. But his relief in seeing me came with a price. *I just can't see being under the roof of a daughter who's living out of wedlock,* he said. Mother stood by without speaking. As though beckoned, Spears came out the door. As soon as we unpacked the car, Spears took Father down to the Kitsilano pub. I had never known my father to go to a pub, and I worried about his opinion of Spears, a worry that increased as one hour stretched into two. When Mother called me to the window, she was smiling. The men were strutting homeward, laughing and talking, unaware of us or of time.

I had almost given up on the idea of attaining a normal life when Spears quit the Keg and began a Master's degree at UBC. Once he had passed his comprehensive exam, he spent the summer at SFU training to become a high school teacher. Woldy, a burly Russian of thirty, bounded into our lives when Spears brought him home after their day in a shared classroom. Soon Cathy joined us, his recent bride who taught English literature at a Vancouver college. They too ate up the cultural events and night life of Vancouver. But at the same time they kept a balance between respectability and festiveness. Their West Vancouver home could be reached by a small wooden bridge that spanned a creek running through their yard, and once inside their door there was always a bottle of wine and a gourmet meal among the antique furniture, flowering plants, and various pets.

With her long legs, broad shoulders, and reputation as a tennis player, Cathy was permanently tanned and elegant. But when we began to share our lives, I discovered our common pasts. Two years older than I, she too had graduated from UBC's English Department. We had both been married to architects and shared in common our grief over not being mothers. They had lost a baby years before during a sabbatical in London. I came as close as I ever had to admitting I had given up on finding the courage to risk disappointment again.

One weekend, Spears booked a table for four in a corner of Vancouver alive with ethnic foods. The Italian restaurant where we ate with Cathy and Woldy had a live band and a dance floor. After eating, Spears whispered something to the lead musician. When the music started, he swept me onto the dance floor in time to "Manha de Carnival" from Louis Bonfa's opera *Black Orpheus*. Perhaps every woman has an evening in her life when she feels endowed with an unreasonable share of beauty before she discovers an ordinary woman staring back from the mirror. This night was mine. Our bodies moved as one and our eyes never left each other's. Over a year would pass before we returned alone to the restaurant, but when we walked through the door the band struck up "Manha de

Carnival" again. It never occurred to me to ponder the opera's ill-fated lovers.

During the year between those two nights, our friendship with Cathy and Woldy evolved into weekends of non-stop conversation full of serious opinions and cotton-candy dreams. Cathy and I told each other the secrets of our relationships, and in one of these conversations I told her about my affair in Cambridge with Tom. As if by magic, he reappeared in the flesh, driving up beside my car on a busy street in Vancouver, just as he had once driven up beside me outside Boston. After we stared from one car to another and then separated in the traffic, I thought I must have imagined him. The story was too preposterous to share, and I shelved it somewhere as I had done with the photograph album. When I didn't hear from Tom that day or the day after, I put my vision down to spring fever.

In May, Cathy tested positive for pregnancy. When she came through my door with the news, I leaped up to hug her. *Don't touch me*, she said; *I might lose it*. She had hidden an oak high chair under their house to avoid her husband's scolding for setting herself up for further discouragement. Other women's pregnancies made me feel as though I was part of something contagious, an epidemic of babyhood. Through friends like Susanna, Carole, and Cathy, I allowed myself to come again to the belief I would eventually give birth. It never occurred to me to be jealous. Lovely as their babies were, I wanted my own. When Lynne gave birth to Jordan, Susanna to Michael, Carole to Daniel, and Cathy to Alexander, a longing for motherhood coursed through my waking hours.

On a sunny afternoon in May as I walked toward the grocery store on West Fourth in Kitsilano, I realized I would be thirty-five in autumn. *With baby making*, my mother had said, *you have to pee or get off the pot*. Mother and Joyce had both given birth to their final child at thirty-six. My time had come. Before I reached Fourth Avenue, I turned and ran home empty-handed. *Okay*, I said to Spears when I caught my breath. *I'll marry you in September*. His light-up-the-day smile suggested our world was about to become a better place. *How about June?* he asked, sliding out from the kitchen nook to hug me. I shook my head – June was the month I had married Corbett. We agreed on July 3 at three o'clock, a lucky number to the Greeks, who also loved stories and children.

Spears busied himself organizing our official divorces while I rehearsed a phone call to Corbett. *I thought we'd marry again,* he responded, moving me with his sincerity and also erasing the need for me to tell him not to come: *I guess I'm not supposed to come to your wedding.* Shortly afterward, a glass vase arrived from the Winnipeg Art Gallery, rich earth colors blown into an oval of greens and blues. He hadn't enclosed a card.

I taught one spring course in late afternoon as Spears and I went about our do-it-yourself divorces with the help of a woman who for a hundred dollars each made certain all paths to legal freedom had been traversed. I sewed my dress in silky sandalwood and wondered when my waistline had changed from nineteen inches to twenty-three. *Just imagine me at sixty-five!* I moaned.

When I picked up my mail at the English Department, mind full of wedding plans, arms full of ungraded essays, I was puzzled by a special delivery package from Texas. *What is it?* the secretaries asked. I looked inside to find a one-way ticket. Tom explained that once he had found me in Vancouver, he had returned to Texas in his new position both as a scientist and a divorced man, and made a decision. I phoned to tell him about my wedding to Spears in two weeks and my intention to have children as he had done years before. He sent us a sculptured bowl, reminding me by doing so of the generosity possible among those who have touched a worthiness in each other.

The night before the wedding two friends sat in the late evening sun peeling carrots. Two others sliced them for dipping. My parents arrived with a side of lamb to roast on a spit in preparation for Greek dolmades. *My son has horseshoes up his you-know-what,* Spears' mother said again, presenting us with gilded pots to hold flowers. Blossoms kept turning up on our doorstep from friends who were determined to keep us from our original plan of stealing an unnoticeable few from every yard in Kitsilano until we had enough to deck the entire yard. The tenants downstairs warmed up their guitars for the party. I bathed Fred and tied a bow around her neck while architect friends filled helium balloons and hammered together a dias which they then covered with their own Persian rug. When the Justice of the Peace turned out to be a disabled middle-aged man on a red moped, we had to smother our anxiety at his climbing onto our raised platform. During the final hours of the night we looked into a starlit summer sky, and I thought of Grandma's line, *Happy the bride the sun shines on this day.*

You promised sunshine, I complained to Spears when we woke up to low clouds. *Can't take care of everything*, he said, his voice nonchalant. We could see my parents, already outside filling pots with flowers, radiating satisfaction at my having another chance at love. My heart ached with pride at these prairie people moving about under a sprinkling of West Coast rain to soften my disappointment.

Father was hanging streamers of silk ribbon from the trees when I worked up the courage to speak. *I know you don't approve of divorce, Dad, but will you give me away today, again?* He looked down at his feet a moment, before I saw a restrained smile broaden into an enormous display of his perfect teeth: *I thought you'd never ask.* It was harder to convince my mother to make the wedding bouquet from whatever flowers she could find in our back yard. *Oh dear*, she said. *I'll have to shut myself in a quiet spot where no one can watch me.* She returned an hour later with a cluster of marigolds surrounded by the white of ocean spray and trails of ivy.

At the last moment, I picked some damp buttercups from the grass along the fence. Making a razor-thin braid behind each ear, I tucked six buttercups into each side. Once finished, I halved a crocheted doily to cover my head and put a matching shawl over my shoulders. Fred came out of the bushes as I finished, shaking dust off herself after rolling in the mud to escape the smell of shampoo. Just before the magic hour, Carole's husband arrived with an eighteen-layer chocolate and rum cake he had baked and iced himself.

Nesting on top were two yellow marzipan birds, one dressed as a bride in a white veil, the other a groom in a black top hat.

At three o'clock I heard people gasp at the sight of Spears. He had dressed next door in our old apartment, but I couldn't see him from where I stood waiting in the shadow of our entrance to the garden. Finally, I moved forward behind Fred in her bedraggled bow and Cathy in her long silk dress to where Spears stood on the Persian dias. He looked like a radiant virgin in his white suit and shoes, a red rose in his lapel and a red and navy hand-quilted tie against his blue shirt. During our vows, large rain drops fell on the helium balloons, causing them to bounce around the head of the Justice of the Peace. Someone flipped open an enormous red and white striped umbrella to protect us from nature's wry sense of humor. Someone else reminded us that rain at a Greek wedding is a symbol of fertility.

In his toast to the bride and groom, one of Spears' friends likened me to wind chimes in some remote Tibetan monastery and Spears to a revolving door in some international hotel, going round fast enough to take everything in, but slow enough to meet all the most interesting people. He ended by saying, *We are celebrating what is best described as a well-tested relationship, an unlikely match, but abiding proof that the miraculous is possible.* When it was time to cut the cake, we gathered around the dining table. The only people missing were the groom and the best man. They appeared with actors' timing, just as the wait became awkward, their grins stupefied and condescending, red eyes glowing with stoned self-importance. *The wedding's over,* Spears called out, raising his glass. *It's party time!* In the morning, I woke up in his arms, each buttercup surprisingly in place.

On my reliable Underwood, I typed fifty applications for possible teaching jobs for my new husband. We sent them to schools in Greater Vancouver and the surrounding areas. Immediately Spears was offered a position as drama director in a high school where he gained a reputation for being able to coax participation out of even the most reticent child. When he wasn't in the auditorium coaching acting techniques, he taught literature and writing. He complained of trying to interest kids in reading, but when they performed the dramas, they did it to sold-out houses and standing ovations. At the end of the day, we shared ideas on how to excite students about their required readings and argued happily about our differing interpretations of poems and stories.

On my thirty-fifth birthday, in September 1976, I had everything I had set out to acquire – an education, a full-time sessional teaching position at UBC, and an articulate husband to father my child. When I opened Spears' birthday card, it ended with

Out with contraception
In with CONCEPTION
(bet your mama never heard you scream like that!).

It seemed a long party had ended and a life of substance had finally begun.

I hadn't become pregnant during the summer as expected, but I told myself missing an ovulation or two didn't forecast a lifetime of empty cradles. One month of teaching followed another until Christmas decorations appeared on downtown streets. As classes ended, we prepared for our delayed honeymoon in the South Pacific. Christmas shopping in Eaton's, I began to bleed without warning. Blood ran down my stockings and into my shoes. I hid in the store's bathroom while Spears bought me fresh underwear and menstrual pads. While I waited, I thought of Corbett and the boat to England.

Spears never mentioned the episode. Instead we plunged into our vacation plans. The night before leaving, my back ached from grading papers. *Don't you worry about a thing; Spears is here to keep us on time,* he grinned, having started to party before I arrived home. I hesitated to relax until his old roommate came over, and the three of us unwound during our dinner conversation. Late in the evening, after several glasses of wine, we tumbled into bed unpacked but with our plane tickets near the door.

At eight o'clock I woke up. Our charter flight left at 8:10 a.m. *Oh gawd, what do we do now?* I beseeched our well-travelled neighbor. *Get your passport and call a taxi*, he commanded, appearing at the door minutes later. By the time I had brushed my teeth, he had packed my bag and was waiting with Spears at the taxi cab outside. *Don't worry about Fred*, he called after us, holding the dog by her collar as the taxi moved down the street. The plane had been fogged in and was now due to take off at ten o'clock. *What'd I tell you*, Spears laughed, raising his eyebrows at the stewardess as she took our boarding passes.

In the South Pacific I had little energy to think about pregnancy. The jungle humidity of Western Samoa smelled like a marijuana garden hidden beside hot springs. I had to search for a bathing suit because it was the one thing our neighbor had forgotten to pack. *No man like you*, a bus driver pointed out as we drove to a famous diving hole. *You too skinny*. A fat wife represented a prosperous husband. Each Samoan woman took up a double bus seat. The king was said to put his betrothed in a cage and fatten her up before their wedding ceremony. *Think you could get off on being locked up?* Spears asked.

Our thatched hut didn't shut out the sounds of pigs being speared for dinner, and my pillow smelled as though it had been stored in a damp basement. Our ten days passed in a fog of humidity, food, and sex. My mind clicked into gear when I swam, partially because our Swedish neighbors had sighted two sharks inside the reef. When our plane home stopped down in Hawaii, the officials wouldn't let us onto the oversold flight to Seattle. We spent our last sixteen dollars on a hotel room with cockroaches in the bathroom and gunshots in the hallway. When we got to Seattle, flights were canceled due to ice, and when we finally arrived in Vancouver by hitching a ride, a rare snowstorm had shut the city down. After the snow thawed, I found my suitcase on the sodden lawn.

In spite of my not getting pregnant during winter, our life took on a pleasureful balance we had not experienced before. *How about a trip to the Okanagan?* Spears asked after classes ended. *We can picnic by the lake and visit my house on the mountain.* He had bought this house with his first wife, Nan, and later lived in it with Linda while he worked in Kelowna. The house was rented to someone who had missed three months' payments, and Spears wanted to see if they had abandoned his place or had simply failed to send the cheques. With Fred and our sleeping bags, we climbed into the cab of the green three-quarter-ton truck he had bought and headed toward the Hope-Princeton highway.

Spears' house was hidden in the trees halfway up a mountain seven miles from Kelowna. The driveway was steep and narrow, but white spruce and ponderosa pine opened onto a rundown cottage sided by purple lilacs. A bush called bridal wreath spread white flowers over a corner of the house. From where we sat in the truck, we could see across the valley to hills stretching toward the horizon in ever-darkening peaks.

As we opened our cab doors, a German shepherd lunged toward us, reaching the end of its chain in an alarming frenzy. A dark and stocky man appeared at the door and sauntered over, his eyes never leaving our faces as he called his dog. *Police dog,* he said without apology. *Bit a guy gettin' in the back seat of the cruiser without an invite.* He patted the dog's head as he spoke: *Just doing his job.* Spears introduced himself after the tenant locked the dog in a shed.

The tenant's expression suggested he was a man inconvenienced in his busy day, but amused by our visit. Garbage spilled from two bins outside the front window, and the living room was empty except for a couch and a coffee table. He pulled out a kitchen chair and straddled it while we sat on the couch. Spears talked in a for-giving voice about the rent. When the tenant got up, we assumed he was fishing his chequebook out of a desk drawer. He returned with things I had never seen except on a movie screen. In one hand he held a roll of money that made me understand the word *wad*, and in his arms he cradled five guns that he laid carefully on the table like a display in a museum case.

I expected country people to own a rifle in case of a skunk with rabies or a horse with a broken leg, but three of the tenant's guns were handguns – small things, taut like angry fists. We looked at them in silence, rather like two prospective buyers and a salesman. After a while, he sat down, thumbed bills off the roll of money, slapped them on the coffee table, and disappeared again. Spears left the money untouched. *Mike's the name*, he said, coming through the door empty-handed as though we had just met. He smiled slightly as he shoved the money our way. Outside we waved good-bye. *I'll evict him by phone*, Spears told me as we drove down the hill. Three months later neighbors phoned to say the place had been abandoned and the Franklin stove stolen, damaging the door frames as it passed into new hands.

As though to compensate for my struggle to understand the scope of Spears' life and to keep personal discouragement at bay, I found a steady satisfaction in students and literature. The university gave me solidity and purpose, a reason for my family to be proud in the absence of grandchildren. Jane's friendship offered me moments of untainted stimulation and gave me the incentive to leave any personal problems at home.

When my parents visited Vancouver again, I took them to the Faculty Club for a dinner of fresh sockeye salmon, dry white wine, and a dessert with melted chocolate around fresh fruit and pastry. Everything was served with china, silver, and linen, the things my mother saved for Sunday dinners. Like Corbett, Spears adored my parents. They responded to his self-mocking stories and relaxed to a degree previously unfamiliar to me. Like Spears' parents, mine thought we were good for each other. In the setting sun of a summer evening, we clinked glasses and fed upon the plenty of a family in its moment of health and promise.

Linda called Spears to say she was in town with *their* four-year-old daughter. His former lover had given birth to a second daughter, born to her and a fisherman a year and a half after Melon's arrival. *It'd be a trip to see the kid*, he said. *Don't surprise me, that's all I ask.* My words sounded reasonable but my stomach was in knots with my wondering how he could bear the suspense. He arranged for us to spend an afternoon with Melon, and I filled the morning changing outfits, hoping she would like me. When Spears returned with their daughter, I barely suppressed my adoration. She showed me how she had worn two dresses and four pairs of underpants to impress us. Her eyes were turquoise, her face piano-key ivory, and her hair hung in thin golden strands. Her clothes were from the Salvation Army, and I could see by the dirt under her jagged nails she needed my help.

Spears carried her on his shoulders around Stanley Park. She kept one hand stretched out to clasp mine. Our eyes kept finding each other's faces and when they did we broke into silly smiles. A four-year-old girl, as pale as a Chinese radish, stared back at me with Spears' face in miniature. *We'll call you Camille,* I said to her. Spears looked doubtful: *You're asking for trouble.* At home I bathed her in bubbles to preserve her modesty. *She's been living in a camper van for months,* Spears told me: *She's seen a lot of bare asses.* I wrapped her in our biggest bath towel, hugging her damp body. *When I dirty I Melon; when I clean I Camille,* she said. *Your mother's going to love her,* I told Spears.

Let's go shopping for a doll, I suggested. *Can we buy one for Crescent too?* Camille asked. While clinging to me as though she feared I was a figment of her imagination, she tried to maneuver me into caring for her sister and mother too, scheming to keep her mother from tears and her sister from being angry. *Let's cool it a little, okay?* Spears suggested to four deaf ears. None of us expected Linda and Crescent to come to the door that night. When I answered the bell, I stared into the chest of a woman almost as tall as Spears. Her large eyes had no laughter in them; everything about her suggested defeat. A younger child, as defiant as Camille was pliable, sat in the crux of her arm. The mother's hair was dark brown and the child's as fair as straw. *I'm Linda.* Her voice was oddly expectant, shoulders curved inward. Welfare and male sympathy had been Linda's means to survival.

I'll get Spears, I said to her and, as I turned, I saw our living room through her eyes, wondering if the furniture Spears had brought with him had once been theirs. When I returned, she had collapsed on her knees, sobbing into an upholstered chair. *Can I help you?* I asked, feeling the weight of her pain, hearing her children at home in our kitchen. Spears was slicing bread, taking his time. *I'll be okay in a minute*, she whispered, head bowed. As she gulped back sobs and wiped away tears, I heard her barely audible comment: *He's so settled down.* I put my hand on her shoulder, unspeakable complexities passing from one woman to another.

Spears busied himself with cups and tea and boiling water until we sat together in the kitchen nook. *Melon's pretty hard to handle*, Linda said as though we'd been discussing Camille's upbringing at a PTA meeting. She stared at Spears the way Camille stared at me. It was apparent she had walked a long way to find daughter and father. Whenever I spoke, I felt like an interloper, a domestic canary among starlings. *Spears will drive you home*, I offered when the conversation grew thin. I had expected Camille to stay behind, and when I watched her walk to the car, the girl looked back, her remarkable likeness to Spears reinforced by their walking side by side. She raised a tired hand in response to my waving good-bye. Within the last hour Camille's expression had changed from expectant childhood to the fearful white of a street urchin.

A week later, I heard a knock at the door. Spears had gone to Montreal for a drama conference and I was just home from teaching a late afternoon class. Linda looked more confident this time, and both children brushed past on their way to the refrigerator. After I explained Spears' absence, Linda began telling me about his visit with her two weeks previous. They had met in the rented room where she lived with her girls. Linda and the children stayed the night with me, sleeping on the living room rug in front of a blazing fire, making me feel an outsider as I tossed and turned in the bedroom I had offered to them. I knew she envied me my life, but as I placed extra logs on the fire and covered my unexpected guests with a quilt, my heart ached at the sight of a woman falling asleep with a daughter curled toward her on either side.

We didn't actually have sex; he isn't into it with me anymore, Linda shrugged. I pictured my husband reaching out for her and then recoiling in disappointment. I wondered what I'd been doing while they climbed under the covers. *My body hasn't changed with the kids, but I could see how much he cared for you by the way he poured your tea.* My hands had begun to shake as they once did when I taught a group of third-year engineers who whistled and threw paper airplanes as I coached them on business writing. While Linda and I talked over breakfast, Camille fed her sister celery stuffed with peanut butter. *I bought those pieces of furniture.* Linda pointed at a marble-topped table and an oak china cabinet. *He paid for them, but I found them.*

I've been trying to get pregnant, but nothing's happened yet. My words surprised both of us in their bid for kindness. Combating this disappointment was my elation over Spears not being able to have sex with her, the suggestion that I held the key to his appetite. *Have you had him checked out?* Linda questioned, before telling me, *It took me two months to get pregnant.*

Cathy came to the door after having earlier interrupted with a phone call. *I'm going to ask you to leave,* she said. *You shouldn't be talking about Spears to Elizabeth. You're just causing trouble.* As though someone had rung a bell to end our session, Linda gathered her reluctant daughters. *I'll have him phone you when he gets back,* I called through the screen door, feeling foolish and angry and relieved. Cathy's ability to act on behalf of our friendship kept me from dissolving. It didn't occur to me I wouldn't be capable of trusting Spears again. We had celebrated only one wedding anniversary.

When Spears called that night, he exploded. *What a fuckin' cunt she is,* he spat into the phone. *You tried to sleep with her,* I sniveled. *Baby, you know I love you.* His voice had pleading around its margins, and my body leaned into his homecoming. I met his airplane in the kind of strap shoes with spike heels I knew he liked but had never seen on me. Spears was like morphine to cancer, keeping up my hope while causing the damage of excess.

My mother and I were sitting side by side in my car, shortly after my parents' move to the West Coast, when I told her about Camille. *She was born in Ontario about four months after I met Spears.* It seemed possible to convey all that the child implied about my husband, as long as I kept my eyes on the road. *You have to remember we were over thirty when we met, Mom, and we'd both been married before.* My mother said nothing. *Anyway, I wanted to tell you he had a daughter with a common-law wife who left him while she was pregnant and she has another child now, although she's on her own again. The girl's four and a half and I've just met her. She looks like Spears.* My palms sweated against the steering wheel.

Like many mothers, mine had a way of guessing her children's truths. Having been through my pain with Corbett and her own with four serious cancers, she had amazed us with a return to health before she packed up her own life and my father's to move out west: *You mustn't let the child suffer for her parents' mistakes.* Mother's voice was as soft as puppy fur: *You know I still have that miniature tea set of yours in my china cabinet, and she might enjoy it.* I turned my face and caught her smiling. We both laughed at my audible sigh and the prospect of a child in my life.

I think we should check out your husband, Dr. James King told me. He was the doctor Cathy had sent me to, the one who had brought her son, Alex, into the world. Dr. King made a woman feel as though her empty womb was on the verge of blossoming, if for no other reason than to please him. He had run me through every available test before he suggested a small operation, a laparoscopy to enable him to see if any obstacle stood in the way of pregnancy. In the hospital room, Spears pushed my visitors aside to sit beside me, his hand on my arm. We seemed to have agreed on what was important.

Your tests don't indicate anything's wrong; everything's in its place and doing what it should. We'll have your husband tested by a urologist, the doctor told me. *There's nothing the matter with him*, I explained: *He's had three pregnancies with three different women we know of, and one of them has a child that looks like his double.* Dr. King was unimpressed. *What about venereal diseases?* I remembered Spears telling me about the hairdresser who had run her hands through his hair and rubbed against him as she snipped and trimmed his shoulder-length curls. He had told me that Linda *freaked out* when he got syphilis and passed it on to her. Dr. King broke the silence: *I guess he can discuss his history with the urologist.*

Spears burst into my office at UBC, uncharacteristically out of breath. *This ain't what you're waiting to hear.* His mouth had a way of forming a straight line when he was angry or defensive. *The doctor wants to tie off some vein that heats up my bloody balls.* My chest tightened: *We always knew you needed cooling down.* Spears didn't laugh. Soon after, he had the operation.

On campus I grew chatty so no one would suspect the drama going on at home. I approached my students with the added decorum of one who holds a confidence. I had a sense of hanging around the edges of life. After Spears' recovery, Dr. King asked us to have sex in the morning and then for me to remain still for an hour before coming to his office. He examined me, taking a sample of sperm from my body, and then telling me to get dressed before leading me into a smaller office where he kept his microscope. *I think it would help for you to see that your husband is up to the task.* I looked through the microscope to see sperm partying their way around a Petri dish. *You're sure to be pregnant this month or next.* When I moved toward the door, he put a hand on my shoulder: *Did you ever think of going to Greece or living in the countryside where there's lots of fresh air and solitude?*

My two-year sessional lectureship was coming to its mandatory close, and I had been one of the lucky graduates to be offered two college positions. At the last minute, when UBC hired me for a third year, I took all three part-time positions to put myself in line for a permanent teaching post. By November, I could no longer turn my head from manipulating my car through heavy traffic between one campus and another. While my bicycle sat as idle as my dog, I hurtled along the road with three sets of notes in my briefcase. Rushing to a final class in New Westminster, I felt the premenstrual ache that alerted me to yet another failure.

Overwhelmed and bewildered, I sought advice about coping with the disappointments and contradictions of medical logic. The psychiatrist appeared as anxious as a trapped mouse. When something fell in his outer office, he jumped a full minute after the sound reached us. I suspected his denials were even more deeply entrenched than my own. The second psychiatrist flirted with me during our meeting. As I left his office, he suggested I bring Spears with me next time. After the three of us spent an hour together, he said Spears would never fulfill the two characteristics I needed most in a partner – loyalty and consistency – and that he wouldn't agree to another appointment unless I separated from my husband.

I felt annoyed with the doctor's opinion, thinking he had over-looked Spears' admirable traits – his easy conversation, his amazing memory, his celebration of life, and his ability to make a woman's body sing. I wasn't sure how a discussion of Spears' faults would cure my neck pain or our infertility. The psychiatrist seemed oblivious to my being almost thirty-eight and having little time or energy left to find another man who was single and sexy. Breaking up with Corbett had taken away a portion of my decisiveness and replaced it with a belief in making the best of what I had.

When Spears realized the average high school student had a shorter attention span than his own, he quit teaching. The administration and his mother argued against his decision, but Spears had already made a plan. It included a cure for my stress and a way to find the fresh air and quiet Dr. King had suggested. He wanted to move full circle, back to the mountainside where he had lived with, in turn, Nan and Linda, back to the shack where lilacs and bridal wreath waited for someone to make a home among the fertile orchards of the Okanagan. We rented a ten-ton moving truck on the last day of July, and our friends helped us fill it. Among my belongings was a letter from Okanagan College inviting me to accept a permanent position with their Kelowna faculty.

There to welcome us in August of 1978 among the old vehicles, broken windows, and leaky roof were deer, porcupine, chipmunks, and endless birds making their homes in a forest stretching for twenty miles behind our house. We had forty-eight hours to unload and return the truck to Vancouver. While Spears and an old friend moved our piano up the steep incline from truck to house, Fred found shelter under a spruce tree and I carried boxes. Exhausted and alone again, Spears and I ate sandwiches and climbed into the old porcelain bathtub we shared with a resident frog.

At daybreak, we piled into the rented truck to make the Hope-Princeton highway before holiday campers clogged the route. Concentrating on the gears, Spears hummed along with me and our tapes as we neared the summit with its majestic view of a lake far below. Suddenly blue smoke and burning rubber caused Spears to swerve close to the rock face and send me crashing into the door. An eighteen-wheeler screamed out of the haze, passing us in the opposite direction. Tucked behind the transport, an elderly couple moved slowly along on the mountain edge. They were unaware of the trucker's foolishness in trying to pass them on a narrow road, oblivious to their being a heartbeat away from the rocks and water far below. I looked over just in time to see the trucker blow Spears a kiss of sweaty gratitude for creating the inch we all needed to live, a reflex that saved five people and renewed my confidence in my husband.

Arriving back at the cabin, Spears called to me from the front door. *Look!* Arms around one another, we gazed at a harvest moon. It seemed to hold a world of promise, bigger than earth, deeper than time. A second chance appeared to offer itself on this fifth anniversary of the day when Spears had first appeared under the moonlight, a stranger in my garden.

Margaret Laurence wrote, *A bird in the house means a death in the house.* Her words played at the corner of my mind after I watched a sparrow slip through the door of our mountain home and batter against our living room window before I could shoo it outside. Her words returned to me when Fred, not yet fourteen, died at dusk. I found her where she appeared to have fallen asleep in a bed of flowers, not making a sound to warn me she was leaving. Spears dug her grave by swinging a pickax against the mountain so I could think of her resting near the apricot tree on the path to the driveway. Corbett had put her in my arms so many years before, and Spears lowered her into the earth. He surprised me by weeping: *You made a man out of me*, he said, resting against his ax. Corbett surprised me by distancing himself, suggesting the loss must be hard for me, but expressing no sadness of his own.

The next day I ended an eight-year silence by mailing a letter of thanks to Corbett's mother, who lived now in Victoria. I remembered her having said she liked my letters from Cambridge because *they say something*. These had been her first words of praise, her hint that living with a silent man carried the burden of a loneliness we both knew well. I thanked her for having given Fred's puppy Cleo a home when Corbett could no longer manage her. Weeks later a large box arrived in the mail with a handmade quilt. I draped it over our bed, its red strawberries and blue background picking up on the notion of the Okanagan Valley as the sunny fruit-bearing capital of Canada. The quilt took the scent of Nan and Linda out of our cedar bedroom and replaced it with the healing power of a dog's love.

My parents drove up to visit in their new brown Chevette. Mother carried Scrawny's cage out of the back seat while Father hauled his toolbox from the trunk. They had come to rescue me from a bedroom without a closet, a living room with holes in the floor that looked onto the mud beneath, and four walls whose interiors had never been covered by insulation. They made joy of the seemingly insurmountable task of creating a home from a shack. Father sawed logs for winter and stacked them near the house. They were our only source of heat, except for the oven and two inefficient wall heaters, until Spears and I installed another Franklin stove. In years to follow, I would always see an orderly stack of wood or hear the crackle of burning logs as a sign that someone cared.

Mice laid waste to our dried goods with their black rice droppings. A pregnant female nested behind a stack of tea towels where she had gathered bits of dog chow to feed her coming litter. In the night, I awakened to the trap snapping closed. When I tiptoed into the kitchen with my flashlight, I found her dead, her furry white belly exposed and rounded. The next day Spears rescued a mouse clamoring behind a cupboard door, a trap attached to its tail. In work gloves, he took the mouse outside and opened the trap to free it. *He's had enough for today*, he said, stomping the snow off his boots.

To Spears' surprise, Linda changed their daughter's birth certificate to *Camille Melon Iris*. She was no longer the butt of watermelon jokes. By this time I had come to see the beauty behind her original name. *Linda got me under a melon moon*, Camille had said, her arms stretching into a large circle. She explained her sister had come from *a crescent moon* and made a narrow swooping curve of her hands. *Linda had two kids because she had two arms*, Camille told me. She made my own arms ache.

Waking from an afternoon nap during one of Camille's random visits, I found her waiting beside my bed. She wondered if I had ever had a butterfly kiss. I shook my head, expecting her to tell me a butterfly had landed on her, my having told her the previous day about the Greek belief that a butterfly landing is a mark of luck. Instead she reached forward and put her face against mine where it lay on the pillow. Silent and warm, she began to move her eyelid up and down so her lashes swept against my cheek, soft flutterings of love. I sensed the gods shining down on us. When she felt my face move with smiling, she stepped back. *That*, she told me, *is a butterfly kiss*.

She taught me too about bathing. I had known bathing with sisters to save hot water and bathing with husbands as a prelude to sex, even bathing with a small green frog as company, but I had never known bathing with a child who was so young her tummy protruded slightly farther than her chest. She was six when she taught me to play a spelling game. I wrote letters in bath bubbles on her back, and then she guessed the words: *dog, frog, log*. At first I rhymed them so she could guess easily before we began to shiver in the cooling water. After the first round, I realized spelling by feel was more difficult for me than for her. When she got an entire series of words correct, we would trade places, and she would spell her words on my back. Often she used names of friends from school whom I didn't know. She would laugh with happiness when she tricked me.

When Camille came to visit in December, I discovered she wasn't yet registered in school. *Mom says you can't learn to knit there.* I took her to the local school for the two weeks before the Christmas holiday. She wore one of the two dresses I had sewn for her arrival, her skinny arms protruding from puffy sleeves. *Why do you hide your clothes under the bed when we go out?* She had begun this habit after I had convinced her she didn't need to bring her suitcase with us every time we left the house. *So nobody can take them*, she told me. *Shhhh*, she interrupted Spears, her finger to her lips. The radio was playing Handel's *Messiah* and she wanted to hear it. I wondered if school would ruin everything.

Linda says she might die, Camille told me one day, looking concerned. *When did she say that?* I asked. *At the airport*, she explained, looking up at me as though waiting for an explanation. I never got used to her using her mother's first name. *Her mom died, you know*, she said. I remembered Spears telling me that Linda's mother had died of multiple sclerosis when Linda was in her early twenties. *She's not even sick*, I argued. In my joy at seeing Camille, I avoided thoughts of her mother's difficulty in parting from her.

When Camille arrived for her seventh birthday, I asked her what she would like *more than anything in the world*. I held my breath, hoping she would say she wanted to live with us forever, thinking of the brass bed, the teddy bear, books, record player, quilt, dolls, and television waiting in her room. *A closet*, she said.

I'd like to hang up the dresses you make me. I emptied the storage closet in her bedroom, dug out the sewing machine, and sewed her a blue velvet jumper and a red velvet cape with a hood. We reread *Little Red Riding Hood* together. The next day I bought her red velvet shoes to match. She found them with her new book, *The Red Shoes.*

On the day of her birthday, I sent her to school with a cake. *They'll eat it*, she told me. *I'll make another for dinner*, I promised. At the end of the day, the teacher called to tell me Camille had collected every scrap of cake left uneaten on the children's paper plates. In the morning I put out her freshly washed clothes but she threw them on the floor. When she reappeared, she was wearing the torn and mismatched outfit she had worn on the airplane. Her skinny arms were on her hips and she was prepared to quarrel. We drove to school without speaking. When I was delayed at work and she was left to stand in the snow for fifteen minutes by the side of the road, I found her sobbing. *What's the matter?* I asked, pulling her next to me and puffing hot air on her hands. *I thought you weren't coming*, she said, wiping her nose on her coat.

Before she went off with a boy her age who was also traveling alone, Camille promised to wave from the top step into the airplane. She had been chatting up a storm since I had taped her silence at the table to show her that silent people are invisible, and I could see her warming up the boy's ear as she climbed the steps. *She likes boys*, I laughed. *Her mother's daughter*, Spears quipped. When she reached the airplane door, she stood on tiptoes to say something to the stewardess. I stood behind the glass wall, disappointed that she had so soon forgotten us. *She's just a kid, you know.* Spears put his arm around my shoulder; *stewardess is all she's got till she gets home.* I wiped my tears on my scarf: *I thought we were her home.*

The following summer Camille took a different approach. *Linda and Crescent are coming with me next time.* She sat on the kitchen counter looking over to where I rolled out pastry dough. *I don't think we have room for two more people; there's not even a*

basement or an attic. Without a second's pause she found a solution: *They can sleep in my bed, it's lots big enough.* We were putting
together an apple and strawberry pie to surprise Spears. *I don't
think so,* I told her. She didn't answer but the color drained from
her face as she banged her heels against the cupboard doors below.
Talk to your father about it, and stop banging your heels, I
snapped. *He doesn't like Linda,* she wept.

The wounds of confusion in early childhood became evident
when I took her to have her hair cut. I had kissed her good-bye
before leaving her with the stylist and looked back to wave at her
in the mirror. Camille didn't see me as I turned, she was already
addressing the beautician from the high-backed swivel chair that
hid her from view. I returned to ask the stylist what time she would
be finished and overheard Camille repeat the reason I had used to
talk her into having her unkempt hair cut: *Mom wants me to have
short hair so everyone sees my turquoise eyes.* My heart imploded
to hear her call me *Mom.*

During our first two years in Kelowna, Spears worked part time at
the college where I taught, while he dug a dry well and added a
porch to our cottage. At work, he organized events in Community
Services and made plans for the new college theater. Once it was
completed, I arranged for a poet to give a reading for my Canadian
literature class. Since P.K. Page had been the first female poet I had
ever heard live when she read at UBC, I wrote to ask if she would
share her work with my class. At the airport we met for the first
time. I was amazed she hadn't aged since I'd seen her years before.
After lunch and before her reading, we visited the women's washroom together. Coming out of her cubicle as I came out of mine, she
asked me if I had children. Although we had not discussed anything
personal, I sensed she had guessed the answer.

I told her about Camille, and she revealed that she had stepchil-
dren too and now wished she had spent less time pondering the
issue of giving birth. Knowing that this famous and beautiful poet
had shared something of my disappointment, I felt for a moment

special rather than denied. Whenever I saw her in the future, her presence reminded me there was grace for those who caught the light in their own creations.

It was an adjustment for Spears and me to live in a small city where college staff and faculty intermingled to a degree impossible at larger institutions and in bigger cities. Everyone on faculty knew who had flirted with young students and who was bedding down away from home. In close proximity and with few secrets, faculty shared their gossip, dinners, books, and music. On campus, I missed Jane in ways our current visits couldn't replicate.

John Lennon and Yoko Ono – already in her mid-forties – had just given birth to a son. I bought their new album and let its music feed my hope. It made me feel young enough to inquire about artificial insemination, especially as Dr. King had phoned unexpectedly from Vancouver. *I just wondered if you'd become pregnant?* he asked. *No news is bad news*, I told him, hoping to lighten my defeat. *It's beyond science*, he said. The Okanagan specialist told me that only ten percent of sperm reaches the womb in normal intercourse, but ninety percent succeeds with the syringe. He agreed that since in vitro fertilization was restricted to women under thirty-five, the syringe was my only choice. He checked out my health and Spears' fertility before giving us a green light to begin.

For our first session, the specialist asked me to come by for a sterile vial to carry Spears' sperm sample to its temporary home in the syringe. *I can artificially inseminate you for three months under the medical act, and if the third try doesn't take, we'll have to reconsider the problem.* With praiseworthy aplomb, Spears filled the vials I took to the doctor on the days my temperature indicated ovulation. We wrapped them in warm towels, as though they were fragile children. At the end of three months, the specialist shook his head and closed our file. *Sometimes these things can't be explained*, he said. We applied to adopt a newborn baby just in time to meet the under-forty age restriction.

Spears moved on to a new job in Penticton, directing a summer school of the arts and making the two-hour round trip daily. I couldn't name the sense I had that Spears was lost to me when, on my birthday, I sat alone on the forest carpet overlooking the valley, knees drawn up to keep me warm. I supposed it had something to do with his staying overnight occasionally in Penticton. Nothing apparent had changed other than a tightness in my chest, although teaching Canadian literature released a new passion, allowing me to forget Spears in the day and prepare lectures through the quiet evenings.

At Easter, Cathy, Woldy, and our godson, Alexander, visited, as many of our friends did during our years in the Okanagan. When I bought Alex a five-foot-tall inflatable rabbit, he fell in love. In spite of his mother's disgust at the lime green toy with its great orange carrot, he hugged it like a friend. After breakfast we walked through meadows and played softball among the sheep. Alex easily fell asleep and the four of us refilled our wine glasses and grew imaginative. *Why don't we each sing a song our fathers taught us?* Cathy asked.

Woldy began with a haunting Russian song, taught to him by his father, who had escaped Russia in the mid-forties with two babies, a wife, and his art books. Cathy went next, singing a lullaby her German father had sung to her and her sister. Spears cheered us with a risqué 1920s song from Hollywood about cocaine: *Have a snort, have a snort, have a snort on me.* When my turn came, I sang my father's train song, about a man dying in a train wreck and leaving behind a message for the woman who would wait in the house he had built them until they reunited in eternity: *Now I leave it to you, For I know you'll be true, Till we meet at the golden gate good-bye.*

During our third summer in the Okanagan, Spears built a retaining wall to keep our lawn from slipping down the mountainside. I overheard the stonemason who worked with him make a comment about the dangers of women *if you don't breed them.* After the spring thaw I planted giant tulips along the lip of the wall. The neighbors called our joint effort a work of art. Finally, a painter changed the random patches of color on our house to a uniform moss green, and we watched our cottage melt into the surrounding forest. An unloved shack had become a cozy home.

Quail marched in small armies past our house, wearing their dark coats. Like the starlings, they never ventured out alone. Steller's jays and doves furled their wings at our bird feeder, and an occasional pheasant or grouse fluttered from the roadside when our car descended the driveway. In early summer a mother chipmunk darted out of the woodpile with five perfect miniatures running after her. They scurried into hiding at the sight of me. I took these gifts as blessings on the house.

When the arts school was in full heat, I spent two weeks with Spears in Penticton. We stayed in the house of a widow without children who had lost her husband suddenly in middle age. She spent her days going through photo albums. Pictures tumbled from tables, sat in stacks on chair cushions, and slipped from kitchen counters. I wondered where a childless widow went for comfort and how she managed to return to these glossy memories.

I registered for a course on writing fiction. On impulse and at the end of the course, I invited the resident author, Aritha van Herk, to come up to our house on the mountainside while Spears stayed behind with his paperwork. She drove to and fro in her white Jaguar convertible, bought when she had won a $50,000 award for her book *Judith*. We stopped for gas midway, and a young attendant wiped the windshield while another looked on in envy. *Where'd you get the car, lady?* he asked. Aritha drawled, *I'm no fuckin' lady, kid.* I marveled at her moxie. *Don't waste time writing letters or putting up with people*, she told me as we sped onto the road. *Just get out of bed and write.* How comfortably she lived outside the bounds of convention, giving birth to characters instead of babies.

When I shared *Judith* with my mother during one of her hospital stays, she said it brought home memories of her childhood on the farm when Grandma was often alone caring for children and animals while Grandpa ran his shoe shop in Winnipeg. *I think she's writing about her own life when she talks about caring for her pigs,*

Mother told me. *It's about finding out who she is by running a farm without a man.* It occurred to me how a woman's life, like my mother's, was determined by the decade of her birth. Her appreciation of literature came naturally, although she had been a woman with little time to do anything other than read sewing patterns and recipes and type up strangers' words. In her letters and notes, I had never come across a grammatical error or a misspelling.

To avoid claustrophobia and satiate our appetite for travel, Spears and I left the Okanagan each year for a month. We read voraciously on these trips, sharing books and enjoying arguments over meaning and theme. I read Thackeray's *Vanity Fair* over his shoulder on a Greek bus when he refused to tear our paperback in half, and we fought about whether the unfaithful George was a villain or an opportunist. We hiked across a mountain in Crete until our feet bled, and found a tiny hotel with canaries singing in every room. While exploring undeveloped beaches on Corfu, we read Somerset Maugham's short stories and Graham Greene's novels. We cycled up to the ruins of Hippocrates' sacred garden and looked out over the sea from the first hospice. I wondered how the sick had let go of their lives in all this Aegean beauty.

Our compatibility changed in Paris the following summer. Before our flight left Vancouver, the stewardess called on the loudspeaker for Spears. As fast as my hand went up, Spears clamped it down. *Why did you do that?* I asked. *I don't want anything to prevent us getting out of here.* After he thought a moment, he spoke to the attendant and she gave him a French book Jane had left for me. During our second day in Paris, we quarreled over an exotic prostitute on a street corner. I asked Spears why a woman so attractive would give herself away. *It's not a gift*, he told me: *It's a business.* I accused him of purposely missing the point, and he turned on the television to watch Wimbledon. *Some day your prince will come*, he called after me as I walked out.

From a nearby restaurant, I watched French families enjoying their daily routines. Sitting near me was the eye-catching woman we had seen on the street earlier in the day. When I declined her offer of a cigarette and asked if I could buy her coffee, she got up from her table and sat across from me. She spoke a little English, I rummaged about for French verbs, and together we managed to carry on a halting conversation. Marie had twelve sisters and brothers in the Caribbean. They were the reason she was working the streets in Paris. Under the make-up was a young girl, perhaps a teenager. Her white dress was soiled around the neck and her hair needed washing, but she was painfully beautiful. I told her I had left Spears in the hotel room because he was watching television. Perhaps she thought he was watching pornography because she told me his other women were for the moment whereas his wife was for a lifetime.

Spears and I arrived home in the Okanagan to find the five baby chipmunks floating belly up in the rain barrel. Like drunks, their thirst had outsmarted their caution, and they had managed to jump into the water when the temperatures soared, but they couldn't scramble up the curved barrel to escape. I picked their small bodies out one by one and buried them behind the house where they had been born. Thoughts of their swimming around and around haunted my sleep. As they had scratched on the sides of the barrel, I had been indulging in petty squabbles with Spears, wandering France in search of yet another air-conditioned art gallery where voluptuous paintings kept me distracted from my barren existence.

In late September of 1981, Spears drove us to Vancouver to stay at the Sylvia Hotel for my fortieth birthday. We met my parents and Lynne and Ken for Sunday brunch at a favorite restaurant. When Spears dropped us off to park the car and we stood sheltered in the doorway from the rain, we realized the restaurant was closed for renovations. Lynne and I also realized our mother's pretence of being well couldn't hide her frailty. We didn't ask about the cancer that had returned for its fifth visit in three decades. Our parents had always practiced action and silence in difficult times. Spears decided on another restaurant within easy walking distance. A revolving room atop a hotel allowed diners to enjoy the mountain and ocean views.

Waiting to be seated, I caught a familiar pair of blue-gray eyes looking into mine. Corbett had driven from Calgary for an architecture conference and had dropped by the hotel to buy cigarettes. The coincidence was both momentous and natural. During lunch he blew cigarette smoke across the table as we ate but no one thought to ask him to put out his cigarettes for my mother's sake. To my parents he was blameless. They had loved him from their early middle age, and they would love him to their graves.

Months had passed since Corbett had last visited me in the Okanagan. Once I had taken him swimming with Camille, and he had commented on the selfishness of kids when she took my attention away from him. Another time he had brought a woman who did her fluttering best to accommodate the indelible ink of my connection to him. Later he phoned to say he had been working in Africa. While there he had watched a baby being born to a woman who by next morning was carrying water home from the village well. Corbett had carried it for her, impressed by her stamina and the new life she had bundled against her.

In January, Okanagan snow fell more heavily than usual, turning the surrounding hills into a white quilt. Spears had trouble getting his truck to the top of the hill. When he turned the final precarious corner, the truck stalled. Hearing the engine, I went to the door to see his fist collide with the windshield. The glass cracked like thin ice on a spring lake. I tried to restrain a laugh, having just organized a surprise birthday present for him, a used Pontiac to keep him safe and comfortable on the highway to Penticton.

After his birthday, Spears caught an airplane for a week-long conference at the Banff School of Fine Arts, and I agreed to join him for the final weekend and banquet. Perhaps it was the mountain air or the relief of being away from all our responsibilities, perhaps it was something that had taken place at the conference, but Spears reacted to my arrival like a teenaged boy toward his first girlfriend. When we spotted each other at the bus depot, his smile lit up the snowy landscape. On the way back to the school in a borrowed car, his humor rose with the altitude. Once inside the residence, he spun me into a first-floor room where we made love among the clothes and suitcases of another guest.

When Spears was offered a full-time position in the performing arts in Victoria, I balked at leaving the Okanagan. I'd spent too many pay cheques transforming the mountain cabin into a home, too many hours patching holes in the floor, making curtains for windows, and learning to garden desert soil. I'd grown attached to the Franklin stove, the log pile, and the stone steps Spears had built to reach the vegetable garden. The thought of someone else at the summer table under lilac trees where we had eaten with friends was unbearable. I needed to rest, just as Spears needed to move on.

I also feared I would be tempting fate to turn my back on a permanent faculty position in times of austerity. I opted to stay behind from September until Christmas, living alone on the mountainside, searching to understand why a life as full as the one we shared felt so empty. My consolation was the Airedale puppy we had bought the summer before when the pain of losing Fred had finally subsided. We called her Chance, and her risk-taking personality made it all the more fitting. When Spears left us for the West Coast, I was taken aback by my unexpected tears and by the puppy rushing to lick them from my cheeks. The longer the dog and I remained on the mountain, the more I wondered what life would be like by the ocean in a city of early springs and prolonged autumns.

At Christmas, Spears returned with a moving truck. I said goodbye to the little house surrounded by bridal wreath, spruce, and cedar, expecting to give up the loveliness of snow for an expanse of ocean. But Victoria surprised its residents with a rare snowfall that December. Colored lights shone from houses clothed in white. Cars skidded into snow piles, and pedestrians gathered to shove them back onto the roads. The snow melted as quickly as it had come, and Victoria became a city of cyclists in woolen mittens and bright toques. Because Spears worked in the arts community, I arrived to an instant community of friends and was surrounded by a cornucopia of theater, music, restaurants, and bookstores.

In the summer of 1982, I cycled to the library or along the waterfront until I reached downtown, where I could sit with a book and lunch at outdoor tables. It was the first time I had enjoyed the freedom to create my own day. An artist friend from Okanagan College had moved to Victoria to work at the university, and we met on campus one day when I heard a canary call from a nearby shrub. A student had set it free from the cage that defined its life. *It will learn to love its freedom*, she said, walking away. In fact, domestic canaries can't forage for themselves. I used my mother's teachings to catch the bird and take it home. It sang from its wicker cage until I thought its heart would burst for joy, especially if we played Bach or Eric Clapton. We called him *Il Buco*, the mouth.

Late in the summer, I locked my bike in front of a small downtown café. Standing in line at the counter, I glimpsed Spears having coffee with a woman who appeared awkward when I introduced myself as his wife. I had no idea why she had been startled. *It's your imagination*, Spears told me later. *Well, I hope I didn't say anything to hurt her feelings*, I worried. I was reading the book my Kelowna students had given me as a good-bye present. Margaret Atwood's *Bodily Harm* is a story of the hardships suffered by a woman who tries to live outside convention. The heroine, a writer, attempts to escape the aftermath of breast cancer by going to South America, where she is imprisoned and molested. *Do you think Atwood exaggerates the cruelty men inflict on women these days?* I asked Spears.

In autumn I began teaching at both Camosun College and the University of Victoria. I told the two department heads my husband and I had completed papers for an adoption. *You can do both things at once*, the college dean smiled. *I have no trouble with that for a sessional position*, the university department chair assured me. On free weekends Spears and I packed Chance and some food and wine in our second-hand camper and drove the back roads of Vancouver Island. In the sanctuary of coastal trees and campsites, we made love amidst the sounds of lazy rivers, eternal tides, and whispering leaves. In the morning we shivered around a fire, hugging our coffee cups, laughing at nothing we could name. Clapton played from our tape deck, and we moved our bodies to his rhythm.

We're being evicted, I told a college colleague in the office across from mine at Camosun. In November of 1982 our landlord sold our rented house, and we had to find a place with a fenced yard for Chance. Moments later, the colleague popped his head into my office: *I know of a house for sale, but it's got a cracked sink.* He shrugged as if to say this wasn't his doing. *My mother's selling it for a friend who's just died.* Without looking inside, Spears and I purchased the property, entranced by its yard of cedars, blackberry bushes, and an ancient apple tree.

The house had been lived in by only one couple. They had lost their five-year-old child and never conceived another. To help relieve the solitude during her husband's absences at sea, the wife had taken in a friend from Scotland. In time this friend helped the wife to bury her husband, and then she went on to bury the widow before falling ill with cancer herself. Neighbors told us she had died of loneliness. When I came upon a collection of licenses from the city pound, I realized their friendship had lasted through many dogs as well. We ripped off the window coverings, and sunshine dazzled the rooms. Everything in the house from hardwood floors to delicate chandeliers had remained untouched since the house had been built in 1930. Our dead-end road, two blocks from the ocean, was called Faithful Street.

In spring we returned to Greece while we waited for the adoption agency to call. Our travels through the Aegean were as lovely as our first trip to Greece had been. We came home to a summer in which my younger sister gave birth to her second son, Luke, and an autumn when Scrawny, the canary my mother and I had once shared, died. Mother considered the bird's initial survival and its long life a miracle. She saw its death as an omen of things to come.

It was in the fall of 1983 that I noticed on a weekend visit that Mother had lost considerable weight over a short time. *Acute leukemia*, she told me. When she was hospitalized in Vancouver, I took the ferry on weekends to my father's home in White Rock. Spears reacted to my exhaustion by being distant and edgy. On Thursday afternoons I escaped my parents' sorrow and Spears' irritation by studying creative writing with Jack Hodgins at the university. His guidance inspired me to corner my sadness in short stories.

When I phoned, Mother reported that Spears had seemed troubled when he visited her in the cancer ward. *It's hard for me to follow everything since chemotherapy, but he doesn't seem to like his job anymore. I guess we all feel hemmed in now and again*, she continued, implying death and a career carried the same need for courage. *Show him a little kindness, dear*, she advised, before we rang off. I found her oddly chatty for a normally quiet woman who had just lost the shelter of her flesh. *It's too bad I can't call her two days in a row*, I complained to Spears, who was watching a hockey game while I stared at the phone. *Why not?* he called back. *She's too prairie, she'd think I was being wasteful, and she'd know I think she's dying.* After the noise of someone scoring a goal, Spears called out again, *Just call her.*

I'm sorry you have no children, she said, skipping pleasantries. *If you want to tell me why you didn't, I'd be glad to listen.* Apparently she didn't believe that I had told her all I knew, including the limited options available to me as a woman of forty. I repeated an abbreviated version. She accepted my explanation, perhaps remembering how long I had kept Corbett's infertility a secret, perhaps making certain there were no wounds she might attend to while she had breath to speak. *Just be happy, dear*, she said before she told me she'd been blessed to have three healthy daughters and a wonderful husband.

On the last day of January Mother died alone in her bed in intensive care even though Father had made a supreme effort to be by her side at all times. The next day I was startled to realize the world still turned and people went about their business as usual.

While I was ironing Father's tie for the funeral in White Rock, Corbett rang the doorbell. He and his parents had come to be with my father on this awesome day, not having forgotten the years we included them as family. When I sat down momentarily on Corbett's knee in the crowded reception in Lynne's home, Joyce scolded me that I must *never do that again!*

Mother's absence changed our family in ways none of us had expected. One of the losses was my father's capacity for joy. Another was my younger sister's steady withdrawal from our family and from her former personality as she allowed herself to be consumed by a new-age religion. My older sister had begun to display an uncharacteristic apathy, a middle-aged weariness, that spread through her life. Preoccupied with Mother's death and Father's loneliness, none of us guessed cancer had begun its relentless journey through Joyce's body and had lit a small fire in my own.

The most unexpected loss came with a credit card receipt I found blowing across our bedroom floor on Faithful Street, dancing in the draft of an open window in late March 1984. *Why were you out of town for lunch today?* I shouted to Spears over the lawn mower, having noticed the address of a restaurant out on the Malahat mountain highway. *You just told me ten minutes ago that you ate at the café across from your office.* It occurred to me as I spoke I might be spoiling some surprise he was planning for the semester's break to cheer me after the funeral. When Spears shut the motor off, wrinkled his brow, and looked down at his feet, my throat constricted.

It was nothing, he said. *Are you having an affair?* I asked in a sleepy voice before I dissolved into wakefulness. *She came on to me like gangbusters,* he responded. *What if I screwed everybody who came on to me?* I shouted. *You're not into screwing around,* Spears accused me, as though I was missing some crucial gene to make me human. *Anyway, I was just having lunch with her today.* I tried to remember the last time Spears had asked me for lunch.

The first counselor I found asked to see Spears as well, and afterward told me I had a stronger core than he did. I wondered why, if this was so, he had all the fun. She asked how often we had had sex the previous month. *Eleven times*, I told her, after a moment's calculation. *You're not unhappily married*, she insisted. The second counselor also wanted to see Spears. She told me he was addicted to addictions and I was addicted to him. After discussing my family, she said he was the same as my sister Lynne – inconsistent and fabricating reality as they went along. She explained I had been brought up to care for my younger sister, and I had transferred this caring to my husband, who was also the entertaining baby of his family. As I left she hugged me and suggested I could do better than live with Spears. She didn't say how a woman manages to be twice divorced in a world where divorced men are often pampered and divorcees avoided.

I took the ferry to listen to my father tell about the bleakness of his week, to fuss over him a little and to ask how his orphaned siblings had adapted to adoption after his parents died. *I can't talk about all that sad stuff now, damn it!* he snapped. *I was just trying to talk about things, Dad*, I persisted. *It's just a matter of luck*, he said, not for the first time. Spears and I had stopped talking about adoption. We hadn't heard from the agency in a year, and we were advised the wait might be long, even though we were well educated and employed home owners who were legally married and under the age of forty when we applied. It occurred to me how little this information described a couple's worthiness for parenting. Spears had grown indifferent to Camille with her outbursts of teenage angst, and I had grown frustrated with her obsession for lewd jokes and boyfriends. A friend had remarked that *God created teenagers so parents could bear losing them*. But Camille was only thirteen.

During one visit Camille stood behind Spears as he sat on a stool talking to me. With her arms around his neck, she rubbed against his back and talked in a high and silly voice. When she left the room my nerves were taut as wire, and I suggested he should advise her about the dangers of rubbing up against men before she ended up on the street or pregnant or both. *You're such a paranoid bitch*, Spears hissed between tight lips. I picked up a small milk jug, threatening to toss the contents at him. As I sat it back on the counter, his knee hit my groin and I rose off the wooden floor. *Maybe that'll loosen a few eggs.* Spears' sarcasm left me as breathless as the blow had. Suddenly Camille was there. *You okay?* she asked, her cheeks ashen. I realized I must have cried out when his knee collided with my pubic bone. *I'm okay,* I told her.

For two days I could barely move or sit down. He never said he was sorry, and we never spoke of the incident. At the end of the weekend when Camille left and the pain remained jagged, I examined myself with a hand mirror. Dark bruising spread like a tainted lotus flower. I began to shake uncontrollably, wishing my mother was alive or one of my sisters accessible. Nothing had ever happened to make me feel as worthless as that image of my wounded womanhood. It stayed in my mind even after I had put the mirror away and sat down gently to write a letter to the adoption agency. I asked Spears to sign it if he agreed we should give up the quest for a child. He signed without hesitation.

When Camille visited months later, she took on the mood of the house. *Nobody thinks I'm pretty in glasses,* she said, waiting for me to make everything okay. *I can't teach you to see the way I taught you to talk,* I huffed, reminding her how I had used a tape recorder to encourage her to speak up at the table. When I saw her face fall, I felt the horror of what I had become in the short time since I had last seen her. *I'll get contact lenses for you when you're older, and those turquoise eyes will bowl the guys over,* I promised. She looked at me with desperate hope. *I'm not exactly popular like you,* she said, frowning when my laugh came out as a snort. We stood side by side facing the hall mirror – Camille distorted by glasses, and me distorted by betrayal.

The eye doctor said Camille bordered on legal blindness, a problem easily avoided with eyedrops at the time of birth. The diagnosis explained why, in spite of her intelligence, she couldn't catch an orange I had thrown her again and again, why she couldn't ride a bicycle easily, and why she sat with her nose against the television screen. Blindness also explained the night I had taken her to see the bespectacled Nana Mouskouri singing in Vancouver: *When do I see her?* Camille had asked afterward. For the musical *Cats* I bought tickets in the front row. *This is the best show in my whole life*, she whispered.

I visited Father the following month determined to save him from the sorrow of removing Mother's clothes from her closet. He still talked of *we*, unable to accept himself as a widower: *We went for groceries yesterday*, he would say out of habit after forty-nine years in Mother's company. Father watched as I packed three boxes of clothes for charity: *You're about the same size, you could wear her things*. I couldn't find words to explain why wearing Mother's clothes wouldn't be desirable or healthy, but I salvaged one fleecy outfit to wear when Father visited Victoria.

On an early May morning, though, I dressed and turned into the hallway to see my mother standing in front of me. She had a look of astonishment on her face. In less time than it took to inhale, I realized I was looking in a mirror at myself wearing Mother's fleecy blue pants and jacket. Her leukemia and my despair had returned us both to the weight of our teenage years, and I had slipped into her clothes as though they had been made for me, the gentle aroma of her body a comfort.

What's her name? I asked Spears. *What does it matter?* He refused to tell me, and I felt an outsider in my own marriage. Over the next few days, I pieced together bits of information about his time away from home, especially his classmates in an evening course in French where he was the star pupil. *A real actor*, the teacher had told me. An image kept returning of the day I ran into Spears after I had taught a class at the university and he was supposedly in the language laboratory listening to French tapes. A woman in a navy suit with a short skirt sat with her knees too far apart, looking up at the man standing over her. At second glance, I saw that the blushing man was Spears. I walked by, pushing open the double doors that led back to my office, closing off the scene behind me.

Trish Dick, I told him. *Aren't we clever,* Spears conceded. I slammed the bathroom door and sat on the closed seat for an hour, waiting for him to knock, wishing I had listened to my mother's warning about divorcing Corbett, forgetting she had fallen in love with Spears too. An hour later I opened the door to find myself alone in the house. *Don't you think you've spent enough time in melodrama city?* Spears asked the next day. *You've known about your affair for almost a year, but it's hot off the press for me,* I yelled. *How could you sneak around when my mother was dying?*

Your mother would have known what to do, Father sighed. *At the end of the day, remember where your home is,* Cathy told Spears. *He's just cruising,* his recently divorced co-worker advised, taking me to a concert up-island. *It's the nature of the beast,* his squash partner said, stopping by for wine and crackers. *He's just another male asshole,* a girlfriend quipped between mouthfuls of salad. *Don't let bitterness change your face,* the French teacher told me. *It's called elevator sex,* Spears' old roommate explained. My doctor smothered a smile when I told him I would have had elevator sex if Spears had asked me. *I cut off my husband's pant legs and the arms of his shirts when he threatened to be unfaithful,* a gentle colleague confided. *He's probably gay,* another female friend opined. *You must work at being naive,* a theater owner shrugged. *It ruins everything,* Spear's mother sympathized, her voice solemn. She showed me a picture of herself when she had fallen in love in her early twenties, sitting on a rock in a bathing suit. How beautiful she had once been.

It's Spears' wife, I announced to Trish Dick on the phone. *Do you want to talk to me or do you want me to talk to your husband?* The receiver slipped from my grasp as my palm sweated. *You have six seconds to decide.* After a full minute, she amazed me with the normalcy of her voice, neither sultry nor syrupy as I had imagined. *I'm five foot ten and weigh one hundred and eighteen pounds, and I'm twenty-eight,* she said, bewildering me by talking about her vital statistics when I wanted to talk about her morality. *Spears is forty-three and I'm forty-two,* I told her, confident she would see I was more well suited to him. *I'll phone back when your husband's there.*

I'll meet you for coffee tomorrow morning around ten-thirty; I'll be finished my first meeting by then, she said. Perhaps she had heard the quiver in my voice. Perhaps she was familiar with the hysteria of betrayed wives. She arranged our rendezvous as though I was just another business appointment she would have to endure. When we hung up, I felt flushed with success, but then something registered to make me sit poker straight on the telephone stool: Trish Dick was younger than my younger sister.

My hands shook as I tried to bring a coffee mug to my lips the following morning. Breakfast was out of the question; I gagged on toothpaste. The dress I selected was red silk and fit me like a leotard. The neckline plunged to where I made certain a new bra produced as much cleavage as its modest B cups could muster. My shoes were all straps and heels in shiny red patent leather with matching purse. I slid black nylons up to a new garter belt and stroked my nails with red polish before I applied blue eye shadow and black mascara. Once my lips and cheeks had a gloss to them, I was ready to roll.

When I slithered from the car, I had difficulty navigating the parking lot in stiletto heels. Trish and I had agreed to meet at a coffee shop attached to a motel known for hiring strippers with names like Lovely Lulu and Perky Polly, talent advertised on its neon sign. Judging by the number of cars, the place attracted a lot of people even in the morning. Men turned their heads, and I gave each of them a slow smile, tossing my long hair as my heels clicked past the tables. The woman waiting for me at the back of the room appeared to be in uniform. Her navy dress was gathered at the neck by a white cowl. A series of pleats fell from her shoulders to mid-calf, where navy stockings rose up from flat shoes. *Are you Trish?* I asked, using the husky tone I'd practiced in the car. *Spears told me you were beautiful,* she smiled.

Looking across the table, I imagined Spears' hands roaming around the flesh hidden under its loose cover. *Where did it happen?* I asked. *Which time?* she retaliated. *Any time.* Perspiration tickled the back of my neck. *In his blue cruisemobile*, she said, using his expression. *I gave him that car to keep him safe*, I confessed, instantly regretting my confession. *Mostly we got together over picnic lunches in your camper*, she went on. *He brought the dope and I brought the wine.* I thought about our funky old camper, the striped curtains I'd sewn, the yellow cushions propped on the padded bench that unfolded into a double bed. *How can I believe you?* I asked. By the time she told me everything I demanded to know, I wanted to gouge the knowledge from my brain, to stand in the middle of the road and let a ten-ton truck deliver me from pain.

It was just sex, Trish said, walking to her car as I stumbled along beside her. *We met in French lessons, and he was the darling of the class, quick and funny. We never talked of love and he broke it off, nothing for you to worry about.* When I didn't respond she went on to detail their sex play, a small grin playing at the corners of her mouth. What woman in her right mind would want love if she could get what Trish got without doing the laundry, buying groceries, or sharing a mortgage? When she realized I was rooted to the concrete, she climbed into her dark blue Ford and rolled down her window. *You're too good for him*, she said. *He's a boozer.* My breath caught. *He called you a titless wonder with a flat ass and a hook nose*, I said, hopelessly happy I had remembered his exact words. When I turned away, my chest quarreled with a desire to turn back, to tell her I was sorry, to be decent. She had dressed to fool me as I had dressed to fool her. Two women who might have been friends if they hadn't met a trickster.

You did it in our camper while my mother was dying, I accused. *Would you have liked it if I'd brought her home?* he asked. *Why did you have to take her anywhere?* I demanded. *We had a connection, that's all. It's what she does*, he explained as the doorbell rang. *Why do I have to end up with all the losers?* He left me to ponder his question while he welcomed his squash partner into our kitchen for a beer.

I changed into my jean overalls, climbed into my Honda, and stepped on the accelerator. The car bounced off the back of the camper. Lights came on along the front porches of Faithful Street. "Manha de Carnival," I thought, and stepped on the accelerator again. I got out to discover I had dented the front of my car and barely scratched the camper. Undeterred, I roared to the front of the van, put my Honda in reverse, backing into its headlights. I could see Spears and his friend watching from our living room window. They looked as though they were taking in a sports event. I walked past them and went to bed. Spears sauntered into the room and turned on the lights, cocky on an excess of beer. *You're just feeling left out*, he told me. *Left out?* I asked. *I was almost forty before I could afford a decent car of my own*, I cried, as though someone else had been at the wheel. After work next day, I drove to campus where he was playing squash, left my car locked in the parking lot, and drove home in the cruisemobile with the extra key.

Jane arrived from UBC with four exquisite coffee mugs from a Gulf Island potter. After greeting me, she pointed to a hyacinth on my mantel: *You wouldn't let it wither, so why do you neglect yourself?*

I didn't consciously decide to stay with Spears. We simply drew back from the trauma, intermittently reaching the same playful heights we had once known, especially on holidays. Perhaps Spears and I both assumed the old feelings would return eventually and bring with them the trust I once had. With effort I believed him when he declared how badly he felt, how loyal he would be, how Trish Dick had been an aberration, a token of discontent in his forties. I sang as I wandered around the house, wondering why he still came home late: *I'm a little teapot, short and stout, This is my handle, this is my spout.*

Camille accused me of not loving her anymore, and I tried to explain. *It has nothing to do with you, sweetie, it's a problem between me and your father.* The three of us were ice-skating at an inside rink when I realized my sensitivity had plummeted with my marriage. After going twice around the rink as a trio, sliding and swaying from side to side in time to the music, I noticed she was skating on her ankles rather than her blades. *Look at you*, I chided. *Stand up straight.* I loosened my hand from hers, shot ahead of them, and swept into a figure-eight. *Watch!* I called. I could feel an old rhythm and confidence in my feet as I gathered speed. As I lifted off the ice, a blade caught my pant leg and I bounced off the boards and onto my knees.

Spears laughed and Camille remained deadpan as he spun her around the circle of the rink. When she caught her breath, she complained the skates hurt her. *No one would feel comfy skating on their ankles*, I told her. The hour ended and we sat together on the bench, taking off our skates. While Spears and I shoved our feet into our everyday boots, Camille sat still and alert, her attention on something I couldn't see, eyes full of tears, feet still in skates. I thought she was disappointed in herself, as she often seemed to be, and I encouraged her that none of us skated easily and well until we had done it a few times. When Spears eased her skates off her feet, she yelped like a puppy. Blood oozed from where her toes were skinned from scraping against hard inner edges.

She had been afraid to tell us the skates didn't fit in case we left her behind. The father who had left her mother behind was now threatening to leave her stepmother, and she saw her tenuous future dissolving. Deferred gratification was something she had never been able to afford, squeezed as she had been between short weeks of being mindlessly spoiled and long years of going without. To her, future comforts depended on our being together.

Although Spears had agreed to stay put awhile if I gave up yet another faculty position to follow him to Victoria, when a job came up at a theater up-island, he came home full of reasons why this would be a great opportunity for us. If he got the job he would have his own theater, a chance to bring in entertainers from across the country and places we had traveled. He promised to do the two-hour round trip without complaining or expecting us to give up the home we had barely finished renovating.

Spears drove off to become the impresario he dreamed of being. He began a classical music ensemble on Sundays, organized appearances by k.d. lang, Long John Baldry, and Rita MacNeil, ran a foreign film society, and commuted there and home every day. In return, I traveled weekends over the mountain road after dark, sometimes taking a friend, sometimes alone, exhausted after a week of teaching, often not seeing Spears except to say hello or to wave at him up in the lighting booth. *Guess who I saw today?* he asked one Friday as we made dinner together. *Who?* I asked, peeling a cucumber. *Trish Dick*, he told me, as though sharing a joke. *Did she come to see you?* I asked, chest clenched. *She was just passing through, and we happened to meet by accident at the opening of a new mall. New boobs*, he announced. I dropped the scraper into the sink and rummaged about through peelings to retrieve it. *How do you know that?* I asked. *She opened her suit jacket and did a little demo.*

My happiest times were when I drove my father up-island to Spears' theater. He allowed me to view things from a different slant, sometimes unintentionally comical. He would often ask a question and then, without realizing, answer it himself: *Why do those ballet fellows wear such tight pants? You'd think they want people to see everything they have. Why does that Baldry guy smoke when he sings? He looks like he doesn't give a damn. Why do they have two intermissions? People just buy alcohol.* Since Spears arrived home long after the city was asleep, Father and I would get up before him in the morning and go down to the edge of the ocean cliff to watch windsurfers challenge the waves or walk through Beacon Hill Park where lawn bowlers played under sun hats.

Everything will work out, Father comforted: *Spears told me it was harder for a guy who's been married more than once to be faithful.* I couldn't understand why Father believed a ready-made excuse that denied the same privilege to women. *Just get him to put his hand on the bible and pledge his loyalty*, Father continued. His trust made me realize how many miles I'd traveled away from home. I thought of Spears' experienced hand caressing a bible. *Some men can be like stallions, they just go from one mare to another if given the chance*, Father advised. I tired of Father's homilies. *I want to be a stallion then*, I told him: *It's less pathetic.*

After Mother's death, I no longer took life or luck for granted.

I wondered if Spears would reach home unscathed from the winding highway. I worried over having been condemned by the comments of two wives who frequented the theater and were married to men on the arts board. They chose to stay home and berate career women as selfish. After making it clear they didn't approve of me on the grounds of my having *decided* not to have children, they told me how they followed their men to *the corners of the earth*. According to them I was a woman carelessly zipping up and down the highway in my own car, neglecting to pack my husband's lunch, and never taking a day off to help him out. They argued that a real woman *caters to her man* no matter how much he asks of her and remains discreet rather than long-faced over his indiscretions. *I guess life is different when you don't like children,* one woman told me as she flounced about serving Christmas cocktails in a red dress. I returned to Victoria with a new appreciation of my teaching life.

The following summer I went to Pearson College where the Metchosin Summer School of the Arts, an hour's drive from Victoria, offered a course by a writer and theater critic. There I wrote out the story of my days with Camille, who flew in from New York State and came with Spears to hear me read on the final night. *Were you jealous of Linda?* she asked, astounded. *I guess I was jealous she had you, and she was jealous I had your dad.* The next day as I swam lengths in the college pool, a woman waited until I pulled myself out of the water to tell me she had found lasting happiness after leaving a circumstance like mine. I wasn't certain how to regard this free advice. Having given all I had to make the marriage work, there seemed nothing left to leave for now.

Almost two years had passed since Spears had ended his affair with Trish Dick, but the experience still defined us as the guilty and the innocent. I often wished we shared space on the same emotional planet where neither of us felt remorse or anger. I tired of friends calling me naive and Spears a womanizer. I also grew increasingly accustomed to shame as though it was a cape of disgrace I had been born to wear.

I had never noticed Rock until late summer of 1984 when he walked into my office wearing shorts and sandals. His thick hair sprinkled with silver and his bronze tan reminded me of my father. His broad shoulders and long lashes over blue eyes reminded me I was alive. Although Rock was considered bright and industrious in his area of expertise, I seemed to have lost interest in matters of the intellect and become charmed by the way he turned his shoulders at a slight angle to ease past others in the hallway.

His presence assaulted my common sense. Trish Dick's long limbs disappeared from my nightmares after I heard him say, *I hate tall women*. I never consciously resolved that a physically appealing man with no wife and children would be a solution to the unlevel playing field with Spears. Instead I followed my hormones and began tucking a flower in my hair each day, filling vases with bouquets for my office window, wearing dresses instead of slacks and blouses. In spite of having no idea how to proceed from nonsensical conversations over the Xerox machine to hot sex in a bachelor's bedroom, I imagined myself a *femme fatale*.

Cathy suggested I ask him for coffee. On Monday I carried some essays with me as I rushed over to Rock's desk to give him the chance to ask me for coffee since I couldn't seem to ask him. As I turned into his office his phone rang, and the sound startled me into dropping thirty-five assignments on the floor. I was squatting near his chair retrieving the papers when a colleague walked in on my humiliation. For days afterward I tried to redeem myself through conversation, comparing the view from my office to the one from his: *Mine is better than yours because when the leaves fall I can see the ocean whereas you look over a courtyard*. He looked out his office window as though he was seeing the view for the first time. *Come see me sometime* ran through my head, but not off my tongue. The next day I discussed the harsh effects of computer screens on the human eye and how it was beneficial for ocular health to stare into the distance every now and again. I mentioned being at an advantage because I didn't have to wear glasses, hoping he would realize I had no need to slip on contact lenses with my morning coffee. At the paper cutter, I was telling him that Aldous Huxley had written about the benefits of eye exercises and looked down to see I had sliced a corner off a dozen essays.

Finally, I slipped a note under his door. While I lectured on Margaret Laurence's *The Diviners*, focusing on the pitfalls of being a woman with independent values in a narrow world, I recalled a friend's advice: *Never put anything in writing.* I considered the students' reactions if Rock published my note in the school paper. Instead he said, *That was quite a note.* We drove to a restaurant for lunch. I drank three glasses of wine before he had finished one beer.

So what are we doing here if we're not going to bed? he asked. My protests and blushes seemed ridiculous in the aftermath of telling him I was forty-four. Soon I found myself exactly where I had fantasized – in a bachelor's bed. At the moment of mutual glory one of his housemates returned, banging doors and making wisecracks. I realized Rock was a person with friends and a kitchen, not to mention a girlfriend who visited on weekends. Having consumed my week's quota of wine in one hour, I could feel a headache coming on.

Startled into the humdrum reality of middle age, I wondered if I would look different in the mirror now that I had crossed over the River Styx. When I stepped from Rock's car and into the calm of home, I was startled by my having worn a wrap-around purple dress to class. In the hall mirror, I saw the flower in my hair flattened beyond recognition. I went straight to the basement and dropped my dress, stockings, panties, and bra into the steadily filling machine. With the flower still in my hair, I sat on the edge of the bed, my energy sapped by an unfamiliar post-coital loneliness.

When I invited Rock for lunch, we ate on the deck looking into the green of late spring and talked about the Queen Charlotte Islands where we both planned to holiday with our separate mates. He didn't suggest I run away with him to a distant island of our own. I watched from the window as Rock drove off and Spears' car pulled into the very spot he had vacated. When Spears burst through the door, I realized he trusted me and always would. He was completely preoccupied with covering his own tracks.

My final rendezvous with Rock was in the front seat of his car. I'll never know whether it would have been an exciting alternative to our earlier meetings. A man with a camera began photographing us immediately after we had exchanged something close to a kiss. The encounter brought to mind tawdry letters in Ann Landers' column. I was no longer certain I enjoyed being the other woman.

The first repercussion came as Spears and I sat on a ferry making its way past the Gulf Islands to Vancouver. One of my students who was also on the boat interrupted my reading to talk about balance, how hard it was to keep an equilibrium between play and work, how important physical fitness was to intellectual effort. When I suggested friends were essential to a balanced life, he asked if I meant *friends like Rock*. Spears didn't look up from his magazine.

Shortly afterward Spears and I left in our camper for our vacation on the Queen Charlotte Islands, having replaced the cushions, curtains, and the spare-tire cover. Our trip began auspiciously when the engine burst into flames before we had lost sight of Victoria, but once we smothered the fire the camper churned back to life. With no itinerary besides getting there, we took a sixteen-hour ferry trip up the Inland Passage from Port Hardy to Prince Rupert and then a seven-hour ferry ride to the Islands. Wildflowers dotted silken sands, small jewels in leafy cups. Hidden deep in the forest, I wrote a card to my father, glancing up just in time to see one of the island's black bears, famous for their aggressiveness and size, within two feet of me. *Fuckin' hell*, Spears hollered, flinging me into the camper. We watched the bear shear off the top of the cooler, rob a three-day supply of food, and leap from table to tree when Spears blew a yellow whistle. It shimmied up the trunk, shedding pancake mix from a bag hooked onto its incisor, yellow flour powdering the forest floor.

Each night at dinner hour Spears and I listened to CBC's Lister Sinclair on our battery radio while we cooked on a two-burner stove, washed dishes under a hand pump, and folded out the infamous camper bed. In the morning, our bodies curved into one, we peeked out from our shared sleeping bag to see mist rising amid enormous trees. Through postcards, I took Father on our month-long journey into the rain forests and Haida settlements. The natives' ready smiles, their longhouses, and silver jewelry, folklore and totems, created a place of forgetfulness.

Just before dark in a remote site, we set up our solitary camp. Our van was unpacked beside a crackling fire, towels strung out on a line, folding chairs down-wind from smoke, and food secured next to a pail of water. I recognized the sound of Rock's four-wheel drive when it came up beside us and then passed on its way to another sanctuary before night descended. Strangers would have waved to each other, but we barely looked across the space between us. Spears commented on the lengths some people will go to make their point.

On the ferry home, Spears disappeared into the bar. *Don't fall asleep*, he slurred as I tucked him into the bottom bunk of our rented cubicle. *Don't worry*, I whispered, opening my book to read in time to the rocking waves. We woke up to a fist banging on our door. *You bloody fell asleep*, he accused me. Our camper sat alone in the bowels of the vast steel hull, a stubborn argument against the ship's crew locking up. *We're coming*, I called out to its dented corners before I began to laugh, finally falling to my knees and holding my stomach at the absurdity of it all. *Get ahold of yourself*, Spears barked. In the morning, he apologized as we set out to drive down island toward Victoria. A worn but welcome peace hovered over us.

When Rock's girlfriend moved to Victoria, she and I found ourselves in the same shower in the gym after she returned from jogging and I came in from the squash courts. I was happy to be dancing fit at the moment her eyes fell on my body in the glare of institutional lights. After I dressed, I mumbled something about being sorry for what had come to pass. *I don't know what you're talking about*, she cut me off. My confession was too coy for repentance, her response too quick for sincerity. I wanted to say that casual affairs are overestimated, bereft of the warmth of social approval and the silk of post-coital sleep.

After my infatuation, I came to believe Spears' promise to be faithful. Surely he too must know the ultimate emptiness of an affair.
I relaxed under the illusion that my life would unfold as other
people's seemed to do. On a night like any other, as Spears and I fell
asleep, the phone rang. Because of the late hour, my first thought
was of my father, alone and perhaps ill. Instead I heard Corbett's
voice. The woman he had been living with was about to have his
baby. *I could see his fist in the ultrasound*, Corbett told me. I felt an
instant and overwhelming joy, perhaps the kind a woman feels
when she hears her husband has regained consciousness after a terrible accident.

What the hell did he want? Spears asked. After I shared
Corbett's news, he turned his back on me: *Why did he phone you
about it?* I thought back to Corbett telling me his woman had a
school-age son when they met. Spears interrupted my thoughts:
Why'd you make me have that operation? His voice was angry. *I
had nothing to do with your decision*, I reminded him. *It was
between you and your specialist.*

The birth of Corbett's son brought together unrelated bits of
my past, making me interpret the world around me with new eyes
and ears. I hesitated to swallow whole the points of view rolling off
the tongues and pens of supposed experts. I wondered where I
might have gone for medical advice if not to the top of the medical
chain in Cambridge. I discovered an article suggesting male infertility from mumps could heal itself in time, though it didn't reveal
how much time. At forty-six I was left to consider that the doctors
who had misdiagnosed Corbett may also have misdiagnosed me.

When Corbett brought his son to visit, the boy was almost two.
Corbett had married the mother a year after the birth, and they
now made a family of four. We kept our day simple, taking the child
to the playground, sitting together in a sandbox. The boy scrambled around the slide, the merry-go-round, and the monkey bars.
He was a bear cub reflection of his father, a powerhouse of curiosity and brawn. Corbett's eyes had always been on me when we were
together, but in the playground they were on his son, heart of his

heart, child of his loins. *I have to watch him,* he said, as though embarrassed: *You never know.*

Something in me evaporated. I lost interest in why Spears often arrived home late and kept friends who didn't include me in their parties, gatherings I preferred to avoid in any case. Instead I put my energy into my students at Camosun College, into visits to Father whose health floundered with mini-strokes, and into playing squash several times a week. I kept Sundays free to reconnect with Spears. Arduous weeks of teaching often ended with my driving up to his theater when I wasn't scrubbing and cooking for my father. My life was in the service of two men and five classes of over one hundred and fifty students each semester. I no longer wondered how I could restore our home to a place of companionship and purpose. Whenever reflection threatened to intrude on my unstable life, I simply opened another novel, taking my imagination to places where no disappointment could wound hidden flesh or corrode small dreams.

Death did not do well in separating my parents. Father simply kept Mother alive in his imagination when she was no longer sitting across from him over dinner. In this way he lost her over and over again, as people do when they grieve. *Can I have this picture?* I asked, discovering a photograph of my mother from their courtship when she was a woman of twenty wearing pearls and a self-conscious smile. *Not yet.* Father shook his head. He chose solitude over the women who pursued him, and I echoed the advice of my friends when I chastised him for wasting his charm on perpetual sorrow. Widows were caught off-guard when his green eyes spoke of suffering, and they imagined themselves young again: *Oh my, your father has such a head of hair.* When I tried to tempt him by repeating their flattery, he was ready with an answer: *Your mother always kept it clipped for me.*

One widow had responded to the church's announcement of Mother's funeral by stopping in front of Father's house a few weeks after her death. She arrived behind the wheel of a red sports car, its top down, wearing a dress to match. I was cutting his hair in front of the big front window, our presence hidden by sheer curtains. *Can you get rid of her?* my seventy-six-year-old father asked, rising from his chair, snippings of silver hair scattering on the rug. His escape into the back garden exhibited more energy than I had seen in a long while. I answered the door in my bare feet, still holding the scissors. The woman appeared to have prepared herself for my father's dimming sight and diminishing testosterone. Tall, slim, and aggressive, she wore crimson lipstick to set off the reddish tint in her hair. *I have no idea where he is,* I told her, tapping the scissors against my empty palm.

Father's confidence returned the following week when he faced a female realtor who had spotted Mother's obituary in *The Peace Arch News*. She assured him that selling his ocean-view property would give him *a new lease on life*. My parents had discovered the property when they moved from Manitoba eleven years earlier. When they had subdivided their ocean-view lot to build a sturdy house where their cottage once stood, Father stared at the rubble: *Took three hours for that damn bulldozer to rip up three years' work.* Mother had told me she had been hemming the bathroom curtains for their new home when the Cancer Clinic called. Father was watching an early football match between the Winnipeg Blue Bombers and the Saskatchewan Roughriders at the moment when their future changed. *Do you want me to tell you now or after the game?* Mother asked. He switched off the television while she confessed to having leukemia, her fifth and final cancer.

The realtor knew nothing of this when she slithered up the steps and greeted Father with an unsavory warmth. He responded with his puzzled look, the one he used with his daughters when we demanded something he felt was beneath consideration. Then he surprised me. An undramatic man for the most part, he shut the door in her face and leaned his forehead against its smooth wood.

Lynne organized a local widow to bring Father dinners made of leftovers from banquets she catered at their church. This aging shepherdess delivered meals to him on the unreliable wheels of her rusty Datsun. Father felt obligated to complain, *Your mother knew when to be quiet.* But roast beef dinners with potatoes solved the problem of what to do with the groceries he carried in from the store when I wasn't there. I pasted notes on his refrigerator door to remind him to heat his milk before he spooned in Ovaltine.

About six months after Mother's funeral, Father lost consciousness. The college secretary brought a note to my classroom, saying Lynne had called for me to come quickly. Father remained locked in his own world for twenty-eight days, picking imaginary insects from the air above his hospital bed and making garbled sounds no one could translate. The doctors found a fracture in his spine, but further X-rays proved it was an old wound none of us could explain. Only once during the month did Father make some kind of sense. I was alone with him at the time, talking softly to him while his familiar but unseeing eyes moved in reaction to a world apart from my own.

Without warning, he spoke lucidly. *Betty*, he said, calling me by my teenaged name, *we miss you.* I knew immediately he was not physically ill. My father had simply gone crazy with grief. He was sick with the knowledge he had lost the woman who had once saved him from the deaths and losses in his boyhood family and, with her, his chance to see himself as normal. I sat by his bed and carried on a monologue about how important he was in his daughters' lives. As quickly as he had lost consciousness, he regained it, tossing aside his bedding, asking me to drive him home.

Once there and without a flicker of disbelief, Father told me Mother had come to him in the night, sitting on the edge of their bed, talking with him as they always talked during their half century of bedding down together. When she glided out of the room, her silk nightie loose around her slender form, he discovered his limbs could not move to follow her. She left him rooted to his loneliness until morning's light freed him to face an empty kitchen.

During summer, Father took me to a Sand Castle Festival at the ocean's edge in White Rock. Artists competed to create statues, sculpting recognizable gestures and facial expressions during low tide. Our favorite was a train with the driver leaning out the engine window and someone waving good-bye from the caboose. After dinner, Father mentioned having something to show me and waited at the door, a sweater over his shoulders, impatient for me to lace up my joggers. We returned to stand wordless above a beach now covered by the incoming tide. No sign remained that anything had taken place on the sand except a few Styrofoam cups bouncing on small ripples working their way up the beach. *Can you believe it?* Father said, both of us staring into the silence that just hours before had been a carnival of activity. It was his way of showing me how the years disappear in the turning of a moment.

When I visited during winter, Father kept logs burning in the living room fireplace to keep me comfortable while I graded essays and prepared for classes. After I cleaned his bathroom and cooked a meal, I made him turn off the sports channel and talk with me as we shared dinner. In these hours together we came to know each other as loving friends with separate lives, rather than simply as wise father and respectful daughter.

Spears and my plan to leave for Asia in June of 1987 gave us an exciting short-term focus. Our trips had always been havens of uninterrupted movement and conversation, a time to renew ourselves in the company of each other. With our knapsacks packed for five weeks and our passports up to date, we flew to Hong Kong. In our two days there, we made friends with an engineer from England who appreciated the company of Westerners after eight months away from family.

I'll never know exactly what happened in Singapore. It had something to do with an altercation Spears and I had over my picking a perfect orchid off the floor of the airport. The flower had been knocked from a display by a passerby and lay at the bottom of the escalator. I attached the lovely blossom to my hair. *You could get us arrested*, Spears accused me. *I suppose you'd rather be with Tricky Dicky*, I quipped. Spears disappeared in the morning, leaving me to ponder the equatorial heat in an enormous city of strangers.

All the emptiness of my life rushed toward me, and I returned to our hotel room to look down on the swimming pool far below. I told myself I would be okay if I went down to join the women who sat by the pool with their husbands and children. Once there I saw the families as insular and preoccupied. A rippling haze obscured my vision as my heart thundered. Sounds of splashing arms and legs seemed distant. When I dove into the pool my vision remained fuzzy. I thought I might be suffering heat stroke and returned to the air-conditioned cool of the hotel. As my head cleared, I watched uniformed police do their morning exercises in a distant garden.

I took out a bottle of tiny blue pills my doctor had given me for the treatment of heart fibrillations, a sensation he attributed to stress. Rolling the bottle between my palms, I thought about a writer who had visited my class and said to my students, midway through his reading, *A broken leg gets more attention than a broken heart.* I learned later that his woman had left him. I thought too of the doctor who had prescribed the pills. He suggested I get a hysterectomy even though I exhibited no symptoms of needing one. *Your spirit's much stronger than your body,* he said, as though he thought my problems would disappear with my uterus. *I like my womb,* I told him.

Thinking back on these conversations in the clarity of a foreign city made me realize what I wanted – to be near a kindly voice, to say to someone how it was after the hollowness of heartbreak, to tell someone who would listen that poets had got it wrong: Heartbreak is not a terrible force, but a nothingness worse than pain. If I couldn't experience a natural evolution into motherhood, at least I wanted to have a normal transition into menopause. Mocking that possibility, however, was the suspicion that perhaps this next stage would bring further emptiness. When darkness fell, I sat on the edge of the bed facing a window, looking into the night.

A stillness fell over me like a net cast into a gentle wind. One hand turned the white plastic top on the bottle and the other held the vial. It seemed better to die alone than to live in public shame. I poured the bottle's contents into my mouth as I had seen men pour sunflower seeds into theirs, head back, jaw slack. They tasted like dusty orange pits. In tribute to some illusion of decorum perhaps learned from a movie or a book, I lay down on the bed and extended my limbs as though standing at attention.

Spears bounced into the room and flicked on the light. *Ready to check out the town?* he asked, gathering his toiletries to shower off from the day's heat. *I've swallowed some blue pills*, I told him, my throat dry as though on the verge of a cough: *Could you come and sit by me a minute?* My voice sounded muffled. *No*, he said, his tone angry. As I struggled to focus, I saw my father waiting for me to come home, sitting where he could see out his front window. I saw his life bracketed by the deaths of those he loved. I heard him blaming himself for being unable to save his mother and sister from the prairie flu, his father from a cough, his wife from cancer, his daughter from despair.

In that lucid moment I knew too that Spears would feel nothing beyond the inconvenience of having to take me home in a wooden box and the excitement of telling an outrageous story to friends. Like a sleepwalker, I went to the elevator and swept down through the vertical shaft, passed the doorman, and opened a taxi door. Spears followed me. *Take me to the hospital*, I told the driver. *Which one?* he asked. *The closest one*, I said, suddenly grateful for the driver's bilingual ear and tongue. Then I sunk into an abyss of nothingness.

When I regained consciousness, a woman in white stood at the foot of my bed. *We almost lost you*, she said. *Can I see the doctor?* I asked, authority in my voice to cover shame. *I am the doctor*, she said. She told me: *You'll have to learn to be more spiritual.* Her tone was hushed as though other people listened. *It's necessary for a woman.* I looked around me at the empty beds, wondering whether I was dreaming. *I'm going home now*, I told her. *It's after two o'clock in the morning*, she warned, looking at her watch. *I'm going anyway. My husband may come if I phone him.* Walking back to the hotel Spears filled me in on the details: *They couldn't get your mouth to stay closed.*

Wandering in the darkness of Singapore at night, Spears and I passed a fortune teller in a narrow lane. He sat at a small table with two rickety stools, his face lit by a coal oil lamp. I turned back to sit on his empty stool and looked into the shadows of his face. *My fortune?* I asked, not knowing if he understood me. He stared into my eyes for a dizzying length of time. *No,* he said. *You must not think other women anything. Not important.* His face was the color of dust, his accent unlike any I had heard. *These things go.* After he spoke, his eyes took on a distant look, dismissing me. He didn't ask for money or appear to notice the bills I placed near his hands.

I became, as the expression goes, *beside myself,* estranged from daily life, a woman on hold. Catching a bus in Singapore, we traveled through Malaysian rubber tree plantations by moonlight. Spears grew anxious, complaining because his seat was too small and the air-conditioning blasted at his head. I turned away from him to absorb the twilight sculptures around us. Morning came in Thailand, and we journeyed on to the island of Phuket.

I hired a Balinese masseuse whose teeth were gone. She knelt beside where I lay on a towel stretched out on the floor. As she placed her palms on my stomach, she asked with a rocking motion, as though in prayer, if I had babies. When I told her by pantomime I had tried to get pregnant but no baby had come to me, she placed both hands on my abdomen, listening for something I couldn't fathom. Her face lost its serenity and her breath quickened. She backed away as though distancing herself from something unholy. As I slipped on my sundress, I watched her from the window hurrying down the beach without looking back.

Beside the white sands of Kos Samui we could hear the waves in our one-room hut with its thatched roof and concrete bathroom. During the day we lunched with two men, lovers who traveled together. The elder one was a pharmacist from the Middle East, his young companion a doctor from Germany. Spears flirted with the tiny woman who served us food, always smiling, teaching her his language as she taught him hers. After two weeks, we flew south to Bali. There we watched dancers move to the haunting sound of

Balinese music, their hands and eyes telling universal stories. We saw elaborate funeral pyres and fire walkers who showed us their crusty soles. Leaving Spears with his book, I explored the countryside on a rusty bicycle.

On our flight to Canada, Spears moved across the airplane aisle to an empty seat and chatted with the stewardess, a young girl who talked to everyone in the same high-pitched tones, keeping herself beyond the desperation of middle-aged men and their frightened wives. I watched as one would a movie, neither angry nor agitated. At home a letter waited from the young German doctor we had talked with over Thai drinks and lunches. Enclosed was a picture of me on Spears' knee, toasting the camera with our full glasses, smiles on our faces. The traveling doctor wrote that he had seldom met a couple as happily married as we were.

My father surprised me by dying of a massive stroke on a Saturday morning in autumn. Spears had left early that day, saying he had appointments to keep, paperwork to do. When I phoned to tell him, no one at the theater had seen him. I sat down to write the eulogy I had promised Father when he thanked me for giving Mother's. The night before the funeral, Spears and I met with Lynne and Joyce and their families at the funeral parlor. The mortician had not been able to hide the massive bruise over Father's left eye where he had always put his hand when he complained of migraines. The ear he used to wiggle to make me laugh was stilled forever.

This day, a decade after his gold watch had arrived from the General Steel Wares Company, my sisters and I looked down on his open coffin to where his wrist held the memento of a man who had been sorely tried but never beaten. I had first seen this handsome timepiece when I visited years before. *Did Mom make you buy it?* I had asked my frugal father. With a look of satisfaction, he reminded me that most workers got a gold watch when they retired after thirty-some years, but he had been robbed of this by the *shenanigans* of new management: *All the oldtimers let go without even a handshake or a thank you.* In his mid-sixties Father had sent a letter to remind the company of the men who had built General Steel Wares by laboring for small wages through the Depression and war years. His gold watch had been his reward for believing in the power of the word. *I told them a fella needs a watch to make him remember the time in his old age.*

Although I didn't see this letter, I had tested him many times and knew he had been blessed with a knack for words. *What does loquacious mean?* I asked when I was thirteen and saw the word in a newspaper article about Janet Leigh. *Talkative*, my father told me, looking up from the sports section. *Define lugubrious*, I demanded when I was part of a drama class in grade nine and had to say the word on stage in the auditorium. *It's slow and sad like an old turtle out of water*, he answered over his tea. What do you mean by *euphemism?* I asked when he said *being pensioned off early* from General Steel Wares was a euphemism for *being sacked. Sugar coating*, he explained. I had begun this game as soon as I could read, continuing it throughout my university years. *Droll*, I said, after reading an essay on modern British comedy. *Humorous*, he answered. *Not a big laugh like you kids have, but one without any child in it.* I always ran straight to the bookshelves with his definitions, and my relief was palpable in discovering he was better than right again. Something important relied on his being clearer than the dictionary. It had meant a passion for words was genetic.

Now his daughters hovered over his open coffin the night before his funeral and talked about the waste of burying a perfectly good watch. *Does one of you want it?* Joyce asked. We three stared again at his arm in the sleeve of his best suit, surrounded by satin. *What about a grandson?* I suggested. *Oh, let's leave it on him*, Lynne urged. Realizing the wisdom in her words, Joyce and I agreed the watch should remain with him, a medal for his uncomplaining labors. The man who had spoken to us across so many shared rooms would now speak to us across the whispers of memory.

I was worrying over the eulogy when I stood at the top of the church steps, but I recognized the man coming toward me. Cousin Charlie from Medicine Hat had my father's face – his broad smile, perfect teeth, and shock of hair. The blond hair that had impressed my mother in Medicine Hat those many years ago now shone as dark as mine and it too was sprinkled with silver. My father's brother, Uncle George, had died from a heart attack four years before while playing his fiddle at his daughter's wedding. The widowed brothers had died at the same age and in the same abrupt way, at a moment when the blood that made them family had stopped its journey. The difference was that Uncle George had been surrounded by music and children, whereas Father had died alone.

Spears left for Vancouver Island before the burial service ended. Not wanting to sleep alone in Father's house, I took a ferry home to find our house empty. After collecting Chance from next door, I lay alone in bed thinking of my father, the man who had started the engine of my life. Eventually sleep came with its kaleidoscope of dreams: Somewhere on the Canadian prairie the spirits of laughter and weeping still wandered where two Simpson brothers had been born more than three-quarters of a century before. I woke to the sensation of being in a small boat adrift on the endless tide of West Coast waters.

Father had ordered a wide marble slab for my parents' gravesite. He had always blown Mother a kiss when we passed the country road that wound down to the cemetery. Above where she lay in her lavender dress, the dates of birth and death had been etched in stone: *1912–1984*. When he and I had visited her grave on Mother's Day, I saw that beside my father's birthdate was a dash and a space waiting for completion: *1909–* . After arranging flowers in the tin cup embedded in the earth, he had stared at the empty spot on the smooth marble and spoken with unusual candor: *Sometimes reading that is enough to frighten a fella.* Two months after Father's funeral, *1987* was etched beside his birthdate.

Father's interest in other women had remained as frozen as the widow's food deliveries, but she had relieved us of worry over his dinners. My sisters and I had expressed our thanks by parking his polished and dent-free Chevette in the elderly woman's driveway. The following month, on my way to the ferry after visiting my parents' grave, the Chevette crossed in front of me at a stop sign. The widow sat where my father once had, peering ahead, hands clamped to the wheel. I warmed to the thought of another widower keeping a vigil at his window, waiting on her roast beef and potatoes.

Two months later, Spears told me he was leaving to house-sit up-island. When I asked him to wait until the earth had settled on my father's grave, he turned away to collect his clothes from the closet. Astonished, I tugged at the back of his shirt: *I don't want to deal with this right now.* He turned abruptly, and the top button ripped his green silk shirt. We both looked at the small tear before Spears' fist hit my chest. I rose through the doorway and into the hall. Fire seared my breast near the space between my ribs. As I gasped for air, Spears lay down on the floor beside me. I could hear him say he was sorry. I tried to catch my breath. *Go away*, I coughed, making an effort to crawl away on my elbows. As I neared the end of the hall, I heard his car disappearing into the distance. When I finally got to my feet, I picked the torn shirt from the floor and, like a robot, mended the tear.

Spears came home subdued the next day. He asked if I would visit him up-island, give him some time while he cleaned up his act. At first I ignored his invitation, preoccupied with my breast where smashed tissue and bruised cartilage argued. The doctor told me to resist the temptation of going to court because the process would be more devastating than the bruise. Two weeks later I looked at my life, empty of parents and children, saw around me friends' houses filled with love and children, and I phoned to ask if he still wanted me to visit. *I was expecting you*, he responded.

A woman's dressing gown hung behind the bedroom door where Spears had unpacked his bags. Her blouse was draped over the back of a chair. When the phone rang, I heard him say, *She dropped by unexpectedly.* As he talked, I tore every piece of her clothing in half, shredding with superhuman strength through collars and seams and buttonholes. When I returned to the living room, Spears hung up, grinning in mock sheepishness. *Why did you ask me to marry you if you wanted to be single?* I asked. *I didn't mean forever*, he shrugged, and then explained his dilemma: *I used to be attracted to you but I'm not anymore.* He said this as though canceling a newspaper. *I know you really love me, though*, he added. Walking out to the car, I saw that his new woman had planted our wedding flowers around a tree, flowers my mother had put together in Kitsilano on the day Spears and I had pledged ourselves to each other. I realized the answer had been there all along – yet another woman, one who worked adjacent to his office.

Under evergreens shadowing treacherous curves, the highway to Victoria was slippery from spring rains. I saw a transport trailer in my rear view mirror, bearing down, horn blazing and a cab light making the driver visible. When I gave him an opportunity to pass, he stayed behind, blowing his horn, keeping tight to my bumper. With nowhere to pull off, I drove faster and faster to separate myself from his blood sport. We careened around corners, up and down mountain turns, his beeping and my terror mingled. When a deer jumped in front of my windshield, I swerved into the oncoming lane. Headlights confronted me, and I drove into the far ditch between trees and rocks. The deer jumped free, the car sped past, and the truck roared into the night. When I came to a rest stop, I vomited until my body shook. Alone in the darkness, I looked up to see a clear sky bright with stars.

One of Spears' co-workers said he had been sneaking around with a lounge waitress named Liv Wackov for over two years. *Wack-off?* I exclaimed. When Spears asked for the exact sum of my father's bequest, my lawyer advised that I would have to give it to him if I wanted to keep the house. *Why would you give him money?* Corbett asked when I called to ask the advice of someone I trusted. *There's a no-fault divorce law now to keep the courts from getting clogged.* When Spears' lawyer asked about the violence, Spears said, *We had a few little hassles, the usual stuff.*

My doctor said I should stay out of court because it would be too hard on my health. Once again he mentioned a hysterectomy. I left his office and walked through the park. The flowering Japanese trees were voluptuous with springtime. I sat by the duck pond, turning my face into the sun, closing my eyes. The peeping of duck-lings broke into my reverie, their tiny webbed feet paddling valiantly to follow their mother. They had learned the miracle of forward motion. I turned homeward knowing I would forgo surgery, find a female doctor, and look forward to menopause.

I called Spears' mother to chat with her for what I thought would be the final time: *I've been traded in like a pair of worn gym shorts.* Clara laughed unexpectedly. *Oh I know how you feel, dear.* I felt jealous when I realized Spears had taken the lounge waitress to meet *my* mother-in-law. *He'll just bounce along*, his mother said; *I've seen him do it before.* Clara had stayed in her marriage because her man was all she had known of love. I had stayed even having known an honest life and having had no children to bind me. Change seemed as difficult to tackle as hardship was to sustain. *You'll have to take care of yourself, dear*, she said. *I told him he'd be sorry. He's going to be a lonely old man some day.* I hung up knowing the courage it took for a mother to speak about the boy she had loved for forty-eight years.

Unlike me, she had accepted that yearnings go unattended with the years. Washing and drying dishes together, she had explained that time once spent is time engraved on a woman's life. She too had allowed her loyalty to be used against her. At a party in her thirties, another woman's husband had asked her to dance. She wanted to tell me she had done it, that she had danced in his arms until the music stopped, that his asking her had spoken of all that might have been, had she been free.

On our last outing together to discuss the division of spoils, Spears and I went to breakfast at a place I chose because it was just on the other side of the duck ponds by way of paths through the park. On this late Sunday morning, sun slipped along the grass and paused on the edge of blossoms. The line for brunch stretched into the street, and we listened to live music coming from inside as we waited. A trio played fiddle, bass, and washboard. Each table had a lighted candle flickering in the breeze from the open door, and when our table came up, it was the best in the house with a clear view of the musicians.

Spears talked about collecting possessions he had abandoned months before. I restrained my annoyance at his leaving behind worn underwear and expecting me to take care of the detritus of his past. As the waitress brought us brunch, the band struck up "Manha de Carnival" from *Black Orpheus*. My breath caught as I unfolded a paper napkin and spread it on my lap. A draft carried a spark from candle to paper. I leaped up, pushed the burning napkin to the wooden floor, and stomped on it. While the band played on, I danced out the flame that had consumed me for a decade and a half.

Frustrated by a delay in the processing of Father's will, Spears called some weeks later. Never one to get to a topic directly, he encouraged me to pity his girlfriend. He told me her two fur coats had been stolen by a roommate, that her former husband had a problem with alcohol, and about her father's journey into madness. *She's poor as a church mouse*, Spears complained, even though she had lived in new houses until her husband of twenty years went bankrupt and she left him. The change from pig farmer's wife to lounge waitress was apparently *difficult for her*. When Spears told me Liv had a son who didn't like him and a daughter who had moved out on her own, my throat tightened at the thought of family.

He said the problem was I hadn't given him enough space whereas she never argued with him. *She's enough woman for me, and anyway, it's just a temporary thing.* A year later he married her in Costa Rica. *I didn't want to disappoint her*, he told me when he disrupted a quiet evening with the need to share his new marital status.

Camille's visit reassured me. I needed to know she had become a part of my life regardless of Spears. Already fifteen, she made me aware I had become lost in time. I had hesitated to talk with her about the struggle for teenagers who become unwed mothers, and yet I feared she might follow her own mother's lifestyle. Linda had four pregnancies by four men before marrying a man who was birth father to none of them. I felt parochial and strait-laced in the face of it all, and Camille seemed impossibly young for a sexual appetite that might welcome an eager and unprotected penis.

We stretched out on the bed, whispering like two schoolgirls. Awkward, I told her to be careful around boys until she was ready for a long-term relationship. I grew up when she responded, *I'm always careful when I have sex, Elizabeth.* Camille had never really been young in the way I had been. She was still on her mother's breast and living in the back of a van when her sister arrived. As the oldest child, she had been expected to take on responsibilities that challenged her understanding. She had lost her innocence but never her willingness.

When Camille visited the following year, her opinions about men had solidified: *We don't have to put up with his shit.* I drove her up to Spears' new house, insisting she keep in touch with him. *He only sees me because you arrange it*, she wept. *You can't divorce your father*, I told her. *He's blood.* When she remained silent, I coaxed: *There's no need for you to choose between me and her.* In saying this, I felt released from the confused emotions I harbored toward Camille's mother, thinking of the adults that had trooped through this child's life. *Our fight has nothing to do with you*, I reminded her, knowing the words sounded comforting but were actually hollow. It seemed to me an observant teenager could profit from the lessons she learned from Spears, the ones my father never taught me. Especially how an affair with the wrong man can take up a hefty portion of a woman's life.

Spears' new wife came home from her supermarket job to discover her husband with his former wife and the child of his relationship before me. With her bags of groceries and a tired face, she climbed their driveway to where the three of us were chatting. As I watched Spears salvage the moment by rushing to carry groceries, I wondered how many times he had invited women to our home when I had been at work. I found myself trying to put her at ease when she reached the house, hurrying away when I saw her dry lips struggle to say something cordial, remembering my own dry-lipped days. When Spears walked Camille and me to the car, I knew by the way he swooped in to kiss us that he was confident he could patch things up. *She'll be fine.* His tone implied it was a virtue in women to endure in silence. When we next spoke on the phone about Camille's mother petitioning him for child support, he told me Liv's daughter was about to give birth. *It'll be the first time I fucked a grandmother*, he laughed.

Relief softened my limbs as I hung up the phone. As the slow sorrow of acceptance took root, I realized Spears had become a stranger to me. A woman alone may no longer love the man who left her, but she can reflect with tenderness on thoughts of herself in younger days. I learned to escape the waste of shame through cultivating blissful memories. I looked back on Kitsilano's spring grass and the stretch of sand where Vine Street slopes into the sea. I thought of Okanagan evenings redolent of lilac, the harvest moon, and a male voice singing about country comfort being any truck that's coming home. In memory's eye, the camper is parked by a river while autumn leaves move in its current and music from our tape deck mingles with the purl of water. I remember love, and forgiveness comes over me like gentle rain.

LOVE IN THE MIDDLE AGES

NOEL CAME to me piece by piece. When I moved onto Faithful Street in November 1983, I was vaguely aware that he and his cousin owned the house next door. I waved from an insulating distance and grew to know them slowly, by inches. During the mid-1980s my eyes were blinkered by the sorrow of losing both parents and the confusion of living and not living with Spears. I often kept to myself, preoccupied with a heavy teaching load and numbed by evenings alone. Chance battled against my solitude, forcing her affections on me at the beginning and end of each day, leading me into the heartbeat of nature when we walked by the ocean. In spite of myself, I would return home in high spirits.

According to dog books, the Airedale was originally bred as a bear baiter because of its courage and perseverance. I eventually learned this characterization was simply a cover for a big heart and a stubborn streak. Exhibiting both, Chance seemed to contrive a series of encounters between Noel and me. Since he felt overrun by pets and I felt overrun by men, our friendship was unlikely. But Chance simply needed an ally, and she found one in Noel's cousin, Lyn. Both unmarried, Noel and Lyn ran their home as a cooperative house, sharing it with nurses, nephews, students, and visiting friends.

Avoiding these neighbors came to an end when Chance needed rescue. Her howling rippled my spine like a fingernail on a blackboard, and I ran outside to see passersby trying to locate its source. As I circled the block, running in bare feet, her whimpers drew me back toward my own yard. Lyn was leaning on crutches on her deck, directing me to the dog's anguish: *She's on the hedge.* And so she was. My forty-four-pound Airedale was tangled in a laurel hedge that was supposed to keep her confined. In an effort to reach our neighbors, Chance had discovered that the hedge's width almost matched its height.

When I went next door to thank Lyn, I saw her up close for the first time. Previously, I had observed her through my window when she sailed down the street in her wheelchair. Inside her home, she shuffled from room to room on a pair of shortened crutches, swiveling from the waist because she couldn't separate her legs. When we talked together in her kitchen, she propped herself against a chair. Unable to bend either knees or elbows, she kept distant enough from the table to rest her hands on it. In this way, she could type, turn the pages of her books, and play table games with visitors. Lyn was a dwarf whose animated conversation and brimming generosity pushed the realities of her condition to the background.

When Lyn asked if I would leave Chance with her while I worked, I hesitated. How could I keep my dog loving me best when this woman was home all day and surrounded by treat-dropping friends? *When you get home from teaching, just open the door and whistle*, she told me. *You don't have to visit unless you want a cup of coffee.* I fumbled for authority, but the guilt that plagued me for leaving Chance alone on weekdays lifted when Lyn promised, *We won't give her sweets.*

We had more than the dog to draw us together. My neighbors too had been born on the prairies, Lyn in Moose Jaw, Saskatchewan, in the same year I was, and Noel in Winnipeg three and a half years later. Noel taught at the same college as I did, although the paths to his Social Sciences lectures and my English classes never crossed. He was as solitary as his cousin was social, as tall as she was short, taking the stairs two at a time in his loose-limbed way. He retreated to his renovated room to grade papers, prepare lectures, and work on his Ph.D. thesis. Neither Chance nor Lyn's cat was allowed in his sanctuary. Once, though, Noel let his guard down by expressing delight over a raccoon's visit. She had crawled from the roof onto his balcony to stare in through his sliding glass doors, returning repeatedly with her two raccoon babies.

After a few coffees in their kitchen, I agreed to join Noel and two of his friends to sing folksongs and play guitar. When Noel's low tenor wasn't harmonizing with other voices, he ran his lips over his harmonica, fingers picking and strumming all the while. In conversation, he had a way of distancing himself with ironic comments that caused me to falter and yet to work at connecting with him: *My favorite Dylan is the one who plays his mouth organ*, I told him. Noel nodded toward me: *Good voice*, he said. I didn't know whether he meant my timid soprano or Dylan's nasal twang.

Around their teak table with friends and relatives, I learned how the cooperative house had come to be. Nimble of mind but feeble in body, Lyn had been unable to leave her parents' home until the 1970s when Noel suggested that they buy a two-story house and share the accommodation, cooking, and cleaning with students and nurses. Dinners were always shared efforts with stimulating chatter. On weekends, everyone snugged together in the living room for videos and popcorn. Sometimes Noel came and sometimes not, keeping a flexible boundary between himself and others, always preoccupied with his career.

After the semester ended in 1984, Noel had surprised everyone by saying he had quit his teaching job at the age of thirty-nine to work with the Hospital Union in Victoria. There he would be able to help people who didn't know how to protect their rights in the workplace. I couldn't imagine anyone leaving an academic position, and our conversations made clear how little I knew of the world outside campus. I hinted too that I couldn't understand why anyone would pick Social Sciences for a career when fiction held all the variations on human nature that anyone could wish to know. *Guess you gotta keep those hands clean*, he laughed.

Except for his musical talent, I had no reason to believe Noel was as wonderful as other people's eyes suggested when he came into the room. I had formed a lesser opinion when I saw him backing a black Buick convertible out of his driveway, top down, and a young woman beside him. *My pimp-mobile*, he said, squinting in the hot sun. I wanted to suggest he cover his receding hairline with a cap, but thought better of it. When I expressed disapproval of big cars, he said he had bought it from a widow for the leg room. Apparently she had discovered that her courage and her legs were too short for her dead husband's car. *We both got a deal*, Noel told me as if that justified steering a gas guzzler down the road. *Why'd you buy a new Honda?* he asked. *Keeping my hands clean*, I answered.

One evening when I whistled for Chance and she didn't come, I discovered a debate going on between the cousins over the dog's rights. Perhaps because Lyn had grown up with dogs and Noel had never owned one, they argued about whether Chance should get away with eating the cat's food. I watched as Noel kicked the bowl out of the dog's reach while the cat meowed from the counter. Noel and Lyn argued along with the cat and dog, neither soliciting my opinion about what my dog should do. I noticed too that once defeated, Chance returned to sit on Lyn's bare foot rather than near mine. *Keeping her backside warm?* Noel asked Lyn.

Noel and Lyn had made an impression on Father when he visited the Christmas after Mother's death. Spears and I were working in the kitchen, preparing the turkey and calling over Pavarotti to talk with my father. As we basted the bird in the microwave oven, we realized how plump it was for three people. Suspecting most friends would be with family for the holiday, we called our Jewish neighbors. Noel carried Lyn over and propped her on her crutches at our table. It was obvious she depended on Noel's agility to carry her stiff body up our stairs and then deposit her at our table between her nurse and nephew.

I was slicing tomatoes and grating carrots for the second course when I heard Noel talking with my father in the dining room. Noel was saying he'd watched Father the previous summer from his balcony, admiring how he topped the enormous cedars in our back yard, sawing off dead branches and removing boughs that blocked the sun. *I've climbed plenty of trees*, Father said, his voice boastful. *She tried to get me up there*, Spears called from the kitchen, emphasizing the *me*, as though the idea was preposterous. *We're a generation of cowards*, Noel agreed.

Noel spoke to my father about politics and Tommy Douglas, the prairie Socialist leader who was a hero to them both. I could hear my father's voice liven up when they talked of Saskatchewan. Noel's sardonic tone evaporated, and his gentleness reminded me that a colleague had told the story of Noel giving a passionate speech for the Faculty Association about applying humanitarian values to support staff. I noticed, though, his passion for fairness collided with his lack of faith in universal goodness. Instead, Lyn lived out Noel's theories, welcoming anyone in need of a cup of coffee or an ear to bend.

Over dessert, Lyn turned to Father and explained how an anesthesiologist had been fooled into thinking her neck was a normal length. The doctor had measured it in his mind's eye and overdosed her for a simple hysterectomy. She had woken up unable to raise her voice beyond a husky whisper. Her permanently damaged vocal chords were the reason she wore an oxygen tank and why she couldn't make herself heard over the clatter of dishes and music. Noel had a way of focusing on his cousin that would silence those nearby if they attempted to interrupt.

She might be small but she sure can talk, Father said next morning. *Her boyfriend's an interesting fellow too.* He was curious about the relationship between a four-foot woman and her six-foot-two inch companion. *They're cousins, Dad; their mothers are sisters.* I shared the gossip about a romance going on next door between Noel and a young boarder who had met him at the college. *Noel's girlfriend is seventeen years younger than him, and Spears says she's sexy.* Father looked confused: *You never know about neighbors*, he said, shaking his head. He needn't have worried because at the age of forty-one and shortly before my father's death, Noel moved to Vancouver to work with the Federation of Labor.

Between random meetings with Noel during his visits to Lyn in the years following Spears' departure, I spent my days among students and colleagues, and my evenings with Chance and friends. Once, when Spears had wanted me to move again, I had told him I was going to *die in this house*. I should have said I was going to *live in this house*, but in those days my imagination had grown as thin as my patience. I came to realize through Lyn and Noel's camaraderie how much sustenance there is in friendship, how much I too needed someone genuine and simply there, how much I needed to stay put.

I was walking Chance the Sunday morning after my final visit with Spears, thinking about how I had tiptoed out when he was on the phone, feeling relieved all over again at the memory of having escaped disaster on the highway home. I didn't notice a woman who passed me on the oceanside path until she turned around. *My neighbors have an Airedale*, she said in a Texan drawl that made me smile. As we puffed our way from the beach to the top of the embankment, I saw she was about my age and anxious in a refined sort of way. She told me she had never adjusted to her daughters spending time with their father. *Teenaged girls belong at home*, she said, meaning *her* home. When she talked about divorce, her mouth tensed and her eyes aged. *Why don't you-all come for dinner with me at the Empress Hotel where I'm staying?* she asked.

The *maître d'* in the hotel dining room was familiar with his guest, but I didn't recognize her when she slipped into the restaurant in a camel-suede dress, hair swept up to show off diamond earrings. Tucking into West Coast salmon, she raised the subject of money. Her ex-husband owned a chain of gas stations in California and the sections of highway connecting them. After abandoning her for another woman, he had set her up in luxury. She thought I should realize how often men put money in Swiss bank accounts and that it takes a mighty good lawyer to discover unrecorded millions. I confessed I had been the one to pay a settlement, and by the time our chocolate mousse arrived, she had realized the futility of educating me about money.

My despair caused my cancer, but I've become empowered now, she drawled with southern femininity. She had just had a new breast fashioned where the cancerous tissue had been removed, complete even to a matching nipple. Thinking of my mother's five cancers in the midst of a happy marriage, I doubted her theory of cause and effect, wondering instead if perhaps disillusionment caused a cancer of the soul. A harpsichord had hushed our talking, and during the performance I felt grateful for my unscarred although recently untouched breasts. Suddenly I was overcome with a need for a temporary escape from the tortured thought that I had made a foolish choice in marrying Spears.

On Monday morning I bought a plane ticket to England where I had been invited by my friend Ursula to visit her home in Cornwall for a month. Noel had come from Vancouver to help Lyn with a newspaper advertisement for another nurse, and he was in the kitchen when I went over to ask if Chance could stay with her while I was away. When I mentioned how much I missed traveling, Noel talked of how he had grown to love England while working as a librarian in London. When he had first left Canada, he had been twenty-two and had worked between Holland and Portugal as a sailor with the Dutch merchant marines. He told us that steering a cargo ship into forty-foot waves and vomiting his socks off had encouraged him to look for work elsewhere.

After Lyn described her camper trip to Mexico and I exclaimed over Greece, Noel talked about his hippie days off the coast of Spain on some Mediterranean islands where he struggled to pay his rent for a beach cottage and buy pipe tobacco. *The high kind?* I teased. When he grinned, we badgered him about his sanctimonious attitude toward smokers, especially anyone who brought cigarettes near Lyn's oxygen tank. It was the first time I glimpsed the child that lived behind Noel's ironic tone.

When we spoke about our former lives and how hard it was to keep trust in people, he reminded me that criminals are *made* not born. I argued that *people are born good or bad*, using the example of my father, who had been *good* even though he had lost his family and gone to a foster home, and Spears, who had been *bad* even though he was much loved by his parents for the twenty-six years he lived with them. Noel suggested I should have got myself a good divorce lawyer. *I had one*, I told him: *She couldn't ignore the law that said I had to divide my assets and buy out his half of the house.* When Noel looked away, I guessed he had heard enough divorce-ranting women to last his lifetime.

With Chance sitting happily on Lyn's foot, I climbed into a plane, sleeping through takeoff, cruise control, and descent, and waking when the plane bumped down in England. Ursula waved from behind a glass partition in Arrivals. She had once been my student and, on our drive south, she told me she had left her husband to his medical practice in the Okanagan and returned to live alone with her cocker spaniel on an estate in southern England. Surrounded by meadows and hedged roads, we talked, hiked, and explored the villages of Cornwall and Devon. She had recently survived an affair with a man half her age who had charmed her onto the Orient Express, made her spirits soar, and then gone to prison. Ursula's parents had lived in the unhappy splendor of inherited wealth, whereas mine had found purpose in labors of love, but in our chatter she and I crossed the boundaries of our different childhoods.

Ursula had access to an apartment in London, where a wealthy male friend took us to dinner and a musical each night. Alone in London after she left, I lined up to get a single ticket to hear Michael Crawford sing *Phantom of the Opera*. As rain poured down after a month of drought and the last of the theater doors began to close, I dumped all but my subway fare into the waiting hands of a hawker. Lights dimming, clothes dripping, I pushed my way into row six, front and center. When Crawford sang, he sang to me, and when he swung out on the chandelier, he looked down at my upturned face. On the subway back to the apartment, I could hear him singing still, even over the hum of accents and snoring drunks. In the morning, I sent Spears a letter to tell him how luxurious my life had become. En route to the airport the next day, I regretted mailing it, bought a present for Lyn, and flew home to my dog.

In Victoria on an early autumn Saturday, exhausted by student registrations and the unrelenting knowledge that I had become someone I never imagined possible – a divorcee twice over – I woke up to someone tapping on my front door. To stop Chance's barking, I padded to the door without enthusiasm. A colleague waited on the front step, morning sun catching the basket in her arms. *I thought you might like breakfast*, she said. She put the basket on my dining table, asked me for a vase for the tulips sticking out from under her blue cotton teacloth, and then brought out four croissants, a bottle of champagne, a plastic container of freshly squeezed orange juice, a glass jar of raspberry jam, and a hunk of aged cheddar.

I was still in my nightie when we sat down at the dining table and my colleague spread food between two plates. After a glass of champagne we started into our pasts: While I had been trying to avoid a second divorce, she was working up courage to leave a man thirty years older than she was, a man who had been an English professor when she was a twenty-year-old student. As we emptied our second glasses of champagne, we questioned motives, theirs and ours, and on our third glass, we got down to the choice between loneliness and living with the wrong man.

Slipping the empty basket over her arm, she left just before noon. We had solved not only our own problems but those of the entire English faculty. No memory of our resolutions remained, only the sound of the door closing as I pressed my head into a couch pillow and pulled a quilt over me. With knees curled under white flannel, I drifted into tipsy sleep with Chance on the rug nearby. When the dog again barked at the doorbell, I thought my colleague had returned for something forgotten. Instead, I opened my eyes on a neighbor: *You and Chance want to come for a walk with us?* she asked, her two children looking up expectantly.

My neighbor and her husband lived with their offspring and orange cat behind a tall cedar fence across the street. I had once imagined living as she did with a son and daughter to take cycling and sailing, a husband to welcome home, and an address that seldom changed. She pushed her blond hair behind her ears while her children waited patiently, and I looked down to see I had used my nightie as a napkin when a croissant had dripped raspberry jam. My big toe stuck to the hardwood floor as I turned toward the kitchen. In the dining room, the cloth was askew, and the champagne bottle on its side, clearly empty. Crumbs and bits of cheese littered the space between place settings. Only the tulips seemed alert. My neighbor's cheerfulness made me realize my breakfasting on champagne was judged less harshly than Spears' benders. Perhaps neighbors are like hockey fans, bestowing their cheers on the home team.

In December Noel returned to Victoria for the Jewish celebration of Hanukah, and we waved across the space between our front steps. During the following week, I sat alone in my kitchen wondering how I would get through another forty Christmases without children or my mother's turkey or a man who came home to love me. Finally, I laid my head down on the circle of my arms, mixing skin and hair with crumbs, peanut butter, and banana peel. A commotion at the door disrupted my self-pity and, before I could put my hands over my ears, I heard carolers singing *Oh Come All Ye Faithful*.

Noel's melodious voice slipped under the glass-paneled door and into the kitchen. I imagined his height and broad shoulders forming a peak in the group – a Jewish man singing carols to his Christian neighbor on the corner of Faithful Street and Cook Avenue. The familiar carols brought back memories of the choir loft where I had sung in my high soprano voice as a girl, of unwrapping gifts under trees that wore the same decorations year after year, of Cambridge where it snowed the first winter Corbett and I were there, and how students ran out to catch snowflakes with their tongues – a Norman Rockwell painting come to life. I thought of Camille and me, of our following Spears and his ax into the woods, looking for the perfect Christmas tree, looking to be family.

Lost in the past and still dressed in the clothes I'd worn to class, I remained on the kitchen stool while the carolers persisted. Between songs, Chance barked to tell me they were there. After a while, someone again pressed the doorbell and a female voice called out *Silent night* before everyone laughed and began to clump down the stairs singing *Ho-oh-ly ni-ight, si-a-lent ni-ight.* I imagined their mouths round with vowels.

The event that finally startled my heart into its former thrum and encouraged me to consider the possibility of appreciating men again began with two female friends and an invasion of rodents. Kenna and I met in the squash court where we struck up a conversation that led to our weekly games and to drives there and home in her red sports car. Jenny came into my life over the Xerox machine the day she wore high rubber boots under a prim jumper to teach in a snowstorm. During this snowy winter, hungry rats moved from Beacon Hill Park into my attic.

I ate, slept, and graded papers beneath their rummaging. Afraid to lure them onto the gluey floors of live traps or pry open metal contraptions that might snap my fingers, I climbed a ladder to the attic and poked my head into must and darkness. There I set out plates of poison from a box marked with skull and crossbones. One false step off a beam and onto the puffy insulation, and I would plummet into the room below. I conjured rats tumbling after me, their teeth and tails intermingled with my flesh. Airedales are rodent hunters, and Chance earned her treats by warning rats away from our living space. For a price far exceeding a dog biscuit, the university's pest-control worker climbed my ladder and came down with a plump rat by its tail. He said he would have to come back for its relatives, but he never mentioned that the vent screens in the attic roof had been shredded by raccoons on their nocturnal journeys.

The rats mocked me with their reproduction. I struggled to avoid sympathizing with mother rats nibbling their last suppers while their young died around them. I moved from room to room with my sleeping bag, Chance padding after me, stench of rat cadavers clawing my throat. The man who installed new screens over the air vents assured me the eaves were now secured but resident rodents were trapped inside. He suggested I cut down the cedar tree by my living room window because its branches created a highway for unwelcome guests. I had always seen this tree as an act of grace, its cedar boughs welcoming me home.

The loggers left immoveable hunks of cedar strewn across the driveway, and Jenny sent her husband to saw through the logs and stack the firewood. I gave him a large cedar log, thinking he would chop it into kindling for his own fireplace. He left behind a clean driveway that restored my sanity. Soon I heard familiar scratchings and smelled more death. In time, the sound became singular, and I imagined a female rat scurrying around, energized by pregnancy and her dream of slick-tailed babies. I longed to cut open the vents and free her, but the horror of teeth and tail won over my guilt.

The stench subsided when I opened the windows and lit a blaze in the fireplace, the chimney sucking up rancid air. A week later, I came home to a dusky odor just inside my front door. The final rat's optimism had been stilled. It was late summer and her smell clung to my front hall as the phone rang. Kenna and her husband had a visitor from California who wondered if I would make a foursome for dinner. I refused him on the grounds of nasal fatigue, promising to go out with the first man who could make a dead rat disappear.

Shortly afterward, he appeared at the door, flute in hand, promising to lure the rats to the sea. I gave him an empty shoe box and a pair of work gloves before leading him to the ladder. At first he called down about the pink insulation, the sloping roof beams that brought him to his knees, and the terrible heat. Then he grew silent. When I called up, he coughed. I could hear him rummaging like a rodent. After many minutes, he came down with pinched nostrils, white cheeks, and a closed box held at arm's length. I dressed for dinner while my California pied piper sat on the front step filling his lungs with fresh air.

The massive cedar that had fallen to the ax had exposed a small tree hiding within its limbs. The young cedar unfolded itself to the light and stood the same height as I did. Weeks later, in the pristine air of the kitchen, I made dinner for Jenny and her husband to thank him for clearing the driveway. He gave me a cedar bowl, light as a summer breeze, strong as a clam's shell, made on his lathe.

In the autumn of 1989, a sorrow deeper than divorce or rats visited the house. My older sister Joyce was diagnosed with inoperable kidney cancer after months of misdiagnosed hip pain, and I made plans to visit her in White Rock, an hour south of Vancouver. When Spears learned of her illness, he phoned to say he was sorry to hear about Joan. *You mean Joyce?* I asked. In a slip of a synapse, he had meshed two wives into one, confusing my sibling with his first wife's sister from a marriage ten years before our own. His and my fifteen years together had disappeared in the arms of his next woman.

Noel was visiting Lyn when I went next door. *She's barely into her fifties, and it's spread from her kidney to her bones*, I told them. Even though I was sad and frightened, I didn't yet believe she would die. *Does she have anyone to help her?* Lyn asked. *Her husband and teenaged daughter*, I told them; *her four sons are married and living in Alberta.* Lyn's eyes misted over as I talked of all that Joyce would miss when her daughter married and grandchildren came. Once again I was reminded that blood of one's blood doesn't always work out the way a childless woman might imagine. Noel listened, his blue eyes tender and boyish: *My dad died of cancer when I was eighteen.*

Then, in mid-November and in the hollow of my sister's pending death, Lyn died of a heart attack. She was forty-eight. *I'll see you tomorrow*, she had promised after tea the night before. Only Chance was aware of the moment when her enlarged heart stopped around two o'clock in the morning. Chance had gouged the front door trying to get out and I had pulled her back to the bedroom. Later, when I gave in, she scampered next door, heading toward the friend who had sheltered her from lonesome workdays for six years. Lyn had kept secret the fact that she slept standing upright to keep her lungs clear. Her nurse found her propped on her crutches, leaned against her wheelchair.

In Jewish culture the dead are buried within forty-eight hours. I busied myself by writing Lyn's eulogy, spending the night reading about the connection between magic and dwarves, thinking about the many people who had been salvaged from despair by Lyn's charisma and her example of courage. Inside the synagogue I glanced at the front row to avoid being overwhelmed by the crowd swelling into the balcony. Lyn's mother, widowed in her seventies, now daughterless in her eighties, stared at the coffin as though she could see through its wooden sides. I skimmed the family pew and stopped at Noel's face. The small coffin with its ritual cloth stood between us, and my hands shook as I tried to hide my notes. He was there, listening intently whenever I needed his sorrowful blue eyes to give me strength against the crush of death.

A eulogy marks a beginning as well as an end, and the funeral connected me with Lyn and Noel's extended family. I learned later they had asked me to speak as a replacement for Noel, who was overwhelmed by shock and sorrow when he got the news in Vancouver, the day after returning from spending Thanksgiving in Victoria. In the cemetery, rejuvenated by fresh air, Noel and I covered our smiles at the rabbi's stern expression when he saw Chance. She sat beside the open grave while mourners filed by and tossed handfuls of earth onto the coffin. Finally we left Lyn to ply her magic from the world of the spirit.

That evening when someone pressed the bell, I opened the door on Noel, still wearing his yarmulke. It emphasized his high cheek-bones, and I felt drawn in by the sculpture of his face. Without warning, he swept me into his arms, standing back slowly before speaking, hands cupping my shoulders: *I wanted to say thanks; my family really appreciated what you said*. He spoke without sheltering me from his eyes, and I could only nod as he turned to leave. *I'll let you know about the wake*, he called up from the bottom stair on his way to catch the ferry back to Vancouver. Then he turned again before he climbed into his car: *It won't happen until after I've organized the house and looked after Lyn's will.* I watched through a gap in the blinds as he drove off. Perhaps he too was wondering how to bear the absence of Lyn's perpetual hope and wise counsel. His embrace had aroused in me a sensuality I had almost forgotten.

For Lyn's wake Noel had hired a folk band to keep spirits high, and a friend from Vancouver to cater the party. She pulled casseroles and cakes from the oven while people moved to the rhythm of live music. I edged from one conversation to another, aware of Noel's presence when he entered the same circle. We talked to everyone but each other. Excusing himself, he took requests to the musicians and passed around gourmet treats. Crossing from his lawn to my own at the close of evening, I knelt under the October sky, hugging Chance until she squirmed away. Noel hadn't spoken to me, not once.

Joyce died in early June of 1990. She outlasted all medical predictions, and we had almost forgotten to fear death when it finally came. As I watched her four sons carry the casket, followed by their father and sister, I could barely keep from calling for them to stop. I knew my sister would return to us in ashes, to be set adrift in the Pacific Ocean.

Held fast within the fire of my wounds, I went to a workshop on healing. The advertisement promised a *Workshop on Empowerment* with a well-known facilitator. Even though my parents had conditioned me to think it unsavory to emote in the company of strangers, I signed up for the weekend on Saltspring Island. I also accepted an invitation to a party in Victoria on Saturday night as an excuse to escape if I felt uncomfortable. On the ferry over, I wondered if anyone would find my personal problems worth hearing or realize the foolishness in my seeking solutions to damage already done.

I was one of twelve women who walked into a sunny old house with a double swing on the porch, a garden humming with bees, and a gate leading down to the sea. Around a dining table of health foods and the aroma of herbal teas, we met our workshop leader, Linda Popov, who encouraged us to relax into introductions. Guests slept together in an attic in rows of single beds, each with a puffy quilt, all of us under the sloped ceiling. I fell asleep to the rise and fall of female breathing. By morning one woman had disappeared.

Eleven of us gathered after breakfast to talk with Popov about our relationships. I was amazed to learn of the sorrows that went on behind the doors of normal people. Complaints ranged from a woman whose husband called the children of his former marriage *my* children and the children of their marriage *your* children, to a woman whose once vivacious and athletic husband had sunk into debt and drugs after their four children were born. Each time I heard the word *children*, I grew invisible.

No one interfered with the speaker's moment, each listener giving up her desire to respond in favor of the speaker's need to be heard. During Saturday's circle I was one of two women who didn't get teary-eyed while telling her own story. Another tearless participant didn't speak at all. Lost in a sea of confessions, I remembered Saturday's party just in time to make the ferry. Once back in Victoria, I knew I wanted to sleep surrounded again by the women in the attic and to wake up to the smell of fresh bread and the comfort of their conversation.

At Sunday dawn I caught the first ferry back to Saltspring Island, and I was at the breakfast table before the others awoke. After cereal, toast, and tea, we made abstract collages of our unspeakable fears and fondest desires, finding humor in circumstances that had seemed insurmountable. Over the noon break, we walked along the seashore, reveling in the company of kindness. In the afternoon, Popov singled out two women to speak with her privately while the rest worked in groups of three. The first was the guest who had not spoken in our circle.

We all heard the scream. It came suddenly and without modulation, penetrating our bones with a pain deeper than words could say. In the safety of Linda Popov's compassion, one woman had turned to face the horror of her father's and uncles' abuses that began before her puberty. Their sickness had entered her and created a woman who remained a stranger to the sweet abandonment of love. The other woman Popov asked to speak with in private was me. My problems had begun to seem irrelevant compared to the others, but she talked to me about being betrayed by my body with each attempt at pregnancy and again by Spears with each effort to build trust. She told me I had been knocked off balance every time I had tried to gather enough strength to leave or to forgive. I had become a replacement for Spears' cat in the twisting pillowcase, wanting out but, once free, too disoriented to walk away. I understood the deeper meaning behind the expression *dizzy broad*.

According to Popov I told my story in a lighthearted way, skimming over my inability to become pregnant as though I was at fault. I confessed to her I feared the other women would ask why I hadn't adopted or expect me to account for what I did with my time in a house without children. I couldn't explain my wanting a birth child to nurse, a family face to tuck under the covers, the knowledge of blood connection that adopted children yearn for when they seek out their birth mothers. I told her I felt I had been overlooked after years of tending other people's offspring in the classroom, being reprimanded for students' failings but hearing parents assume all the praise for their children's accomplishments.

We sat on the double swing, partially shaded from the sun. She talked about the difficulties of attempting to break through lengthy disappointment alone. I explained that *I have to keep my problems from students, and only one of my colleagues has experienced a divorce.* As I spoke, I felt vaguely ashamed of everything I was saying, as though pitying myself without adequate cause. Popov told me that ongoing burdens have a way of changing people without their realizing. As she spoke, I realized how bitter and angry I had felt in recent years about my unbalanced life. She suggested that *secrecy can be a way of hanging onto a wound rather than healing it.* Father had taught me to keep secrets, and I had difficulty letting go of a lesson I had acquired from the man who had never let me down. Yet others had found undeniable release in confession.

I took the weekend into my future by becoming friends with two women in the group. On the ferry going home, they told me they had considered me lost when they saw me staring into space, *so skinny and sad*. I looked out over the water, amazed at the loveliness I had missed. These women were both ten years younger than I, athletic, attractive, and mothers of young children. They swept me into the chaos of their homes where complications were not a cause for shame but a force to grow by. They asked me to sing with them in the Victoria Choral Society, and Tuesday nights grew into music therapy. When I raised my voice to celebrate the Christmas *Messiah*, I was held fast within a communion of song.

Weeks later, an affectionate letter arrived. Linda Popov wrote about her delight in my having returned to the workshop and our having met each other. I felt humbled by her warmth and strength. I knew then that my loneliness had less to do with divorce than with losing my place among women. It was not Spears I missed, but the woman I had once been before I grew disillusioned. Grazing my memory was a woman once young who had sold her soul for a child she never held.

Noel maintained that he loved Vancouver for its big-city energy – the traffic and subliminal buzz hovering beneath the pollution, the very reasons I preferred Victoria. He also treasured his solitude. I imagined him swallowed up by crowds and choices, and I doubted I would see him again. But he surprised me on a Saturday afternoon when he was in Victoria to visit his mother who came from Winnipeg every year of her widowhood to spend autumn and winter with her sister, Lyn's mother. I was in his former kitchen, having befriended the newlywed couple who now rented his house. Chance was under the table, having somehow managed to be adopted by these people too. Suddenly Noel was at the door, inviting us to his nephew's birthday dinner and a movie.

When I noticed how easily he related to his nephew and young tenants, it occurred to me that at forty-four he might prefer to play in the garden of youth. Lyn had told me Noel suffered a lingering heartache from years with a Fine Arts graduate who was close to his age, a woman Lyn had befriended. Experience had taught me that the price of mistakes is dearer when people are past their youthful optimism. I had felt awkward and distant with the men I had dated since Spears, and I wondered if Noel too felt uncomfortable with women since his breakup.

When Noel's tenants moved to eastern Canada, an architecture student in his early forties came to live next door with his gray cat. He introduced himself as John and asked if I would help him carry a wicker couch into the house where Chance could no longer make herself at home. John looked like Rudolf Nureyev with his wolverine face, dancer's body, and strong lean hands. He kept fit doing construction work to pay for his design courses. I relaxed in his asexual company, and we began a summer friendship – eating out, watching old movies, taking day trips, and enjoying our radically different definition of a normal relationship. Passion seemed foreign to him, and he appeared not to notice either attractive women or men.

John had sauntered over to my deck to share coffee and the morning paper when Noel returned to Faithful Street in early August. When he strolled into his own back yard and saw his tenant on my deck, he came over to discuss house renovations. Seeming in good spirits, he played the role of the benevolent landlord. In Noel's presence I was aware of the breeze pressing my summer dress against my body and blowing my hair off my face and shoulders. Somewhere between our designing a mobile wall that opened up onto the deck and our comments on missing Lyn, Noel told me that Bob Dylan was coming to Vancouver: *I have two tickets and an extra bedroom. Want to come?*

A certain excitement took hold as I drove with Chance from the ferry to the outskirts of UBC's campus, where I had grown into a career woman between marriages. I had seldom mentioned Noel to friends. He seemed capable of disappearing into solitude if anyone inadvertently betrayed something he held private. But on one occasion I confessed to a colleague that I felt awake in Noel's presence, and he replied he always found Noel's intelligence impressive. Try as I might, I couldn't think of one *intelligent* thing Noel had ever said to me, and I wondered if that was because he was most comfortable talking politics, labor unions, and second-hand cars.

Before the Dylan concert, we went to dinner at an Italian restaurant where a jazz pianist dangled a cigarette from his lips while his fingers massaged the keys. Over pasta and wine, Noel and I talked with surprising ease about teaching and music, perhaps energized by our doing something alone together for the first time. The tablecloth was red and white checkered cotton, our wine white and dry, and someone proffered an ashtray just as the ash fell from the pianist's cigarette. It was a night I might have imagined if I had dared to think on the future.

Excited about the concert? Noel asked, large hands beating time to a Dylan tape, tapping the wheel of his second-hand Buick. *He's a poet*, I said, thinking about seeing Dylan with The Band in an unforgettable concert in Seattle in the early seventies. The audience had responded like puppets, moving as one with the music's energy. I saw him again a decade later when he played in Vancouver and a stranger in the row behind vomited on my hair. As Noel and I looked for parking in the chaos of cars, I wondered if I had grown too old for rock concerts. Dylan, lost in a mumble of introspection, convinced me he had aged as well.

With Chance, we ended the evening walking under summer stars in Noel's sleepy neighborhood. Smells of blossoms and newly cut grass filled me with unspeakable happiness. *I'm allergic to grass and strong perfumes*, Noel announced. Astonished, I asked how he could be allergic to springtime. He thought a moment before he told me he hadn't been thinking of spring but about a woman he'd been dating whose perfume made him nauseated. *Maybe it was cheap*, I suggested. *I doubt it*, Noel laughed; *she owns a house on the waterfront and drives a Jaguar.* I told him that among my environmental friends, *perfume's been relegated to grannies at the opera.*

Noel didn't speak while he pulled out the sofa bed in his spare room and passed me clean sheets. When he began stuffing a pillow into its case, he mentioned the stuffed turkey we had once eaten with my father and Lyn. *Are you still celebrating Christmas now that you're on your own?* he asked. I tucked the corners of the bottom sheet the way I had been taught three decades before as a student nurse and told him I would celebrate by singing with the Victoria Choral Society. Together we wafted the top sheet onto the bed and covered it with a quilt. *I'll be singing Handel's* Messiah, *with over a hundred people. Come hear us sing when you visit your mother and aunt, if you want.* I felt a mild blush on my face at the cheekiness of mentioning an event three months away.

As he turned to leave, I struggled to keep his attention: *Do Jewish kids ever feel left out over Santa and presents?* Noel bent to plug in a floor lamp near the door. *My dad once bought me a toy car when I was the only kid on the block with nothing to show for time off school.* I wondered if his soulful eyes had played havoc with his father's heart too. *It didn't help your taste in cars,* I countered. *What's the matter with my car?* he asked. *It's an old person's car,* I told him. *I am an old person,* he laughed.

I heard his footsteps on the floor above and imagined him climbing into his own sheets in the bedroom next to his study, both rooms with the dormers I had loved since childhood. Chance had been restricted to the back porch at first, but now she lay on the floor beside me. With my hand idling on her head, I thought how the hurdle between the sexes grows higher with passing years, especially between adults who drink with discretion and know something about one another that enhances their friendship with things cerebral and spiritual. There was nothing left to do but get into my flannel nightie and go to sleep.

Noel's question about Christmas kept me awake recalling two years before when I had moved toward my first holiday without parents, a husband, or plans. My squash partner, Kenna, had invited me for Christmas Eve dinner. Her burly husband sliced turkey while she and I set the table and talked about West Coast earthquakes. *Don't worry, Elizabeth, if there's an earthquake, we'll dig you out*, her husband had called to the dining room. Twice alone at home I had heard the chatter of china and felt the terror that comes when the earth moves. It was no small thing that friends had promised to be there if the earth's plates quarreled under me.

In spite of Christmas dinner with other nurturing friends and a ski holiday coming up, I longed to see the face of family. My older sister, cranky during the two years her undiagnosed cancer had been spreading to her bones, expected her extended family to gather and it had grown too large and unruly for my jagged nerves. My younger sister had become a born-again Christian, her naughty humor replaced by platitudes and prayer, but I missed her and the generous spirits of her husband and sons. When I phoned to ask if I could visit during the break, Lynne suggested I could come over on Boxing Day when they returned from their island cottage. When I arrived, she was at the bus depot and returned with two old sisters from New Brunswick. These widows had left their snowy farms to spend Christmas together in Vancouver with their journalist niece whom Lynne had met through her music concerts.

Eight hungry people were now gathered for dinner, but no one had thought to buy groceries. Lynne escaped kitchen duty by playing her grand piano with her younger son, Luke, beside her on the stool. Whenever she touched the keys, she enhanced the festive mood with her fingertips. On this late afternoon, tranquility settled on the faces around her. Ken and his eldest son, Jordan, disappeared into the basement and returned with some potatoes, frozen peas, and a salmon they had caught on a father-son trip to the Queen Charlotte Islands. I served wine and asked the sisters about their lives. The widows spoke of drafty windows and long winters without the men they had depended on for more than half a century. In the kitchen, Ken and Jordan thawed and barbecued the salmon, baked potatoes in tinfoil, and steamed peas.

Father had always put chocolates under the Christmas tree, and I had intended to leave a box behind for Lynne. When the old aunties looked expectant at the end of a surprisingly good meal, I dug into my knapsack for the box of Turtles hidden there. After I served tea, I pulled back the waxy divider to expose yet another layer of caramel and nuts smothered in chocolate. The first auntie brought one clenched hand forward and then another, her eighty-year-old fists quivering in indecision. I wondered if cramps from a faulty heart had curled her fingers. Her eyes rolled up to meet mine before she opened her hands. Melted chocolate and soft caramel stretched from palm to fingertips. Watching her sister's revelation, the other aunt freed her own fists to show that she too was keeping her chocolates hidden for the hour bus ride home. I wondered if Lynne and I would lean into each another's lives again when dementia robbed us of our recent past – of her marrying religion and my divorcing a second time.

As the niece gathered her aunts into their coats, one of them turned to exclaim over Lynne's cooking: *Imagine her putting all that together!* Her sister, glassy-eyed, nodded agreement. They proved the adage that people see what they look for: No man had ever bent over a stove in their farm kitchens, and therefore no man cooked. We bit our tongues over my brother-in-law's unappreciated labors, but no one contradicted the women, not even my nephews. Young as they were, they knew how to keep a momentary truth alive for two old widows heading into darkness.

The holiday proved so restorative that the following year I felt more adventurous and flew south with my champagne-breakfast colleague and her partner. In Mexico City a woman nursing her youngest of three on a paved street reminded me of Camille, and I bought a doll from her. Later I climbed the Pyramid of the Sun and, discovering it was considered male, ascended the Pyramid of the Moon. At the gate, I bargained for pyramid earrings to send Camille. On Christmas Eve, heat swallowed the three of us as we joined a current of humanity in a city square with row upon row of red-suited Santa Clauses on raised platforms lit with colored bulbs. We watched child after child scramble onto the knees of identical St. Nicks. When smog pinched my throat, I longed for prairie snow and West Coast rain. Sleepers in the dormitory coughed into their pillows as my colleague and I fell asleep with our Mexican dolls propped beside our beds.

On New Year's Day, my friends and I went to mass at a local cathedral, humming carols on the way and enjoying the unfamiliar combination of Christmas celebrations amid desert heat. Inside the cathedral's cool stone, the music was ancient but vaguely familiar as organ music tends to be for those who spent their childhood Sundays in church. A sacred essence passed under portals as an old world entered a new year.

Afterward, I sat outside on the stone lip of a fountain, watching children and parents push open the massive wooden doors of the church and squint into the morning sun. As sudden as the sun had been to those who came from the dark cathedral, Bing Crosby's voice broke into the courtyard singing *I'll Be Home for Christmas*. Flooding out from two gigantic speakers, his voice carried with it an image of my father turning up the radio when I was a child. After dinner he would croon along with the melody as we washed and dried dishes, mother humming too as she put leftover turkey in the fridge. I had been slightly embarrassed by the way they lost themselves in this promise of a homecoming. Now, I was surprised by tears and the realization that a part of myself would always be home for Christmas, no matter my age or the country.

When I awoke in Noel's guest room on the Sunday morning after Dylan's concert, it took a moment to realize where I was. Relieved to be in the here and now, I hurried into my clothes. Noel, in his jeans, was reading the newspaper, his long legs stretched away from the table, his hand clutching a mug called *Lefty*. When he saw me notice it, he pointed out that Leonardo da Vinci was left-handed too. *Coffee?* I nodded and sat down across from him. Sun shone on my shoulders, and cool tiles pressed against my bare feet. Noel was stroking Chance's head and I was experiencing the drowsy sensation of wanting to stay where I was.

After walking Chance in Stanley Park, we drove to Granville Island to browse over its cheese and herb stalls and to sit outside with caffè lattes balanced on our knees while a violinist played for coins. Later, we cooked dinner to Wynton Marsalis's trumpet, happier with the serenity of CDs than the uncertain promise of a rock concert. At dusk we lined up to see *The Company of Strangers*, a movie about a group of elderly women whose bus breaks down and who become stranded in the countryside. Before their rescue, they discover things about themselves that leave them richer in spirit than before. Noel leaned over to whisper, *This is the best movie I've seen for quite a while.* I looked back at the screen to see the beauty of aging females for the first time since knowing Spears. Old women's faces alive with revelations.

On Monday morning, before I drove to the ferry and Noel left for work, he wrapped me in his arms as he had after Lyn's funeral. It happened as easily as slipping into a summer lake. I had been inching my way all weekend toward his broad and waiting shoulder.

On the cusp of autumn, Noel sold the house on Faithful Street and returned to Victoria to organize a garage sale. Friends and neighbors gathered in his driveway, bringing their own castoffs to sell along with Noel's. I asked why he had allowed his former tenants to leave his basement full of their sleeping bags and paraphernalia. *Some of them didn't have anywhere else to put it,* he explained. The expression *bleeding heart* crossed my mind, but instead I remarked that *each snowflake is unique.* Noel veered off into sociology, my least favorite subject after animal abuse. He suggested that a lot of parents warp their children's attitudes. I pointed to Lyn, who had refused to be a drain on people even though she couldn't speak above a whisper and who had tolerated the ignorance of strangers who treated her as though she were helpless. *Always exceptions, like your father and mine,* he agreed.

When I asked what his father was like, he said, *Fifty when I was born, and he always tucked me into bed when I was a kid.* Warming to his humanitarian view of fatherhood, I tried to impress him with my knowledge of one of his favorite topics – third world need and industrial world greed – by mentioning Mexico: *We slept in a women's dormitory where South American refugees lined up for food and beds.* Noel was taken aback: *Has anyone ever mentioned that you jump from one topic to another?* He turned away when strangers arrived to look over the sale tables. *Half of my friends say that – the male half,* I called after him.

Feeling thirsty, I went in search of a glass of water. Noel's kitchen was empty and I stuck my upturned face under the faucet, splashing my shirt front. Through the window I saw Noel's former girlfriend arrive. They sat together on the front step, and she began massaging his shoulders. I slipped out the back door and returned to my garden with a book, blanket, and Chance. I leaned against my favorite tree and looked up at the few remaining apples. I had meant to prepare for class; instead I thought how ridiculous I was, lacking confidence about everything from motherhood to men. Never able, it seemed, to learn from friends who had taken risks to get what they wanted.

Joan, for example, a Fine Arts instructor, was my best friend during our time together in the Okanagan. Neither of us had children to keep us home, and we lunched, skied, and played squash between classes. She carried with her a quirky kind of luck. Wherever there were lush grasses, her keen eye homed in on a four-leaf clover. Sometimes I would pluck it from her fingers to see if she had tricked me by attaching a fourth petal. Other times I would bend with her, searching furiously until I glimpsed her hand slide with intent toward yet another prize. Eventually her luck divided us.

Before we met, Joan had undergone a partial hysterectomy and the removal of two non-cancerous tumors. I wondered why she had saved her womb at the risk of later surgery. After her teaching assignment in Italy and my move to Victoria, she visited me, arriving exuberant and bursting with a secret. I guessed she was moving to Florence or had fallen in love or had won an international competition. After my twentieth guess, she told me she was pregnant as a result of a short-term romance. Until she told me this, I had held to the belief that romantic love and the illusion of continuity counted for something in the overall plan of creation. As I wondered at the odds of her giving birth to a healthy child at forty and finding contentment as a single mother, I remembered the clover.

Another person more knowledgeable than I on the topic of reproduction was Paul Barker, the physicist who had come from Oxford to the University of Manitoba in the sixties and befriended Corbett and me. He and Carolyn had married after many years together, and his story made sexual ecstasy irrelevant. In 1979, he visited the Okanagan on his way to a conference in the States. At the airport, we recognized each other immediately, another decade of life locked into our familiar faces. At ease with him as always, I told him my frustration in trying to have children.

Paul shared his experience without hesitation. *Two times, two kids – that's the lot,* he said, clarifying the difference between fertility and virility. In all their years of cohabitation, he and Carolyn had experienced only two awkward encounters and had been rewarded with a daughter each time. Eventually his wife had joined a Buddhist nunnery. *I dream all sorts of awful stuff when the girls are away, like their being hit by a train when I'm not there to save them.* He laughed, but his eyes spoke of worry.

As I drove back alone from the airport a week later, I wondered if too much sex, rather than mumps as the doctor had suggested, had lowered Corbett's sperm count. Corbett had been twenty-one when we married, and sex had happened for us as naturally as falling asleep and waking up. We had paused for sex in the Vienna woods and between swims as we toweled each other dry in prairie summers. We had seen it as the privilege of married love. Exhausted sperm was an even greater likelihood with Spears. In the presence of an attractive woman, abstinence hadn't been on his agenda.

My theory about a high sperm count reflecting a dull sex life hit the skids when a friend told me she and the scholar she had married had indulged in marijuana and sex every night for three months before each of their children was born. They had sucked up stamina and stimuli from lighting joints. Even when a mouse ran across their two bodies in a holiday cabin, they had refused to be deterred.

Their healthy daughters shredded my idea that I had had sex too often rather than too late.

I was brought out of my reverie by Noel calling to someone I couldn't see about packing it in and taking a shower. Closing my book on the same page I had opened it, I suddenly remembered a counselor observing, *You always allow men to choose you rather than making the choice yourself*. I shook the grass from my blanket before I called over the hedge: *Do you want to come here for dinner?* Noel counted the heads around him and agreed five of them would come over to help me cook. *Sold everything except this stuff for the Salvation Army.* He pointed to a brass bed frame and several boxes of lamps, curtains, books, and tapes. *Where will you sleep?* I asked. *Lots of floor space*, he motioned with a sweep of his hand. When dinner guests finished off the pasta, salad, and wine, I admitted to having a cedar-lined guest room in my basement. *It's like sleeping in a hope chest*, I said to no one in particular. Noel appeared not to hear me. The conversation turned to the recently departed tenants who had moved away less happily married than when they moved in. *Marriage keeps lawyers in big bucks*, Noel said. Knowing from Lyn that his parents and siblings each had an enduring marriage, I contradicted him: *Your family seems to do well by it*. I gathered up plates for the dishwasher as two guests stepped out on the back deck to smoke, one of them Noel's former girlfriend.

Noel went outside briefly and then returned as everyone else left. We took our wine into the living room where we broke up some kindling before lighting a fire and sat together on the rug warming ourselves even though it was a mild evening. He told me two lawyers were moving in next door, one of them pregnant and the other planning to renovate the house into a bed and breakfast. I didn't understand what he meant when he said my eyes were changing *from red lights to green lights and back again with confusing regularity. Stop and go*, he said, glowing slightly from the wine. He must have seen a green light when he kissed me.

In the morning I woke up having been reminded of the pleasures of the flesh. By noon he was gone, and the only evidence of his spending the night was my ruffled bed and a quilt on the floor. *We wondered what took you two so long*, one of the dinner guests quipped as I passed her in the grocery store later in the day. Not certain what she knew, I smiled and continued along the vegetable aisle.

Noel didn't phone. As one evening stretched into two weeks, the silence in my bedroom rose to a crescendo. I kept my disappointment secret, remaining steady each dawn by stepping onto the damp wooden boards of my deck. Nature's rhythms helped me to prepare for the day: A hummingbird sipped from a drop of water on the end of a knot of twine. Green-back swallows fluttered and swayed on the clothesline. *You're okay*, I repeated to myself, raising my face to the morning.

On the surface, I had adapted to living alone, to having no one notice whether I returned at night or got up in the morning, no one to tell if I had a day of disappointments or pleasure. I was keenly aware of Lyn's absence, but Chance steadied me, in spite of her growing arthritis and loss of hearing and sight. Unlike Noel, she was simply there, our spirits intertwined.

I hadn't forgotten the time, after Father had died and Spears had disappeared, when I sat on the couch incapable of listening to music or voices, hearing instead a pressing silence, sensing my capacity for thought lift away. Cliché became truth: *I'm losing my mind*. The experience was momentary, but I didn't want to sink into a fathom of nothingness again. Before the newspaper hit the doorstep and Chance barked in response, I tiptoed onto the deck, my bare feet alive to the dewy wood. A breakdown, I reasoned, would happen only if I wasn't paying attention.

Noel phoned on a Monday night two weeks and a day after we had made love. He called from Vancouver to say he'd flown to Montreal the morning he left my house. He had gone to visit his paternal aunt and uncle, a sister and brother each in their own apartment and in their mid-eighties. Negotiating his way through my attempt at indifference, he told me he had bought his ticket before the garage sale and had gone from my place directly to the airport. *You could have called me from Montreal*, I said, trying to gain ground before we hung up. *I didn't feel up to it*, he said, without further explanation.

Noel talked about his family instead, even though he was usually reluctant to share his private life. His aunt had seen her youngest sister shot in front of their house in Austria and years later lost the middle sister in a concentration camp. During her own escape from prison, this aunt had become separated from her husband on a train. Years later, they found each other, but by this time he had a new wife and three children in Israel, having assumed his first wife had died as she had assumed he had done. Noel's father survived because his parents had sent their first-born to New York in 1926. *He came here alone at thirteen*, Noel explained, *and after the war my aunt followed with her younger brother*. When Noel's father died at sixty-eight, the aunt had accelerated her friendship with Noel, establishing herself as her nephew's mentor and the family intellect. *She speaks five languages*, he told me, his voice proud, his tone asking that I respect both the horror and the accomplishments of his father's family while forgiving his own silence. *My father was my heart parent too*, I said.

Do you want to drive down the coast with me? he asked, picking up on a conversation we had once shared about the coastline between Vancouver and San Francisco. *I'll think about it*, I said, evasive. He smoothed over my awkwardness with a few days' grace: *I'll see you this Friday, and we'll talk*. I tried to muster some anger, but found myself dancing around the living room, Chance's front paws clenched in my hands, her tail wagging to the rhythm of my heart in spite of her stiff limbs.

Noel took the stairs two at a time on Friday, carrying long-stemmed roses in a white box with an enormous red bow. Chance mingled her legs with ours as we greeted each other. After a walk to the ocean, we made dinner together and shared the wine he had tucked in his jacket. Happy and relaxed, I excused myself, intent on making him feel up to calling me next time he took an airplane. My past had taught me a thing or two.

What're you wearing? Noel asked, his voice tinged with disappointment when I returned to the living room and interrupted his thumbing through *Maclean's* magazine. The simple answer was a black negligee with small buttons down the front. Something about my being in my forty-ninth year made me reconsider what a woman on the brink of bed and middle age should wear. *What happened to your blue jeans and T-shirt?* he asked. With his arms around me, he admitted disliking anything that reminded him of women shivering on street corners or holed up in downtown rooms. As he talked, he pulled the slinky negligee over my head and ruined forever my plan to let it slip seductively to the floor. I snuggled against the warmth of hard flesh, realizing how much younger in spirit he was than many men his age, a dormant corner of my libido bursting into life.

We spent alternate weekends at each other's houses. One person ferried over while the other made dinner and put clean sheets on the bed. *Yours are always in the dryer as though you almost forgot,* I complained. *Just want you to know they're fresh,* he grinned. An unexpected liveliness crept into our conversations. We compared his Jewish upbringing to my Protestant one, his refusal to marry and my two failed marriages, his disillusionment with the academic world and my being enamored by it. *Sometimes I feel a lot older than you because I'm twice divorced,* I admitted. *You're less cynical,* he countered. *Being three years older makes me three years wiser,* I said. *Four,* he corrected. *Three and a half,* I said, trying to sound less earnest than I felt.

When we discovered we both had a passion for health foods, foreign films, Scrabble, hiking with the dog, and reading the newspaper, weekends sped past. Noel said Scrabble was a number game and set out to prove it by using one letter strategically placed to make a large score. I argued that winning depended on words but lost too frequently to be convincing. He had my scores added before I could begin counting and I caught him with misspellings before his hand could reach the dictionary. *My mother beat my father at Scrabble and pool,* I told him, beginning each game with confidence, sauntering off to make popcorn and to open wine. Surprised when he took the lead time and again, I thumbed through novels to find seven-letter words. *Just a lucky night,* he said at yet another win. *You always beat me at squash too,* I complained. *My arms are twice as long as yours,* he said, stretching out his left arm against my right one.

I tried to find out about his previous women, but he protected their privacy with frustrating loyalty. He never asked about my past. *Did any of your girlfriends have a perfect body?* I asked. He hesitated: *The first woman I lived with taught me a Playboy body doesn't make a relationship,* he confessed. *What happened?* He seemed distant when he spoke: *She got too dependent, asked me what she should wear before she got dressed in the morning. It drove me nuts. I broke it off after a couple of years of thinking for both of us.* I thought how easy it would be to slip into trusting his decisions. *You can't have it both ways,* I said, reminding him about the fate of my nightgown.

Do you think I have perfect breasts? I asked, brazenly confident from Corbett's innocent praise and Spears' experienced evaluation. *I've never seen a breast I didn't like,* he responded, a grin playing at the corners of his mouth. Chance's tail moved like a metronome as she padded along beside us, deaf to our words, but alive to our pleasure. I watched our feet moving side by side along the ocean walk, my taking three steps to every two of his. *Why don't you wear sandals on sunny days?* His feet, like his hands, were long and attractive, but he hid them in boots.

Why do you put red paint on your toenails? he retaliated. Like Corbett, Noel disliked artifice. *It's sexy,* I argued. *Says who?* he shrugged. When I asked who he thought was the most beautiful of my girlfriends, he reluctantly chose two – an athletic and soft-spoken blonde without a drop of paint anywhere, and a brunette colleague whose eyes and laughter burned as brightly as her intellect. I had once thought I monopolized the natural look, but I had strayed toward eyeliner and hair coloring after Spears' wandering eyes reminded me I had lost my youth. Noel's negotiating skills swung into gear: *You wear your nails bare and I'll wear sandals over my socks, okay?* He intertwined his fingers with mine as we continued walking. *Socks?*

At home we listened to "As It Happens" on CBC radio while washing and slicing vegetables. I heard Noel's voice over the interviews and the running faucet: *Do you think we might be a little bit in love?* He turned to cup my face in his hands. *Maybe,* I agreed, suddenly shy. Romance struck us as the sweetness of a flower might strike a hummingbird – a fragile communion hovering, reaching, touching, backing off to begin again.

A fiftieth birthday marks a crossroad in a woman's life. The syllables of the word *men-o-pause* imply a time of pausing from men, and I assumed I would reach that stage in a year or two. I wondered if Noel and I were moving into something one of us would regret. At thirteen, Chance too was passing into another time, still high spirited but less flexible. If I had to carry her, she was rigid in my arms but on weekends, she melted into Noel's large hands as he maneuvered the steps. When my key turned in the lock, she would struggle to stand on stiff limbs, and I saw in her the passing of my own time as well. The veterinarian said she had arthritis. I too felt inflexible, longing for Noel's company yet slow to accept the promise of love that had corrupted my spirit in past years. Midweek, at the moment of waking, I would move toward his body and find the bed empty. I wondered about the point of living with a man once the time for having children had passed.

Noel and I never talked of becoming permanent partners, but a history of acquiring marriage proposals made me fear his asking in spite of his belief that legalized love was an oxymoron. I teased him, making a sweeping motion with my hand as I spoke: *Is it normal to have all this without a legal commitment?* Noel looked up from stirring vegetables in the wok: *Who's normal?* We both laughed, imagining ourselves happier than the norm. Without conscious thought, Noel and I began to share each other with friends. Becoming a couple in the eyes of society is a reckless way to stay single.

When I asked a close friend why I felt lonely for Noel even when I kept busy, I meant the question to be rhetorical but she surprised me by responding: *When you're single, busy is easy. Doing nothing is the thing that's hard to do alone.* Less emotionally volatile than I, she didn't go to pieces the day she walked in on her man showering with another woman. She waited until he left her for yet another lover up-island and then took up bird watching.

We seldom talked of offspring, my assuming she had done her stint of mothering with seven younger siblings, but she surprised me again by saying she too had hoped to have a child. The comment led to our admitting a fear of running into former lovers who had sparked this unfulfilled desire. We each had a history with a man living within an hour's drive. While Corbett had evolved into something akin to a favorite brother, no longer under the same roof but still linked by deep affection, Spears had given me cause to be cautious, familiarity extracting the same balance my friend applied to birding – distance and recognition.

My friend's resolve was tested when she drove up the highway to visit her grandmother, parked her car, and stood at a red light on the way to pick up groceries. Only vaguely aware of the man beside her, she stepped off the curb and then realized she was walking beside the person who had broken her heart. As she moved ahead of him, she must have inadvertently reminded him of her shapely legs and what we called her alley-cat ass. He called after her, suggesting they meet. *Okay,* she agreed. But at the far curb, she turned back: *No, I don't think it's a good idea.* Walking off, she didn't look over her shoulder.

It was a Sunday morning and London Drugs was almost empty when Noel and I went in to pick up some photographs. As we lined up at the cash register, we came face to face with Spears and his new wife. Although Noel appeared indifferent to their presence, I nodded with an awkward smile, unable to resist glancing at his woman. They seemed world-weary, and when I looked back at Spears, he blushed as though feeling the same indefinable surge of emotion I had felt. Perhaps he imagined me in grief rather than in the company of a man. Perhaps he had described me to his new love as a woman unable to cope well without him.

Outside the store, they walked ahead of us. Spears had one hand on her shoulder and the other carrying a plastic bag. As suddenly and wordlessly as we met, we parted again. I felt tainted by my gullibility, by her having known what my husband had been up to before I did, by his having preferred her to me. *She doesn't even like literature*, I grumbled. *That's not the point*, Noel said. We drove in silence until he lifted my hand from my lap. *You okay?* I wasn't sure how to respond, and he filled the silence: *It's Spears' loss, you know.*

I'd been thinking about the difference between reality and romantic illusion, the temptation to imagine Spears and his woman as a hot item, forever free of mundane chores and everyday needs. Glimpsing them in the context of loose change, plastic bags, and tired eyes erased in an instant the picture I had carried for over two years. It taught me what I knew as fact but hadn't realized as truth – old lovers confront passing time too. Without seeing a former lover in the raw light of daily tasks, we risk keeping alive the destructive energy of love's illusion.

Noel stopped at a corner store and picked a bundle of flowers from a pail sheltered by an awning. I watched him tuck the flowers under his arm, reach for his wallet, and disappear inside. When he crossed the street and opened the car door, he held a bunch of orange tiger lilies, the emblem of Saskatchewan: *For you.*

I had celebrated my forty-ninth birthday with the Argentinian custom of giving instead of receiving, inviting friends over on a Thursday night to share wine and a cheesecake that took me two days to make. At fifty I walked into a small restaurant on a quiet residential square to meet a friend. Eleven female colleagues called out a chorus of *Surprise!* On the phone, I described the lunch, balloons, and cards to Noel, saying that a public fifty seemed a bit daunting, that I had wanted to slip into its cloak without being noticed and yet I didn't want my half century ignored. He laughed: *That doesn't surprise me; it's impossible.*

Noel took me to San Francisco as a birthday present. When he left his house for the Vancouver airport, I left mine to catch a small plane to meet him there. On the highway just outside Victoria, steam billowed from my radiator, and my Honda collapsed after thirteen years of untroubled service. After rolling the car into a ditch, I coaxed Chance into a taxi. The driver hurried us to the kennel and then the airport. Noel and I met in the Vancouver terminal, where we listened to an elderly couple fight, flinching as the old man smacked his wife's bare legs with his cane. We flew to the city of romance and stayed in a posh hotel where air-conditioning and sealed windows denied us an ocean breeze or the sound of salt water crawling up and down the beach. The next day we wandered around galleries, bookstores, and funky restaurants, coming back to our room to discover candles and a closed door can create a paradise anywhere.

During the weekend, I happened upon an article about healing touch. The writer claimed that a healer's hands never touch the patient's flesh and yet their hovering presence transfers health from the strong to the weak. Noel unwittingly brought credibility to this theory. Initially I had connected his hands with the excitement of sex and the comfort of safety, but they also began to convey a commitment we never spoke about. Each December, I was reminded of healing hands as I stood on a stage and sought out Noel's familiar face in the audience before the Victoria symphony and the choral society launched into Handel's *Messiah*. He would slip in at the back of a packed house when he arrived from the ferry, his hand rising discreetly against the wall until he was certain of my seeing him. I was searching again as I had once done from the choir loft in Westminster Church to find my parents in the congregation.

Noel's hands brought another message too. The effect of his grip on Chance also worked on me. After grading essays to "Saturday

Afternoon at the Opera," I rejuvenated myself with a nap. Noel sat on the edge of the bed, pressing strength into the small of my back while I drifted into sleep, knowing I would wake later to a spine and muscles free of pain. Like Chance, I felt no harm could come to me when I was at rest under the pliable stretch of his fingers, the breadth of his palm.

In spite of this comfort, I noticed a dip in my energy, a need to nap during the day to last out the evening. I tried various positions when I worked, carrying essays onto the deck for a change of scenery, marking in lots of ten in different chairs. Still the weariness persisted. I wondered if the safety net Noel cast had allowed me to acknowledge something I had been in too much denial to feel before – a need for a break from the classroom. While he caressed my back, he coaxed me to work fewer hours. *I can't get anywhere with my students unless I give them some individual attention*, I snapped, angry at being unable to keep up with him. When my mood shifted, I told Noel stories of how my students had helped to fill the void that comes with being childless, giving me the sense of being useful and appreciated, of making a difference.

On top of my teaching assignments, I had organized and chaperoned two student exchanges in the years between men. Taking students to Montreal and then Cape Breton, I revelled in a chance to express maternal caring without stepping out of my professional role. These students between the ages of nineteen and twenty-five were the ages my children would have been if Corbett and I had been able to conceive, and I enjoyed the twenty-four-hour responsibility as a renewal of lost dreams. I came to understand why mothers are often tired and frightened or moved by unexpected affection and blessings.

The Montreal chaperone shared my pleasure. Childless and born in the early forties, she too had been raised in a time when *liberation* meant the end of a war in Europe. Together we entered a world of perpetual present tense where youthful energy filled a space that had been haunted by disappointments. A memory of nestling among hay bales on a red sleigh while two plow horses pulled us through the French-Canadian countryside remained with me. The animals' breath rose in clumps as they crossed the frozen landscape to where we collected maple syrup and spun candied letters in the snow. Montreal's smoky jazz clubs had reminded me of Spears, but the silence of Notre Dame turned me inward as the countryside did. It was always the same – the past looming like a rogue wave and then subsiding as the present claimed me again.

When the Quebec students came to Victoria, I took them to rugged corners of the island, creating a sense of freedom as we shared the tidal pools of Botanical Beach and the ancient rain forests on the West Coast. Students were required to love the outdoors whatever their pasts had been. Noel saw my nurturing instincts in a different light: *You're too responsible, a little dictator*, he accused. I drew a sunnier picture as I thought back on rosy cheeks and exhausted smiles: *A benevolent dictator*. Colleagues gave lectures to the visiting students, and we all discovered a wealth of academic knowledge in the college. *I would have asked you to share some sociology if you'd stayed in teaching*, I told Noel. He looked doubtful.

I did an exchange to Cape Breton as well, encouraged by my transformation in the company of Quebec's students. When our plane landed in Halifax, we climbed into a smaller one to reach Cape Breton. Atlantic winds rocked us like a canoe against waves. Students ignored the pleas of the stewardess, popped open their safety belts, and huddled around my seat. The plane landed in the deepest snowstorm of winter, bagpipes and haggis welcoming us. We plunged into a week of coal mine tours, home-cooked meals, fiddlers, and skiing. Students who had never had their feet in ski boots stopped my heart as they soared off jumps and down the slopes. When the Maritimers left their snow behind, they arrived to Victoria sunshine on a perfect March day. Joggers were out in shorts, and daffodils and tulips colored the roadsides.

At the end of a day of wildlife and logging tugs on and around Newcastle Island, I refused to join the class for a house party, begging off because I had to sleep if I wanted to accompany them to lectures and a rock concert the following day. Shortly after midnight the doorbell and Chance's barking woke me. Two Victoria students were speaking at the same time as I opened the door, bragging that they had fished two drunk Cape Bretoners out of the sea. Before I could rid myself of the horrific thought of phoning a Maritime parent about a drowned child, I learned their rescue was followed by a less successful adventure.

One of our own students had fallen off a porch and landed head first on a concrete patio. Although the two emissaries promised he was alive, they confessed he'd been taken away by ambulance to emergency, unconscious. I called the hospital, certain it was a prank. Emergency staff assured me night shift doctors were checking his vital signs. The student's girlfriend was in the waiting room, vigilant; I was in my nightgown stunned. He came to the rock concert with his head bandaged like Frankenstein's monster, showing off a circle of fresh blood to prove his heart was beating.

My students made me aware how relationships between the sexes had changed. These were children whose parents had fallen in love in the late sixties and the seventies, many now divorced. They took for granted they could sleep on each other's shoulders without being coupled. They no longer marched two by two into the ark of marriage with thoughts of houses and babies. Unlike my generation with its future guaranteed by education and idealism, the youth of the late 1980s had plans for travel and temporary jobs before they figured out what to do with their lives.

I had experienced intimate moments with individual students who had allowed me to glimpse their vulnerabilities, the part of youth that teachers overlook when they mistake despair for delinquency. One student had abruptly left his seat during a final exam, dropped his foolscap on the front table, and walked out. I checked my watch and saw that only twenty minutes had passed. Annoyed by his lack of effort, I flipped over his exam and discovered a suicide note. In an instant I was back in Singapore in the claustrophobia of hopelessness. Having no idea where the student had gone and knowing I would invalidate the remaining exams if I left, I grabbed a passing faculty member on his way to the bathroom and left him on duty in my place.

Clutching my car keys, I set out to come between my student and whatever desperate act he might be considering. Perhaps he had lost someone to an accident or a new infatuation. No one answered when I rang his buzzer at his downtown apartment building. I roused the manager. *You onto a drug bust?* He winked at me. I explained my position. *Teachers don't wear no blue jeans*, he shook his head. *You're a cop, right?* I explained teachers wore whatever was handy at exam time, then remembered the faculty library card with my picture on it. The manager looked disappointed. Mike had moved, but the manager hadn't ask for a new address: *The kid paid his rent and nothin's broke.* During a sleepless night, I paced the house.

The missing student called my office the next day to tell me he'd spent the afternoon drinking and the night sleeping it off. I yelled into the receiver about his self-indulgence and irresponsibility. When he didn't respond, I hung up and marked an *F* beside his final grade.

A year later Mike stopped just inside my office door, as awkward as a student about to begin an oral presentation: *You made me different*, he said. *I'm at the university now.* A river of emotion dammed in my throat. *Bet you're a good mother.* I didn't trust myself to respond. After Singapore, I too had discovered the waters of life still ebbed and flowed through other people's caring. *Thanks*, I managed to say but he was already gone.

Recalling classroom memories, I began to discover broader definitions of *mothering*, meanings that extend beyond pregnancy and birth. Young males too proud to admit to tenderness sometimes confessed to their computer screens in the college lab. Their thoughts on the page and my eyes absorbing them added up to more than either of us would have created alone, proof that both writer and reader are necessary to keep the dimensions of a story alive. We struck a bargain: They would teach me what they knew about computers while I taught them what I knew about writing.

I walked from screen to screen, discussing their grammar and composition and they countered with technological tidbits while they wrote on the topic of a significant life lesson. They had to clarify their lesson with a story of where they had gained their new awareness. My meager computer skills gave one student from a small city in the interior of British Columbia the confidence to examine his surprise in discovering his mother's beauty. He drew a word picture of their farm and the woman who didn't talk about affection, but whose life revolved around caring for the chickens, the cows, and her family. At the end of his essay, he admitted he hadn't appreciated his mother's gifts.

When we went over his paper in my office, I asked him if he would do me a favor. *Sure*, he said without hesitation. *Give your essay to your mother for Christmas, okay?* He looked at his unlaced shoes. *No way*, he said, taking an audible breath. *Okay then*, I sighed, *how about leaving it for her to find when you come back here after the holiday?* I could see the hint of a smile as he folded his paper and put it back in his binder.

Noel had a similar epiphany about his father as this student had acknowledged about his mother – an absent parent transported through the grace of love. He often talked of his father's gentleness and the fear of death that stalked the house when his father was diagnosed with esophageal cancer. For ten years Noel was helpless against his father coughing; *He told me he wouldn't always be around, but I didn't want him to leave.* I recalled my own father's irrational upset when any of us coughed from a chest cold we had caught at school. *I was eighteen when he died on the operating table in Rochester. We didn't even get to say good-bye.*

Noel's tears surprised us both, brimming over and rolling off his cheeks. *Sorry*, he said, breaking off a paper towel and wiping his face with a great swipe as though clearing away years of sadness. *Everyone was away, but my brother came home from university to tell me.* I asked why his teachers hadn't helped him, thinking of the student whose mother had abandoned home when he was thirteen, leaving behind the idea that his messy room was the reason she had gone away. When at nineteen he told me his story, I had wondered what education was all about if it could offer knowledge on nouns and verbs but nothing about a mother's vulnerability. *My teachers never knew*, Noel said. *I dropped out of school when my father died and went to live in Alberta with my sister for a while.* Suddenly he brightened. *Her kids were babies then. Graduate school was great too, lots of feedback there.* We sat awhile in silence, absorbing the upheaval of family deaths, words left unsaid, mysteries weighing on youthful shoulders.

Noel hadn't been to his father's graveside for thirty years, whereas I found comfort dusting off the leaves and grass that accumulated in the crevices where my parents' names were etched in marble. *I didn't go to my grandmother's funeral, even though she loved me without a glitch for over three decades*, I confessed, remorse clogging my throat. *Loads of guilt over that one.* It occurred to me we didn't have to keep these mistakes in denial anymore, now that we had shared the worst of it. *Let's go to Winnipeg; I'll find my grandparents and you can visit your father. We'll go together.* Noel looked doubtful: *Sounds possible.*

After my own father's death, I had begun to reread Margaret Laurence's book *The Diviners* to share with my literature class. Having suggested to students that they would find the story relevant and appealing to various ages and lifestyles, I reopened its pages to refresh my knowledge. In spite of my feeling vulnerable over the recent funeral, I was soon mesmerized again with her story and reminded of my parents' early lives. Mid-page, I began singing the lines of a verse Laurence included from "The Wreck of the Old Forty-Nine." How, I wondered, could I so easily put music to lyrics I had never seen? Why, I asked myself, did the tune to these unfamiliar words fit both line length and mood? After pondering the possibility that I could not do a repeat performance, I sang it again. Soul perfect.

T'was a cold winter's night,
Not a soul was in sight,

And the north wind came howling down the line;
Stood a brave engineer,
With his sweetheart so dear,
He had orders to take the Forty-Nine.
She kissed him goodbye
With a tear in her eye
Saying "Come back quite soon, Oh sweetheart mine"
But it would have made her cry
If she'd known he would die
    In the wreck of the old
        Forty Nine.

I was singing the first verse of my father's car song, words I had read on the page several times before but never been open to recognizing as an introduction to our family's traveling anthem. Perhaps a moment comes when a reader unconsciously readies herself for something not yet carved into thought, but peculiar to the soulful longings of the subconscious. My father's death denied me the chance to share this discovery with him or to ask if he had ever heard the introduction to this tragic tale of separation. Together the two verses tell about those born to know the sorrow of an early goodbye. The song spoke to me not only of happy days of our family singing together as we cruised along in my father's Chevrolet and of my parents' farewells when my father set out for the Saskatchewan prairie to sell fridges and stoves, but also of the unexpected grief that would come to mark each of our lives. Joy made keen by a knowledge of sorrow, sorrow enlarged by preceding joy.

After four seasons of commuting, I moved to Vancouver for the summer to teach Canadian literature at UBC. I didn't think of repercussions, preoccupied with renting my house to two European musicians who had come to instruct and perform in Victoria, and excited about returning to old friendships on campus. After a brief illness and some medication, Chance's health returned, and we hiked her daily through the forest trails surrounding campus.

During one walk, Noel told me my office building was across from that of his old girlfriend, the woman who had broken his heart years ago. *Did you love her?* I asked. He didn't look at me when he said, *I thought I did at the time.* He waited on the path and took my hand, as though pulling me along behind him. *She took a Fine Arts degree.* I thought he might be reassuring me I wouldn't run into her in the English department. In a voice softer than usual, he said, *She had lovely hands.* I slipped my hand out of his and tucked it in my jeans pocket.

When I asked what had ended their years together, he told me about their second holiday in Cuba. *It didn't compare to the first time; she was sullen and withdrawn.* Suddenly, he seemed to discover the answer: *We were too much alike, and it just didn't work out.* A pause invited reflection on the end of my own marriages: *I've been a fifteen-year woman both times.* Noel turned to me in mock alarm: *Don't tell me you're going to leave me when I'm sixty.* I corrected him: *Sixty-one.*

During this summer of perfect weather, we spent weekends at outdoor folk festivals, played tennis before the sun softened the asphalt, and drove up and down mountain roads shaded by forest and rock. I spent mornings reading aloud snippets about the arts from the newspaper. Noel hushed me as he read about politicians with names I knew only vaguely. We drank our coffee at the open kitchen window as we had after our first night together in different bedrooms. At the end of the day, we knew there would be someone around to make light of our mistakes and praise us for our triumphs.

Noel gave me a place to be young again, and our affection was contagious. After watching me plant flowers on the deck, a neighbor whispered to him, *Hang onto her, she's a good one.* Certain of ourselves, we laughed at the idea that he had the power to imprison me or turn me out. Lost dreams fell by the wayside in favor of new ones. Days passed, barely distinguishable from one another under persistent sunshine and starlit nights.

Noel met my friends when they invited us for dinner, and I met his when we barbecued on his deck. My academic buddies were still in their old relationships, mostly in tenure-track university positions, but no one rubbed salt in the wound of my being twice divorced and at a college. Jane, the special friend who had stuck with me through my Okanagan days and the turmoil of Victoria, met me for lunch every day on campus and invited us to her home where Noel could meet her man. Cathy and Woldy welcomed Noel and me to their West Vancouver balcony where we could watch ships and sailboats move into the night. Spears and I were godparents to Cathy and Woldy's son, Alex, now a teenager. We were all more sedate a decade and a half after the boy's birth and my second wedding. *Noel's a really nice guy*, Woldy told me when Noel was out of hearing. I wondered if he was assuring me that I was not being led astray this time.

Perhaps because Cathy and I had once shared an intense desire to be pregnant, perhaps because they had adopted two children to keep Alex company, the topic of my adopting a child came up. The next morning Cathy phoned to say she thought it would be too hard on me, *especially your back*. We laughed over my disregard for circumstance and age, and at her having taken me seriously. Cathy and Woldy's lives had changed drastically after their adoption of two fetal-alcohol syndrome children, a brother and sister, aged six and four. Neither had been prepared for the chaos of children who had not been born into love as Alex had been.

I had gone to visit them on a lonely weekend just after Spears had left, taking a gift of placemats decorated with a coyote howling at the moon in each corner. During dinner I drank too much wine as I talked about being at the strange crossroads of growing to hate the man I had loved. Emotionally frail, I drained one glass and then another as I described the agonies of being a woman betrayed. Their adopted daughter interrupted by standing on her chair and declaring with frightening authority: *Mommy, Elizabeth is drunk!* I spent the night with my head in the toilet. Neither Cathy nor Woldy gave up on their two adopted children, and I was grateful they didn't give up on me either.

Other women friends had been adamant about my adopting a child – either for or against it, as if all women and all babies were the same. The adopting mothers I knew had added an adopted child after giving birth to others, as if to round out some imagined perfection. Camille had taught me that having several children in the house eased the problem of entertaining an only child. But there were exceptions, among them friends who had three children before they adopted a baby from an orphanage in Vietnam. The infant had crossed the Pacific on the last commercial flight from Saigon just as the war there escalated. They never spoke of the bravery and kindness that began their infant's journey, nor did they hide their feelings of satisfaction about their youngest son. They simply put their success down to luck and the nurturing they distributed equally among their children. Their example made me wish I had been able to confront the problems of infertility with a realistic and adventuresome perspective on adoption and a faithful man.

My father's attitude about adoption had been similar to this couple's, but ironically with less regard for the difference an adoptive parent can make. He told me the success of adoption is a lottery that depends on the child's personality being compatible with the parents'. Perhaps my friends' realization that luck plays a role allowed their expectations to foster a successful match. Father had come by his belief when his two sisters were adopted into separate families. Although both girls went to families that were kind and financially comfortable, one sister ran away and the other was devoted to her adopted parents. Perhaps adoption of children who have known their parents is a risky business. The process demands courage, wisdom, and generosity, as well as the belief that any child is a gift.

Sometime after Noel came into my life, I realized that my anguish about being childless had lifted, although remnants of longing remained. The change had crept in unaware, but it was brought to mind when I was jostled by a phone call that interrupted an evening of grading papers. A male voice pronounced my full name. I hesitated, suspicious of telephone soliciting. He asked if I was listed with the Adoption Registry in Victoria. I confessed to having applied for a newborn more than a decade before. He asked if I was thirty-one years old, and my imagination churned in search of a response. Had my birthdate been mistyped and then misunderstood? Such is the dark side of hope. Almost simultaneously, I realized a person born in the early forties would be thinking about menopause, not cradles. I hung up wanting to hang on.

In autumn, after I had returned home to teach at the college, Noel found a house on the waterfront in Victoria. So spontaneous was his joy that he leapt into the air on a busy street and clicked his heels together. He suggested I move in as soon as he signed the papers and promised to join me in a year when he could leave his job. The house was on a secluded piece of property most people would envy, but I imagined myself looking out at the dark ocean from Monday to Thursday, alone with Chance, who could no longer scramble up and down rocks. I imagined living without the neighbor across the street who had been born in her home and had kept watch for seven decades over the families she had seen evolve around her. I imagined being without familiar shopkeepers who had unwittingly coaxed me through empty evenings with their simple recognition.

Terrified of hope and crippled by fear, I dug my heels into Faithful Street and stayed put. When Noel let the moment pass, I appreciated again his healthy willingness to let the rose bend of its own free will toward the sun of its choice. He had gone as far as he could and he left the rest of the journey to me.

Noel is not tempted to socialize as often as I am. He does well nesting at home with dinner, music, newspaper, book, or TV sports. Perhaps that is why he preferred the anonymity of the city and I liked the coziness of a familiar street. We responded differently to a heavy snowfall on our first New Year's Eve in Vancouver. Long-time friends, architects who fourteen years before had built the altar platform for my wedding to Spears, invited Noel and me to celebrate New Year's Eve with them. I believed we could maneuver the snow and two bridges between Noel's house and their home atop a steep hill in West Vancouver. I suggested chains on his tires. But Noel proposed a quiet dinner at home and a hike in the surrounding snow.

These friends had been a part of my life with Corbett at the University of Manitoba, and later they invited me to stay at their apartment in Cambridge when I returned alone to visit. Still later they befriended Spears when they moved to Vancouver. We had all been prairie born, and I wanted to introduce them to my new prairie man. But I'd made the mistake of warning Noel his left-wing politics might not be welcomed. He directed his blue eyes into mine to say he might consider partying but he wasn't about to change his politics. We sat for a while at the window, peering into a snowstorm that brought the city and our evening to a standstill.

Having not planned dinner at home, we searched through the cupboards for pasta, vegetables, wine, and candles. Swallowing his last mouthful, Noel left the room and came back wearing a toque and scarf. He could get ready faster than Chance when the word *walk* was in the air. We pulled on wooly socks, heavy boots, and jackets before making a path where snow had erased the boulevard, curb, and sidewalk. I followed him down a single track in the center of the road, acknowledging he had won the argument without saying a word.

Everywhere in the neighborhood, people opened their doors, waving from porches while snowflakes floated to earth. Lovers with blankets around their shoulders leaned over apartment balconies, and families tossed and dodged snowballs, shouting to one another and to us. We moved aside to let cross-country skiers pass. Two children pulled their grandparents on a toboggan while a golden retriever leapt around them, his tail sweeping the snow. Chance's days of leaping were over, but she plodded behind us. *I think she's remembering the Okanagan*, I told Noel as she buried her nose and then came up for air, tail wagging. *I think she likes Vancouver*, he replied, grinning his sardonic grin.

When whistles and horns announced midnight, Noel reached

into his jacket and brought out a bottle of champagne and a glass from each pocket. My glass slipped from my mitten into a pillow of snow and came back ready frosted. The snow stopped falling, and stars came out one by one. *I'll phone them in the morning, okay?* It was a rhetorical question, an attempt to have some input into the evening's events. He stared into the blue-black sky. *They're lucky people*, I told him. *West Van and ocean views?* Noel asked. *Not that*, I huffed, resenting his real estate summary.

At home, we stopped at the bottom step to brush off the dog and kick snow from our boots. When I returned to the subject of my friends, he fell backwards into a pillow of snow, exasperated by my persistence. *She thought being a mother would interfere with her career, but when she changed her mind in her forties, she had two of them on cue. If you're interested in real estate, you might wangle an invitation to their island home off Lion's Bay.* As I spoke about their good fortune, I recalled waking up in their cottage to the sounds of the four of them giggling in an adjacent bedroom.

Noel remained silent, his legs and arms splayed to make an angel near the bottom step. *You're a good listener*, I told him. *Just making up for my mother*, he said, affection in his voice. *Does she chatter like me?* I asked. *She puts a lot of ineffectual energy into fretting about family stuff.* His voice became serious as he brushed the snow off his jacket and jeans. *Do you always keep one foot in the past?* Noel had put time limits on my complaining about Spears, giving me until noon and threatening to change the hour to dawn. *Do you think people get their just deserts?* I asked, thinking of my unsung womb. *Maybe sometimes*, Noel said, unlacing his boots while the history of the Jews made a ghostly appearance to contradict him.

I flopped down beside his angel and flapped about in the powder. When I got up, I could see how small my angel was beside his. *Why don't we go upstairs and make our own New Year's party?* he asked, a gentleness in his voice. The next morning I woke up to Noel's arms pulling me into the curve of his sleeping body and the sounds of water dripping from eaves. A thaw was on the move.

During that winter semester, rain came down day after day until my back yard became a swamp and city sewers spit back at the gods. I opened my basement door to see the concrete floor move in the darkness below, water swirling around my bottom steps. With rubber gloves and boots, I stepped off what I thought was the final step. Water poured over the boot tops, numbing my feet. When I looked around, I saw the blue canoe floating toward me like an old friend, followed by an aluminum cauldron. The ropes attached to each had become entangled, creating the illusion of a canoe towing a plump dinghy. Climbing in, I paddled with rubber hands around the basement.

The cedar guest room was partially submerged, and I could see only two-thirds of the washer and dryer. While consoling myself about material things being replaceable, a slide floated past, and then another. They were from a box of honeymoon pictures of Spears and me in Western Samoa. Like our marriage, they had become unglued, warped almost beyond recognition. In the sanctuary of the blue canoe, I stayed afloat.

Noel and I spent our second springtime together in Turkey. While we explored Istanbul and the seaside villages, we learned the rewards and pitfalls of being together twenty-four hours a day. Our Istanbul hotel looked onto the Blue Mosque through a window we passed on our way to the garden and breakfast. Before the heat of the day discouraged adventure, we wandered into the chaos of traffic – donkeys, llamas, and car horns. Together we coughed our way through exhaust fumes and cigarette smoke on a bus to the Mediterranean beaches. Noel reminded me he had wanted to fly. We toured historic buildings in all their tiled beauty and walked down country roads to find restaurants serving dinners of yogurt and eggplant. In the countryside women worked at their looms and men herded sheep; in the cities men puffed on hookahs and women walked in pairs. We wandered along endless beaches, took a boat to see Cleopatra's Baths, and drank Turkish coffees in small marinas.

A torrent of rain caught us in an interior village, and we ran for shelter under the awning of a restaurant where the owner waved us up to his covered balcony. He told us he wanted to practice his English, and his wife made us lunch while he sat at our table. Without warning, he began to berate the Jews. As I struggled to keep calm, I felt Noel squeeze my knee under the tablecloth, his face expressionless. The owner warned us about a Jewish conspiracy to take over the world. According to him, Masonic lodges in America were organizing the downfall of Europe.

I had never experienced bigotry before except against the Aboriginal peoples in North America, and no self-respecting adult had condoned those cultural slurs within recent memory. The young wife working behind a booth appeared to be a teenager though her husband was clearly middle-aged. Now and again he would order her about in guttural tones without looking at her. *Can she sit with us for a moment?* I asked. *Women want too much*, he said.

When we left the restaurant, I asked Noel why he hadn't argued. *We'll never convince him of anything.* He sounded impatient. We walked aimlessly for a while as the sun came out and our positions reversed. *Now I'm uncomfortable about it*, he said. *I should go back to tell him I'm a Jew and he's an asshole.* He turned toward the restaurant. *No, I'm the one who's wrong*, I coaxed. I looped my arm through his to keep him with me. *I'm afraid; think about the way he treated his wife.* Noel appeared not to hear, so I tried humor: *She was toweling off a bunch of carving knives behind the counter.*

He leaned on a stone wall and stared at his shoes, overwhelmed by ancient history: *Sometimes I think things are different since my aunt's time, but there's always reality waiting to clobber you.* Noel shook his head as though to shake off a memory, and then pulled me toward him, cradling the back of my head as I leaned into his shoulder, our knapsacks growing heavy on our backs. *Let's get out of here.* He turned toward the bus depot, walking away while grabbing my hand. The sun had reached its zenith and steam was rising off wet stones.

I was born blond, blue-eyed, and long-legged, Noel said, as though that explained all his problems. *Good thing you lost your blond hair*, I joked, trying to make him lighten up. When we climbed on the bus, we were separated but I could hear him speak French to a tourist seated next to him and German to the man across the aisle. Finally he closed his eyes and drifted into sleep while I remembered the times I had shuffled off Noel's sensitivity. Now I fantasized pulverizing the restaurant owner, scratching his eyeballs out with my fingernails, and then stealing his wife away to a new life in Canada.

Noel carried a classic Turkish rug under one arm for the last week of our month away. *Don't judge Turkey by one jerk*, he told me. We regained our equilibrium by waving to sheep herders from the bus, talking sign language to wide-eyed children, and devouring food served by friendly waiters who practiced their English. On the plane home, we were overcome by the beauty we had left behind in Canada. *I worked on my Ph.D. in California, but I always knew it wasn't home*, Noel said. *I studied Hardy and George Eliot because I didn't think there was enough Canadian literature to cover a graduate degree*, I confessed.

Alone on the commuter plane from Vancouver to Victoria, I gazed over the Gulf Islands below. The airport bus dropped me off three kilometers from the house, and I realized how seldom I walked around my own city as I had done in Istanbul and all the villages we discovered. With my knapsack on, I sauntered through the sunny park where a jogger called out as she passed, running backward for a moment so I could hear her: *I took English from you four years ago, great class!* she yelled. Only two things were missing when I arrived home – the face I had grown accustomed to seeing and the dog, who was still next door.

After our month together, Noel and I planned small escapes to keep the mood alive – weekends when we cycled to favorite cafés or rented kayaks to paddle out of reach of newspapers and phones. On Noel's birthday just before the spring equinox, I took him to Saltspring Island and a log cabin on a small peninsula with signs asking guests to keep their dogs leashed around the deer and rabbits that Chance no longer cared to chase. For my birthday just after the fall equinox, Noel booked a bed and breakfast hidden among trees and overlooking the water on Maine Island.

Tired from a busy week, we locked up our bicycles, put a match to the kindling in the fireplace, and filled an ancient claw-foot tub to the brim. Once I had joined Noel in the water, I had an after-thought and tiptoed dripping to the large sliding doors between us and a view of the ocean. When I threw my weight into opening the heavy drapes, I faced six smiling strangers, their legs over the edge of a Jacuzzi tub we hadn't noticed before. *Surprise!* one of them called out as she lifted her glass.

On a winter Wednesday in Vancouver, while I graded papers in Victoria, Noel treated Cathy and Woldy's son, Alex, to a Canucks hockey game for his seventeenth birthday. Noel was gearing up to share godparenting duties as the possibility of our moving in together slid from idea toward agreement. Cathy and I had always shared a joke about my predictable presents: *Oh dear, poor Elizabeth*, she would say when I produced yet another duplicate of something she had already bought for Alex. Noel's offering of hockey tickets had lifted the burden of finding an original gift off my shoulders.

Four days later, on the Sunday before the first *Messiah* concert of the Christmas season, Noel had slipped out to see a friend while I reviewed a novel for my Monday morning class. The phone rang and my hand went to my chest to massage a sudden and inexplica-ble pain. Letting the book fall shut, I jumped off the couch and rushed to the phone table. My throat was already constricted and the world moving in slow motion when Cathy spoke.

Alex had died in an accident at Whistler Mountain the night before. *It can't be true*, I said, wanting her to take back the words. *The policeman cried when he told us*, she whimpered, as though confirming the news. He had gone for a weekend of skiing with their neighbors. The two boys had been walking the dog before bedtime. The snow was deep and the tennis bubble, a mountain of white, rose in temptation. Between their climbing up and their turning to slide down, a small fissure opened wide to swallow them into space. With their beds and parents waiting, the boys fell through the canvas roof to the concrete below. Only one boy got to his feet.

At the funeral, traffic officers organized the crowd. With no pews left unoccupied, unseated mourners shuffled by to hug Cathy and Woldy at the front of the church and then left by a side door. Loudspeakers had been set up to relay eulogies and music to those outside West Vancouver's United Church. Students lined the walls so that parents could sit. Noel and I watched from the pew behind as Woldy swayed and then sat suddenly beside Cathy and their adopted daughter. There was an audible intake of breath when their adopted son, recently returned from living on the street, wandered up the aisle in his plaid flannel shirt as though looking for family. All the sorrow of the world seemed to walk with this fifteen-year-old boy who had been born into suffering.

After years of waiting to have a baby, and seventeen more of loving the boy who finally came, Cathy and Woldy now listened to good-byes for the child who was supposed to outlive them but had died before finishing high school. Noel and I sat next to the parents of the boy who had survived the fall. Their despair was palpable in spite of their own son's life being spared. Students pushed back to allow one of Alex's classmates to pass, long white shirt hanging loose as he walked to the pulpit and pulled his guitar from its case. When his fingers found the heart of Bach's "Prelude Number One," we relaxed into contemplation. Woldy's brother took up his violin. Mouth grim, hands shaking, he played "Lo How a Rose Is Blooming." Two Native drummers chanted at the open doors of the church as we followed the coffin to the hearse.

Alex had been on a kayaking team and, after Christmas, friends and relatives gathered at a kayakers' waterfall deep in the Squamish forest, home to squirrels, coyotes, and eagles, along the Mamquam

River on the way to Whistler Ski Resort. At Cathy's request, I stood on a rock and sang new lyrics I had put to old music, my song drowned out by rushing water where Alex's chums paddled into the waterfall and returned unharmed. His ashes were placed in his punctured kayak and covered with carnations before being set adrift. The blood-red flowers bobbed on the surface as Alex's remains moved into the current with the sinking boat.

Some memories are too beautiful to forget, too heavy to bear. In one memory of Alex, Cathy sits in a rocking chair in my living room in Kitsilano. She tells me she is pregnant and I can feel the heat of her happiness across the space between us. Hers is the story of a mother who never complained about her son, keeping alive for me the possibility that motherhood was as joyful as I had imagined. In another memory of Alex, Woldy reaches to close the lid of his son's coffin. It is the night before the funeral, and for a moment his great Russian head rises as though toward a vision. A father's keening fills the room, a cry of extinction acknowledged. He brings the heavy wooden lid down over a space softened by a baby's quilt, over the silence of his son.

In yet another memory, the expression *viewing the body* takes on new meaning. Even with the lid forever closed, I see in my mind's eye Alex's sweeping hair and full lips above his thick neck and paddler's muscles. His long legs stretch to fill a space wide enough for one in this final bed, and I realize Alex will not taste the sweet temptations of women. He moves toward flames and ashes, remaining and not remaining seventeen. In death, Alex has left a gift for me – the knowledge that Noel stays close by, his willingness to be there unquestioned, his grief transformed to compassion.

Visiting Cathy and Woldy months later, we four walked after dinner under an almost clear night sky, invigorated by the exercise and the stars. Cathy and Noel were lost in conversation, far behind Woldy and me when he stopped mid-sentence and whispered, *Look!* Woldy pointed to where a coyote had appeared from the trees and stood on the road below us. Its head was raised as though to howl as the moon slipped out from behind a single cloud. When its sleek shape disappeared into the shadows, we felt the presence of Alex among us.

Noel and I got along well on land, but the water tested our compatibility. He has cursed me twice in our time together. The first occasion was on our way toward open waters in a sailboat, following the cardinal rule not to put the sails up until we had cleared harbor. But what does a sailor do when the motor breaks down and currents push the boat with unstoppable force? We moved down a narrow passage, a seaplane revving for takeoff behind us, a passenger ferry looming into dock, and a half dozen drunks engulfing us in their waves as they zoomed past in a rented powerboat. I froze while Noel's hands struggled with the motor and his vocal chords went into overdrive: *Get off your ass and fuckin' help me or we're in trouble!* I was reminded how long it takes to actually know a person well.

Family is important to Noel, and his interest in his nephews and nieces, their careers, marriages, and eventual children comforted me. The first of many family gatherings Noel took me to was the wedding of his sister's son in Toronto where guests ate and danced in the ballroom of the King Edward Hotel, and where his Montreal aunt assured me Noel had been visiting her when he disappeared after our first acquaintance in the bedroom. This glamorous and festive family celebrates every birth and marriage as though it is the first. In spite of my history of failed marriages and Protestant parents, I was welcomed into their fold.

Noel's mother, Lily, is in her nineties and still spry. She accepted me in spite of my not being Jewish and my insisting on having all the things she didn't have – career, bank account, car, study, phone, and two previous mothers-in-law. *I don't care*, she said; *my son is happy.* She had established her own brand of independence at the age of nine as the smallest child in her classroom. An older boy had called her a dirty Jew, and she grabbed him by his red locks and flipped him to the ground where she beat him until he said he was sorry. The teacher told her to stay after school, but Lily rose to her four-foot height and walked out when she learned the boy would not be scolded too.

Lily's call on a day Noel returned from a trip to Ottawa centered on her fear that she had suffered a heart attack. I suggested her sister phone the ambulance service: the attendants would have equipment to help her. When Noel rushed to her side, he found his mother and aunt flirting with the ambulance drivers. In the hospital the doctor confirmed a heart problem but she came home to cook up a storm and carry on a robust social life. The next time she called for Noel, I had just hung up as he came through the door. *Maybe you should eat and collect your wits before you go*, I suggested. *She's my mother and I'm going whether you agree or not*, he called over his shoulder as he closed the door behind him. He wouldn't allow his mother's lack of patience to create the same pattern in himself. Family is family in spite of a wide range of personalities and expectations. Feelings of respect and trust had overwhelmed my need for control by the time he returned home. I was part of the family now.

When I asked Noel why he had never married, he thought a long moment before he told me a part of him had never settled into the idea of permanence, that having come through the sixties, he saw marriage as an institution to make lawyers rich and love irrelevant. *One woman asked me to father a child with no strings attached*, he laughed. Another woman had caused him to consider the idea of permanence but not the legalities of it. Another had shared his love and broken his heart. *The timing was wrong*, he confessed. *Besides, marriage and children are two different things.* He referred to his goddaughter, whose parents had shared a long and fulfilling bond but never considered legalizing it. As my attachment to Noel grew simultaneously less and more – fewer questions and greater trust – I began to understand how it might be possible to love a man without bearing his children.

After three years of commuting, Noel gave up his job and sold his Vancouver house. Once his clothes were unpacked, he set out to find a home I would like better than the one I owned and had lived in with Spears. He accused me of having a disproportionate sense of allegiance: *You're more loyal to your floorboards than people are their lovers*, he accused. I decided each house the realtor showed us had some fatal flaw, in spite of ocean views and spacious rooms.

Okay, Noel finally agreed. It happened on a day I least expected it, after he had taken me to a log heritage house where the waves crashed up toward an enormous front window, a place where I felt my commitment to Faithful Street waver slightly, but not enough to move: *It's too far from the college.* After a subdued drive home, he said, *All right, we'll stay put but we'll renovate – new bedroom, new kitchen, new bathroom.* When we divided the cost, I discovered Noel had overpaid. *That's to stop you from going on about Spears taking your inheritance.* Hell may have no fury like a woman scorned, but Noel had more negotiating skills than a fox in love with a rabbit.

When we moved out to allow renovations to begin, we regained the childlike excitement that we had encountered during our first summer together in Vancouver. For three months, we nestled with Chance in a small sublet apartment across from Beacon Hill Park, until the builders completed the additions. When we returned to Faithful Street, it was to a new home with a Canadian maple kitchen, two private studies, and a bedroom where no one had made love before us. We expected, at last, to live happily ever after.

How can I have lung cancer when I hardly ever smoked? I demanded. After six months of my coughing and visits to the doctor, Noel had insisted it couldn't be an allergy. The doctor finally agreed to an X-ray. When the results came back, weeks later, I was diagnosed with severe pneumonia. After another round of antibiotics and X-rays, my doctor read off a word I had never heard before – *neoplasm*. When she looked up, I read her face: *Cancer?* I phoned Noel on a payphone, surprised at myself for crying in a public hall between the doctor's office and a drugstore. *I'm coming to get you*, he said to me. *No, I have my car*, I argued. *Take a taxi, we'll get the car later.* His voice was firm but tender. I began to whimper over having forgotten my X-rays: *I'm supposed to take them to the hospital tomorrow.* I hung up before Noel could ask, *Where are you?* When I drove up to the house, he was standing in the driveway.

A boyish-looking respirologist in the emergency ward suggested a hospital procedure that would diagnose my condition with certainty. *Do you think having no children can cause cancer?* I asked. He looked doubtful before he smiled at my skipping from lung to womb. *Are you a smoker?* he asked. *I just came from playing squash,* I told him. The woman in the next cubicle moaned behind her curtain while I explained that I had smoked occasionally at parties and for a brief time immediately after both my divorces, at UBC for the first year because I was nervous, but never in the college where I had worked now for more than a decade. He raised his eyebrows, smiled openly, and asked again, *Are you a smoker?* I tried to think if there was a way I could avoid such a label. *I had a girlfriend I used to see on Friday nights quite often, and we smoked together in her kitchen while I sat on a stool and she cooked.* I didn't tell him she had died of a melanoma two years earlier.

Did your parents smoke? he asked. *Of course not!* I declared. He said twenty cigarettes a day were necessary to qualify as a smoker. *How about happy herbs?* His eyebrows went up as he took notes. *A little in the old days with my ex-husband, but not often.* When he didn't tell me what I wanted to hear, I bargained: *I can't have cancer because I've got someone special now and we've just renovated, and I got a big grant to study for a Ph.D. in Canadian literature, my favorite subject, and my dog is old.* The doctor dodged this logic: *You can't go home today because I've registered you for a bed; it's against the law for us to keep it for you if you leave the building.* I thought of Noel and Chance: *What about my car?* He pocketed his pen and turned to leave: *We take care of these things.* When he drew the curtain closed behind him, I hopped off the table, dressed, and walked out the automatic doors to the parking lot.

Driving home I convinced myself someone had made a mistake. *It can't be*, I insisted to Noel, *I didn't smoke even one cigarette a week, if you average it out.* His voice was soft when he responded: *Just forget the guilt. I'm coming with you from now on, every step of the way.* I pushed away thoughts of his suffering the heartache he had gone through with his father's cancer. *We'll take Chance for the ride back to the hospital, okay?* He had his coat on and the dog at the door before I could make up my mind. Minor surgery confirmed the diagnosis. I returned home on antibiotics to control my pneumonia. A more invasive biopsy came back showing clear lymph nodes. *The cancer appears to be confined to your upper right lobe and that makes surgery a possibility, but not a certainty*, the respirologist advised. *Scans don't show everything.*

The surgeon warned of the risks: *You'll find quite a difference in breathing after the lobe goes.* Knowing he was a skier, I told him I'd see him at the top of Whistler Mountain after it was all over. Just before surgery the respirologist came by to say they'd be checking with dyes for a spread of the cancer after they opened me up. Just in case. *Will they saw you open?* a friend asked, perhaps hinting that I reconsider the operation. Noel ran between his new job, our old dog, and the hospital. *I guess I smoked a bit*, I confessed. *Don't beat yourself up*, he repeated.

Two months later, in mid-February of 1995, I was rolling down the hall on a stretcher, feeling like a prone bystander, listening to the murmured reassurances of the anesthesiologist. When I returned to consciousness, the first thing I saw was Noel's face expressing relief at my recognition. He told me I would still have two lungs when I had beaten the cancer. It took a moment to understand his message. When the surgeon came by, he explained the cancer had metastasized to my pulmonary artery, where lungs and heart connect. Inoperable. Morphine dripped into my bloodstream every six seconds, and both arms were immobilized to allow the deep incision to heal. I could tell by the nurses' false cheer and averted faces they knew of the failed surgery. I could tell by the doctors who visited with humorous stories to relay that they knew

I was absorbing a challenge. I had to look to Noel's eyes to rid myself of doubt.

Noel took me home without asking permission. He propped me in a borrowed wheelchair, helped me into his van, walked me the few steps to the end of our street where I could look into the park, and then tucked me in our bed where I could see the garden. Chance settled herself on the floor beside me. A friend brought me Alice Munro's *Open Secrets*, but on morphine I forgot what had happened at the top of the page by the time I reached the bottom. I had my own open secret: a fear of cancer cells looking for new places to ravage – liver, kidney, or brain. Drugs made me hallucinate about a second invasion of rodents, these ones so huge they overwhelmed Chance when they lurked in corners of the room.

Jane arrived from UBC as she had done when Spears betrayed me. She carried a trunkful of frozen homemade stews, chilis, and soups to our freezer. When Noel came home she ordered him to read the newspaper while she made dinner from the ingredients in her cooler. After filling the dishwasher, chatting with us, and staying the night, she returned home on the early-morning ferry.

Two oncologists took over treatments after the incision had healed, each with their own poison. Noel took time away from his career to sit with me when the doctors gave instructions and shared horrifying statistics. He questioned them and took notes to share with his doctor nephews. He sat by me in the hospital when a soft-spoken oncologist administered chemotherapy by slipping a needle into the back of my hand. The brew dripped into my vein with a buzz of warm electricity.

In time I convinced Noel to return to his office so I could read instead of feeling guilty about keeping him from work. The circle of patients in the room captivated me. In spite of our different genders, cancers, degrees of fitness, and fears, we agreed on the unspoken need to remain up-beat as medications seeped from bag to body, doing their best to cripple cancer cells before they escaped into unsuspecting organs. After treatment, I was feeble but well. Two days later the tidal after-effects of chemotherapy hit me. My sole task then was to get well in time for the next treatment, drinking lots of water with my anti-nausea pills.

Chance and I began taking slow walks along the oceanside. Strolling with a friend in the third week, I decided to forgo pills in favor of more fresh air. At the end of his busy day, Noel found me on the couch unable to lift my head or speak. When he discovered I had ignored both the doctor's instructions and my promise to look after myself, he resorted to the vocabulary he had used mid-harbor on the sailboat: *It's all I asked you to do – to get off your ass and take your pills. I can't be here every fuckin' minute.* I could hear him but dehydration, nausea, and shame kept me from defending myself. *It's okay,* he said, suddenly slipping onto the floor beside the couch, sliding down as though anger and affection had collided to push him over.

Morning and night Noel carried the dog up and down the stairs, and evenings he cooked organic dinners and kept our small world together with his big-hearted charm. Bedtime was my favorite moment, a time when I lay beside Noel with the knowledge I had made it through another day and that it would be hours before he would leave for work and I would begin my struggle alone again. I was grateful to be able to love someone, to feel ensconced in the trio of him and me and Chance. In time we found ways to celebrate our love without moving my arms too much, without either of us endangering the incision that stretched from a place where my collarbones meet to just above my belly button.

To prepare for radiation, I was fitted to a mold that would keep me bone still. Then I was tattooed on the inner curve of my right breast, under my left armpit, where the radiation would focus its lethal fire. When I returned to the cubicle to dress, I saw the indelible mark, no bigger than a freckle. It covered the heart of my cancer, the spot where I had been struck years before. In the claustrophobia of the dressing room, I had a long moment of despair before I remembered Noel was only a phone call away. If doctors couldn't understand the price a woman paid for being barren, they would never heed the loss that comes of being wounded by someone who had promised love.

Alternative therapists healed me while the oncologists destroyed my cancer. Each therapist I visited encouraged me to take whatever curative help the medical profession could offer while they refilled my storehouse of spiritual and physical strength. Acupuncture, yoga, and massage taught me that a person can tip off balance until she is ripe for illness. No complementary therapist offered a quick fix, just a slow and continual process toward higher ground. Acupuncture unblocked my meridians, freeing me to enjoy a sense of well-being. Yoga took me through the sutras and asanas that lead to breathing in the present tense, connecting the inner person and outer universe through stillness. Massage smoothed away tense thoughts and cramped muscles. I came to think of these treatments as a form of making love to the secret person within. Each in its own way returned a wholeness to my being and confirmed my belief in the outdoors as a cathedral of wellness.

Noel crossed the half-century point in March while I was on chemotherapy. The doctor allowed me to skip that week's treatment. From bed, I organized friends to bring wine and beer. The woman who had catered Lyn's wake agreed to fly to Victoria, and when I told her there would be one person to feed for each of Noel's fifty years, she said, *No sweat*. Someone stuck birthday balloons in the front lawn but Noel moved them to the back yard. He hinted he might go out for the evening. *It's a small party*, I told him, adding that I needed to take my mind off my prognosis and promising to take afternoon naps without protest. After he tucked me under the quilt, my thoughts drifted around paper plates, borrowed glasses, and homemade food. I woke up remembering I had forgotten the birthday cake.

All the bakeries in town were near closing and refused to begin baking a cake to feed fifty people. I dressed while scheming how I could persuade a friend to bake a cake while the guests munched at the buffet. Before I could ask, the phone rang. It was a bakery I had called earlier. They had at-the-ready an enormous carrot cake for a Scotsman's birthday. Dates had been confused, and his celebration was for the following weekend. When I agreed to take it, he confessed: *The icing's blue and orange plaid.* I paused. The girlfriend who picked it up called from the store: *Do you know about the colors?* Near the end of the evening, a colleague encouraged me to come into the dining room for the candle-blowing ceremony because Noel was suffering from a bout of shyness over his plaid dessert. After he made his wish, blew out the candles, and slipped a knife into the moist carrot cake, I watched from a horizontal position as friends ate to the last crumb.

Waiting in a bottom drawer were our tickets to *La Bohème.* Puccini had written his famous piece about bohemians in 1895, a century before I underwent surgery, chemotherapy, and as much radiation as flesh, bone, and blood can bear. Attending the opera became a dream that would mark my having strength enough to dress up, eat at a restaurant with friends, and stay awake. Noel had refused to take anyone else, and I was pleased by his faith in my being able to go. My imagination was caught up with the death of Mimi, a seamstress coughing her way toward her last fling in the snow, and Rodolfo, the poet, inconsolable for wasting himself in reticence because he feared his imminent sorrow. We ate in a garden restaurant under the stars with two other couples. *It gives me goosebumps to see you recovering*, one woman said, baring her arms to prove the effect.

When the curtain lifted on Paris with Rodolfo singing to Mimi, he was worrying over her cold hand. Noel squeezed mine without looking at me. I had to swallow my tears, thinking how he had massaged my hands and feet when the fireplace in our new bedroom couldn't melt the icy fear and nausea. I had never presumed to mention Noel's fear of losing me, but I had come to realize his affection said more about his capacity for tenderness than my deserving it. My self-esteem had risen with my remission from cancer, as though love and health connected in ways not explained in medical journals. Though Mimi dies coughing, the opera's catharsis cleared our spirits, as it does when music comes home to the soul.

Since Noel and I were now both in our fifties, I wondered whether we were suffering a mid-life crisis in reverse – running toward home rather than escaping it. The idea of people remaining together because they needed each other had always hinted of weakness to me. But the simple fact was that no one other than Noel would do: I needed him. A glimpse of death had come with a gift of truth: *We only have two choices*, I told him. *I'm for aging*, he said.

I will never know if the opera inspired Noel's marriage proposal. It may have been the book I was reading, propped as I was against a pillow with Ann-Marie MacDonald's *Fall on Your Knees*. Noel didn't actually fall on his knees except in a metaphorical way. I hesitated at first, certain he was teasing, and waited for him to repeat the offer. When he didn't, panic stirred in my belly. He was holding out the chance to move into a marriage where no one would ask the baby question that had corroded my spirit for a quarter century. We celebrated over dinner and under the covers. Noel suggested June for the ceremony. I countered with May because it was sooner.

By that time I was in the midst of writing a book in response to a publisher's phone call. He had read a newspaper article I had written suggesting the need to augment conventional therapies with alternative ones. He asked if I would write the story of my journey with cancer. Noel planted the seed for the book's title when I talked to him about wishing I could have perfected something before I became incapacitated. He suggested I perfect hope as an alternative to fear. A manuscript called *The Perfection of Hope* grew while I organized a wedding dress in silky harvest tones. Together Noel and I made our invitations, wrote in private our vows to each other, and planned a gourmet wedding lunch with a chocolate cake covered in fruit and eucalyptus leaves. We planted a Japanese ornamental cherry Cathy and Woldy had given us, *our Alex tree*, in the yard and picked up our plane tickets for a month's honeymoon in Tuscany. On May 11, I left sickness and sorrow behind to carry a bouquet of calla lilies into a white Daimler and drive to an oceanside lodge where two trumpeters summoned across the space that divided me from my man.

Although Noel's love of subtlety pervades our relationship, I am no longer capable of thinking of a man in terms of obedience. Somewhere between leaving Corbett and living with Spears, I learned to speak up. Self-defence came automatically at mid-life, and Noel complained that when we had a difference of opinion, I talked for both sides as though he wasn't in the room. During one altercation, he said, *If you want to listen to my point I'll be in the bedroom.* For an hour afterward he read in his chair while I considered the damage done by my impatience and his stubbornness. Finally I walked down the long length of our hall: *So what's your point?* I asked. Neither of us could keep a straight face when we realized how easy it was for him to win out over my curiosity, how hard it was for him to stay angry, and how difficult it was for either of us to remember what we had argued about.

However, driving up to Whistler Mountain at Christmas, we confronted other truths about each other. Noel and I were trapped with two hundred motorists on a highway too slippery to move forward with any speed and too dangerous to turn back. No one dared stop to fasten chains to tires because there was no place to pull off in the sudden storm. Local radio gave us news about an overturned bus ahead, ice hidden under fresh snow, and poor visibility. We were warned to be patient. More snow was predicted in Whistler Village, where the highway patrol had blocked cars waiting to descend, leaving the out-going lane clear for the ambulance and police. Those of us climbing the mountain ascended the rises one car at a time. As Noel and I inched ahead, the bus in front of us began to slide backwards. *Heavy metal* took on new meaning as snow swirled about us and the bus slid past a hand's breadth away. I tried to forget that I had survived cancer to risk a relentless snowfall on a road bordered by a cliff edge, high above a raging river.

Noel stepped on the gas and plunged into the night, swerving around the bus and into the passing lane where an ambulance had sped by moments before. Without comment, he overtook angry drivers who shook their fists at us, passed the overturned bus of radio fame, and finally came to a stop several kilometers farther on. *You could have killed us*, I screamed. *Well, I didn't*, Noel said, wiping his nose on his ski glove. *Everyone's mad at us*, I shouted. *Who cares?* he snorted, his eyes on the road where he squeezed between two crawling four-wheel drives and stayed put for the rest of the climb.

My anger resurfaced on the ski lifts when I realized the altitude affected my breathing. Unable to ski more than half days, I sat alone in the lodge full of resentment at Noel for insisting on waiting at the bottom of every run to see if I was still on my feet. I felt discouraged at my audible huffing and puffing as I lagged behind. After asking if I would mind, Noel stayed on the slopes until the chairlift closed and returned with enough energy to make dinner, beat me at Scrabble, and take the dog for a walk.

After a week, however, our affections had returned to a high pitch and we packed for home in the glow of a satisfying time together. *Look at the snow falling*, I called to him as he toweled off from showering. *Just relax*, he called back. By the time we had driven to the highway, the road was barely visible. *You're not going for it, are you?* I asked as we moved forward over an unmarked expanse of white. *Can't turn now*, Noel said. If turning required a view of the road's shoulders, he was right.

The temperature dipped and the wipers froze in position while snow smacked the windshield. I covered my face with my ski gloves. When I peeked, Noel had his long arm out the window, skimming off snow with his gloved hand. *How can you see where the road curves?* I gasped. *It doesn't help for you to be freaking out*, Noel snapped. *Even a search plane couldn't find us*, I whispered. After two terrified hours, I spotted a temporary sign warning of black ice skimming the apparently clear surface in the distance ahead.

I can't handle that again, ever! I shouted, breathless and exhausted. *We're okay now*, he said, yanking off his toque and wiping perspiration from his forehead. At the first gas station, he pulled off and we discovered we had led the last five cars down the mountain before police set up a roadblock. *You're just lucky*, I said, slamming the van door on the way to the bathroom. I kept silent afterward, uncertain whether I was furious at Noel for taking a risk or at myself for not trusting the gods to keep me alive regardless of danger.

The slow process of growth, of confronting old wounds and hurts real or imagined, left residual pockets of static in me, disappointments running on idle, upsets overflowing into Noel's hearing. The episode that stilled my angst centered on an outdoor fireplace in the middle of the back yard, built by the previous owners more than half a century before. Made of beautiful stones, it had been in disrepair since I had moved into the house. Every year the same stray rocks and brick lay among the autumn apples and damp grass. As springtime unfolded, I left Noel sticky notes to remind him to fix it or to phone a stonemason. He never retaliated by asking why I hadn't hired a handyman before he came to live there or why I hadn't learned to mix cement myself.

After promising he would fix it in his own time, he refused to discuss it further. His silence drove me crazy, and I worked into various conversations reasons why he should set to with a little muscle to restore this bit of heritage in our yard. No response. In summer I decided to cover it with an enormous flowering plant. As I heaved the pot into place, I saw that each brick and stone had been firmly cemented. When I ran my fingers over the repair, I could feel by its dryness that it had been fixed for weeks. *Why didn't you tell me?* I asked. Noel looked up from his newspaper without speaking, a sneaky grin moving across his face.

As autumn took over the back yard, a resignation about our sixteen-year-old dog pervaded the house. *She's confused*, the veterinarian told me after he had checked her over. *She's still got all her teeth*, I bargained. *Well, it's up to you and your husband.* Noel and I sobbed with abandon when we said good-bye to Chance. *Never going through that again*, Noel said days later when we dared to talk of it. *You'll feel differently after a year*, I promised. *Not a chance*, he said without recognizing the irony.

A year later, in 1996, Noel was annoyed when I ordered a standard poodle from a breeder in Nova Scotia. She had played in the Boston symphony before she became an emergency room doctor and began breeding horses and cream-colored poodles in the Annapolis Valley. I purchased a puppy without confessing my remission from cancer to her and without confessing my plan to Noel. Instead, I sent a chatty letter to the other side of Canada, enclosing a wedding picture in which Noel and I look like a couple in need of a smart dog to subdue them.

Like most women, I erred on the side of knowing exactly what my husband needed, and Noel needed the puppy he had never been allowed as a child. How else could a man with Austrian blood learn to loosen up, shed his reticence, and laugh from his belly? When Noel balked, I told him studies had proven dogs helped people survive terrible diseases, *cancer, for example*. I argued they force a person to exercise, nap, eat organic, keep ice cream down to a weekly binge, and live for at least fifteen years beyond expectations. I sent a cheque to Dr. Kathryn Diefenbach the morning after he said, *I'll think about it*. A month later Noel was with me at the Vancouver airport picking up a puppy who had been locked in the bowels of an airplane for seventeen hours, while a snowstorm raged across Canada. Before we reached home, Noel had been loved into submission by a blonde we named Sophie. She adored him more than any living thing except the occasional squirrel.

Noel's adeptness at negotiations were piffle in the face of Sophie's determination. To keep up the illusion that she had his best interest at heart, I resorted to subterfuge. When she ate the strap from his Italian sandals, I waited until it reappeared, amazingly intact, at the conclusion of her digestive cycle. I told the Italian shoemaker down the street that the sandal was a souvenir of our honeymoon in Tuscany. When she chewed the leg on the coffee table, I bought her knuckle bones. When she and Noel walked at six in the morning, I stayed in bed, saying I would walk her after work. I declined to feed her in case I slipped out of remission, fearing she would starve from Noel's forgetfulness unless he got into the habit.

All the while Sophie and I played a game together. We pretended to love Noel more than we loved each other. By the time Sophie was a long, tall one-year-old, Noel was clearly in thrall to the dog, making a fool of himself over her without help from me. When she turned two years old, I decided to let the truth surface gradually, so we could enjoy the dog as equals. I tried feeding her, but she turned her head away from the lamb and rice in her bowl, waiting to hear Noel's voice tell her it was *okay*. I took her on walks and watched her rush home to check every room, anticipating his return from the office. She sat at the window looking toward the driveway where he had driven off with luggage for a business trip. In summer she followed him onto a sailboat as though she had been born with sea legs, happy to be rocking with the waves as long as he was nearby.

In turn he refused to leave Sophie behind on *my* birthday or to return to Whistler when our condo outlawed pets. He bought her an international cage even while I balked at such expense. *We might take her to Europe*, he said. Clearly, Noel was Alpha, I was Omega, and Sophie was smack in the center, where poodles thrive. Just when we three had grown accustomed to one another, the breeder wrote about coming to the West Coast. Considering her medical expertise and fearing she might hear about my first book, I wrote to confess I was in remission from lung cancer. She replied immediately: *If you were "nigh unto death" I would still give you a puppy, and if Sophie's future is ever uncertain she can always come home to Fairhill Farm.* When I shared my relief, Noel looked down to where Sophie was looking up and simplified things: *She's not going anywhere and neither are you.*

Sophie sent us in search of a new ski hill that would accept dogs, and we found the perfect lodge at Big White ski resort in the interior of British Columbia. Since the Monashee mountain range isn't as high as Whistler's, I assumed the altitude would be less and the skiing easier on my lungs. But I hadn't taken into account that we start at sea level when we climb to Whistler. The smaller mountain was in fact higher up, and my breathing was still as audible as the rescue Ski-Doo.

Mid-week when Noel bundled up to walk Sophie before bed, I watched them from our third-story window as they chased each other around snowdrifts. She stuck her head into the high drifts or disappeared altogether while Noel, with his long legs, bounded through the snow. I sulked at my respiratory system excluding me from their playfulness and lay down on the bed thinking about the disadvantages of husbands and dogs.

When Noel came through the door, his eyes were sad. I never thought to ask where Sophie was. Instead I watched him pull off his jacket and come over to stroke my face as we often do for each other when one of us feels lost. I realized my terrible need for him as we stared into each other's eyes. As I relaxed in the comfort of his company, he vanished. Stunned, I looked around the dimly lit room and breathed deeply to still my heart. Kicking back the quilt, I ran to the window. Nothing moved outside except endless snowflakes in lamplight. It was as though no one was alive but me.

As I turned back to bed confused and frightened, the door opened and Sophie bounded in, shaking snow from her thick coat. Noel followed, scolding her and laughing at the same time, his cheeks red, his knees snowy from where he had fallen. I waited for an explanation. Finally I bit into my pride and asked why he had suddenly disappeared. As I spoke, I remembered a friend whose cancer had metastasized to the brain, causing her to experience instant replays of events as the tumor invaded her frontal lobe. Yet even before Noel answered my question, I knew I had experienced something else, a vision rather than a symptom. It left me with the message that it is possible for someone to love me even though I could no longer keep up.

Noel and I always brought along two of the many quilts Corbett's mother had made for me after we had reconnected during my illness. Sophie's smaller quilt was patterned with mischievous dogs and trees heavy with pears and apples. Noel and I pulled up our big Joseph quilt, the cloak of many colors. In the calm of their sleeping presence, I thought how forgiveness comes with time and understanding. Thanks to Mrs. Corbett's generosity, a torn crazy quilt that Mother and her sisters had made as farm girls now hung on the wall over the bed I shared at home with Noel. As sleep came on Big White Mountain, I resolved again to be mindful that the worst dangers seldom lurk in obvious places.

When Hamlet said, *Nothing's either good or bad but thinking makes it so*, he was seeking escape from guilt and confusion. New to deception and overwhelmed by ideals, he was young and tormented. Paradox becomes more understandable in middle age when lessons unbidden calcify into half-truths, and opposites co-exist in reality. Cancer, for example, taught me to grasp hope when none seemed possible. Divorce redefined love as a renewable resource. Infertility gave birth to humility and the slow transformation of the worst imagined fate into an acceptable one.

In a book on people who lived to celebrate their hundredth birthdays, one woman gives credit for her longevity to the fecundity that blessed her with thirteen children. Another woman had no children but five marriages, and she considers her active love life reason enough to delay death. Perhaps both women thrived on the change new faces bring. But my eyes caught and held the last page. Here, the only centenarian living alone and cooking his own meals leaned against his fence when the shutter clicked him into posterity. In his left hand an unfiltered cigarette burns as it has since he was ten years old.

Eventually, I wondered if I would have to steel myself once again when my girlfriends became grandmothers in their late forties and early fifties. It wasn't so: I had not created a space in my imagination for grandparenting and could not grieve where I had never imagined joy. The inner voice that once called for children had become barely audible, echoing from a distant place whenever a mother showed off her newborn. Like the pain of a severed limb, my yearning for children came from empty space. I felt its ghost in moments when a child lifted arms toward a parent or turned away in spirited independence. The memory of my wanting to give birth remained alive, but I no longer felt keen disappointment over the loss of a dream.

I think instead of my father's insistence on second chances and of my gift of a miraculous third chance in Noel. I relive a small part of my childhood when I see Noel lace his fingers together and rub one thumb over the other as my father once did, contemplation and wisdom moving together. My father's refusal to be moved by trends or tempted by insincerity repeat themselves in Noel's values. Father's love for Mother taught me to expect a shared devotion from a husband, and I have found it, better late than ever before.

Men are unaware of the dreams they inspire in women. My father, unsuspecting, taught me the lasting nature of unconditional love; it saved my life in Singapore. Through Corbett I learned to take devotion to its zenith and to know later the value of appreciation and forgiveness. Spears taught me to trust in the sensual language of music, which restores the spirit after loss. In the safety of Noel's affection, I reinvented the word *offspring* to mean the birth of imagination, the regeneration of the soul through writing. Stories and babies both demand a concentration that takes more effort and back ache than expected, and just when the burden seems too heavy to carry, they surprise their creators by taking on lives of their own and offering a reason to believe in tomorrow.

Just before our third wedding anniversary, Noel and I returned to Winnipeg for the marriage of his brother's eldest daughter. Before the service, he drove us past our childhood homes on our way to the Elmwood Cemetery. His family had lived in a two-storied house in a treed area of the city. The wartime bungalow on Clifton Street was smaller than I remembered, more humble than a child's unworldly imagination could register. I couldn't fathom how a family of five with maternal grandparents had lived there in relative comfort. My heart constricted with a painful joy before Noel drove on to yet another part of Winnipeg where a map marked the spot of my grandparents' graves.

After reading row upon row of small memorials flush with the ground and surrounded by an acre of old elms, I found none with the name Eva Blore. An almost forgotten chill came on the wind, whipping my hair into my eyes. The futility of searching for a grave unvisited for a quarter century hovered as I wandered through the stones of this enormous cemetery.

Eva? Noel called. *Is it Eva and Ernest Blore?* He was on his haunches, clearing away grass to expose a gravestone no bigger than an upturned cake pan. *Always Remembered.* Her name was followed by 1882–1975. Grandfather's shorter life from 1880 to 1953 reminded me of the years my grandmother had lived without the man she consistently and irrationally loved. I slipped to my knees in the damp grass and cleaned the remaining grass from their stone. *Thank you so much*, I whispered to the earth, to the man responsible for my being born Canadian, and to the woman who followed him here and loved us all for simply being family. *Thank you*, I said aloud to Noel as he cupped my head against his shoulder, waiting while I cried until I was hollowed out.

After the wedding and visits to friends, we drove in search of the Jewish cemetery. *This is it*, Noel said several times along the highway, looking closer at the entrances, then driving on. At Bnai Avraham he turned in. The graves were larger and far more ornate than in my grandparents' cemetery, but the trees had not yet grown high enough to protect the cemetery from highway noise. We walked up and down the rows, each with a wide gravel walkway. Small stones had been left on the monuments to mark the number of visitors.

I spotted his family name and, with a sense of repaying one gift with another, I called out. But before Noel could reach me, I saw that the first name was wrong. We were looking for the same name engraved on my father's stone – *Robert*. Something reminded Noel of his visit a third of a century before, and he pivoted and stopped before the tall and handsome stone that covered his father's remains. I closed my eyes, wondering if I could capture a sense of the man who had carried Noel to bed as a small boy and inspired us to keep a promise we had made when we first discovered love.

I had come to believe through my parents and grandparents that dying meant a final joining, not an eternal separation. But this notion of reuniting after death was challenged by Mordecai Richler's story *The Summer My Grandmother Was Supposed to Die*. Richler complicates the hereafter for those who marry more than once. Through the voice of her grandson, readers learn how an elderly Jewish grandmother clings to life beyond scientific possibility, bewildering her doctor and inconveniencing the extended family, especially the boy's mother, who refuses to abandon the old woman to a home.

When the grandmother finally dies, a rabbi shares the folklore that has given her such power over death: *It's written that if a man has been married twice he will spend as much time with his first wife in heaven as he did on earth.* She had refused to shed her mortal coil until her dead husband had spent the mandatory seven years in heaven that he had spent on earth with his first wife. The thought behind the tale is startling for those of us who have remarried. Am I destined to spend thirty years in heaven moving again toward Noel?

What would fifteen years in the afterlife with Corbett mean to me now? In the days of our marriage, a real man was an amalgam of the strong silent Gary Cooper, the inflexibly sexual Marlon Brando, and the boyishly inarticulate James Dean. The young women of the movie screens were always dependent on a man's love, their very decency defined by it. Born during the Second World War and moving in behind the front lines of feminism, I was too prairie to be bold, too young to be independent, too old to ignore changing roles. But I still trust in Corbett's affection, surpassed now by his immediate family, but simmering nonetheless, a new softness occasioned by fatherhood and age. Our bond is stored in the far reaches of our once being Man and Woman Invincible. For no one else could I be a young bride intent on her husband's career, loving his body, and struck by his talents. Although we searched out our separate suns, our roots remain forever side by side in timeless prairie soil.

When I try to conjure a life in heaven with Spears, I grow confused. So much of our time together lacked the spirit of marriage, the root of faithfulness that gives home precedent over whimsy. In the wake of our eroticism, I discovered that ultimate sexual pleasure takes a meeting of mind and spirit. Perhaps in our afterlife we might shine in our separate corners, two contestants who can appreciate a great round that ended with both fighters standing. Perhaps then we might reawaken in each other the lyrical and literary and dwell in a house where carnal pleasures do not staunch the flow of friendship.

Noel and I have plucked abundance from a street where we once ran our separate ways. I have begun to take our affections for granted. I know my contentment is a luxury and a dangerous pastime, risking my heart again for the spirit and flesh of connectedness, for the soporific sweetness of trust. Having loved before, I am aware one never recognizes the zenith of affection, the moment after which everything pales, except in memory.

A man has to be worth it to a woman. His love is meant to put a shine on her moments of grace. He must answer her yearning and yet remain a mystery. Noel is my prayer that cancer will not visit our house again. Deeper than chocolate, more soothing than ice cream, he stimulates my appetite for days yet to come. Noel's only competition is Sophie, but he understands now that a dog's affection opens the human heart. After all, it was an Airedale who fetched this final man for me.

Now, in our tenth year together, the Big Dipper drenches us in stardust. With our bathrobes tossed over deck railings we sit outside, up to our necks in steaming water. Sophie, alert on the step, guards us from intruders, her coat luminous against the twilight.

From the deep and round of our cedar tub we inhale the smells and hush of nightlife: Birds ruffle feathers among dark leaves; raccoons undulate along fences; maple and birch raise shadowy arms. On the deck, the bird feeder has been topped up for dawn and the potted plants watered against tomorrow's sun. Within reach on our gnarled apple tree, delicate petals rest in their journey toward bloom. They forecast the last of summer's bounty.

The text of this book was set in Sabon, Jan Tschichold's interpretation of Garamond, originally released in metal by Stempel in 1964 and later digitized by Adobe. Renaissance letter forms and large x-height make Sabon ideal for book setting.

Book design by Ingrid Paulson